PASSING THE SOUTH CAROLINA

End of Course Exam

in

ENGLISH I

(2005)

Yvonne W. Culpepper

Zuzana Urbanek

American Book Company
PO Box 2638
Woodstock, GA 30188-1383
Toll Free: 1 (888) 264-5877   Phone: (770) 928-2834 Fax: (770) 928-7483
Web site: www.americanbookcompany.com

ACKNOWLEDGEMENTS

The authors would like to acknowledge the technical and editing assistance of Marsha Torrens.

The Formatting Department gratefully acknowledges the assistance of Mary Stoddard in the preparation of this book for publication.

The cover of this book features a picture of the Angel Oak. The Angel Oak is a living oak tree in John's Island, South Carolina that is over 1.400 years old, and is believed to be "the oldest tree east of the Mississippi." The tree is 65 feet high and has a circumference of 25.5 feet. Its area of shade is 17,000 square feet, and the largest limb has a circumference of 11.5 feet and is 89 feet long.

ALL RIGHTS RESERVED

South Carolina EOC English/Language
Table of Contents

PREFACE

Passing the South Carolina End of Course Test in English/Language Arts will help students who are learning or reviewing material for the EOC Test. The materials in this book are based on the testing standards as published by the South Carolina Department of Education.

This book contains several sections. These sections are as follows: 1) General information about the book; 2) A Diagnostic Test; 3) An Evaluation Chart; 4) Chapters that teach the concepts and skills that improve graduation readiness; 5) Two Practice Tests. Answers to the tests and exercises are in a separate manual. The answer manual also contains a Chart of Standards for teachers to make a more precise diagnosis of student needs and assignments.

We welcome comments and suggestions about the book. Please contact the authors at

American Book Company
PO Box 2638
Woodstock, GA 30188-1383

Toll Free: 1 (888) 264-5877
Phone: (770) 928-2834
Fax: (770) 928-7483
Web site: www.americanbookcompany.com

ABOUT THE AUTHORS

Yvonne W. Culpepper holds a BS from Columbus (GA) State University, a post-baccalaureate teaching certificate from Kennesaw State University, and expects to complete her MA in professional writing at KSU in August 2004. She has taught high school English and has worked extensively with college students developing their writing skills.

Zuzana Urbanek is a professional writer with more than 20 years of experience in business, education, and publishing. She has taught English abroad as a foreign language, and in the US to native speakers and as a second language. Her master's degree is from Arizona State University.

TEST-TAKING TIPS

1 **Complete the chapters and practice tests in this book.** This text will help you review the skills for English/Language Arts: Reading. The book also contains materials for reviewing skills under the Research standards.

2 **Be prepared.** Get a good night's sleep the day before your exam. Eat a well-balanced meal, one that contains plenty of proteins and carbohydrates, prior to your exam.

3 **Arrive early.** Allow yourself at least 15–20 minutes to find your room and get settled. Then you can relax before the exam, so you won't feel rushed.

4 **Think success.** Keep your thoughts positive. Turn negative thoughts into positive ones. Tell yourself you will do well on the exam.

5 **Practice relaxation techniques.** Some students become overly worried about exams. Before or during the test, they may perspire heavily, experience an upset stomach, or have shortness of breath. If you feel any of these symptoms, talk to a close friend or see a counselor. They will suggest ways to deal with test anxiety. **Here are some quick ways to relieve test anxiety:**

   - Imagine yourself in your most favorite place. Let yourself sit there and relax.
   - Do a body scan. Tense and relax each part of your body starting with your toes and ending with your forehead.
   - Use the 3-12-6 method of relaxation when you feel stress. Inhale slowly for 3 seconds. Hold your breath for 12 seconds, and then exhale slowly for 6 seconds.

6 **Read directions carefully.** If you don't understand them, ask the proctor for further explanation before the exam starts.

7 **Use your best approach for answering the questions.** Some test-takers like to skim the questions and answers before reading the problem or passage. Others prefer to work the problem or read the passage before looking at the answers. Decide which approach works best for you.

8 **Answer each question on the exam.** Unless you are instructed not to, make sure you answer every question. If you are not sure of an answer, take an educated guess. Eliminate choices that are definitely wrong, and then choose from the remaining answers.

9 **Use your answer sheet correctly.** Make sure the number on your question matches the number on your answer sheet. In this way, you will record your answers correctly. If you need to change your answer, erase it completely. Smudges or stray marks may affect the grading of your exams, particularly if they are scored by a computer. If your answers are on a computerized grading sheet, make sure the answers are dark. The computerized scanner may skip over answers that are too light.

10 **Check your answers.** Review your exam to make sure you have chosen the best responses. Change answers only if you are sure they are wrong.

Over the Plate

1 For most baseball fans, the essence of the game boils down to the relationship between two players: the pitcher and the batter. **2** If the pitcher can find a way to get the ball past the batter and into the catcher's mitt or to get the batter to hit the ball to one of his teammates, then the chances of winning are great.

3 One way a pitcher attempts to control the game is through the deft use of several pitches, thrown at various speeds, from various angles, and with various amounts of spin on the ball. **4** The spin, coordinated with speed and delivery, can make the ball move several inches or almost imperceptibly during its flight to the plate in an attempt to make the batter swing at the ball with less than total force and confidence.

5 What makes a ball move? **6** First, the pitcher uses motion to transfer the momentum of his body into the ball. **7** He does that by creating a "wind up," rocking his weight back and forth until he thrusts it in the direction of home plate. **8** This transfer is called sequential summation of movement; it is the same principle that a booster rocket applies when it shoots a satellite into space. **9** The sequence starts with the movement of a large body mass that leads to the transferring of momentum to a smaller one.

10 In major league baseball, pitchers stand on a mound, higher than anyone else. **11** The height and angle of delivery are enhanced by this position, allowing the pitcher to place more force on the ball. **12** This force has two elements: thrust and spin. **13** The more coordinated a pitcher's momentum is, the more likely that high speed will accompany a pitch. **14** But the kind of spin that is placed on the ball can have an equally pronounced effect.

15 Generally, the pitcher grips the seams of the ball in ways to enhance spin. **16** Some pitchers become well known for perfecting some type of pitch. **17** Most coaches tell pitchers to attempt to throw with as much downward motion ("over the shoulder") as possible to enhance the spin. **18** The high pressure placed on the ball by the grip and the force works in tandem with the low pressure on the bottom half of the ball caused by the airflow to put the ball into motion.

19 As it turns out, the actual curve ball goes through only about three inches of actual deviation from the pitcher's hand to the batter. **20** But, because the batter is several inches below the pitcher, the ball can move over a foot from his perspective. **21** But it's not an illusion. **22** The ball does "curve," and it becomes more difficult to hit because it is no longer in a straight line and is, in fact, slowing down at a greater rate than the normal "fast ball."

23 Can you say "Strike"?

1. Which of the following definitions of the word "tandem" best explains how it is used in the passage?   Rd 3.3

   A. a two-wheeled carriage drawn by horses harnessed one before the other.
   B. a team of carriage horses harnessed in single file.
   C. a tandem bicycle.
   D. an arrangement of two or more persons or objects placed one behind the other.

2. Where would this passage most likely be published?   Rd 1.5
   A. in a magazine for young baseball fans
   B. in an encyclopedia article about the curve ball pitch
   C. in a book about famous baseball players
   D. in an instructional manual for baseball players

3. What inference can the reader make about learning to throw a curve ball?   Rd 1.8
   A. Only professional baseball players can do it.
   B. It takes a lot of practice.
   C. It is usually the result of a botched fastball pitch.
   D. Once learned, a player never forgets how to throw one.

4. Which of the following words is closest in meaning to the word "momentum" as it is used in the passage?   Rd 3.2
   A. force   B. direction   C. speed   D. size

5. Which of the following words best describes the author's tone in the passage?   Rd 2.2
   A. cynical   B. neutral   C. nervous   D. bold

6. Which of the following is a correct revision of sentence 8?   W 1.5
   A. This transfer is called sequential summation of movement: it is the same principle that a booster rocket applies when it shoots a satellite into space.
   B. This transfer is called sequential summation of movement—it is the same principle that a booster rocket applies when it shoots a satellite into space.
   C. This transfer is called sequential summation of movement; it is the same principle that a booster rocket applies when it shoots a satellite into space.
   D. Correct as is

7. Which sentence interrupts the logical progression of ideas?   W 1.2

   A. sentence 3   B. sentence 10   C. sentence 13   D. sentence 16

8. Which of the following words is most similar in meaning to the word "deft" as it is used in the
   passage?   Rd 3.2

   A. slow   B. skillful   C. careful   D. sneaky

9. Which of the following is the best way to combine sentences 21 and 22?   W 1.4

   A. But it's not an illusion; the ball does "curve," and it becomes more difficult to hit because it
       is no longer in a straight line and is, in fact, slowing down at a greater rate than the normal
       "fastball."

   B. But it's not an illusion, you see the ball does "curve," and it becomes more difficult to hit
       because it is no longer in a straight line and is, in fact, slowing down at a greater rate than the
       normal "fastball."

   C. But it's not an illusion- the ball does "curve," and it becomes more difficult to hit because it
       is no longer in a straight line and is, in fact, slowing down at a greater rate than the normal
       "fastball."

   D. But it's not an illusion: the ball does "curve," and it becomes more difficult to hit because it
       is no longer in a straight line and is, in fact, slowing down at a greater rate than the normal
       "fastball."

"Vets Continue to Care for Oil-Covered Birds"
by Jessica Flathmann

The Island Packet, Hilton Head, SC   Wed. Dec 1, 2004

Veterinarians continue trying to save about 10 oil-covered birds collected last month along the Georgia and South Carolina coasts, but most of the birds coated after a spill off Tybee Island didn't survive.

The birds were injured by a cargo ship leak Nov. 17 that put 1,000 gallons of oil into the Atlantic, said Coast Guard Lt. Anthony Quirino.

Heidi Stout, a veterinarian with Tri-State Bird Rescue and Research, the Delaware-based nonprofit organization called in to rehabilitate the birds, said 41 birds had been brought to the group.

Quirino said about 90 percent of the birds came from the Georgia coast. Only about five percent were from South Carolina. The number of birds found dead and not brought to the center isn't known.

The group hasn't received birds since the weekend and doesn't expect to get more, Stout said.

"We're optimistic that all the oiled wildlife have been retrieved," Stout said. "We're not anticipating at this point any more oiled wildlife."

The group hasn't yet released any of the birds. Stout said the animals were hard to save because they were mostly loons.

"They are an extremely difficult bird to rehabilitate," she said. "Loons are diving birds that don't spend much time on land. They don't have a tolerance for a land-based fungus, which kills them easily. And treatments against the fungus aren't always successful."

Stout said the surviving loons are living in above-ground pools while they are rehabilitated. She's not sure when they will be healthy enough to return to the wild.

Oil ruins the weatherproofing on the bird's feathers. After the oil is cleaned off, the birds still must preen themselves so their feathers are protective again, she said.

"They have to realign all their feathers—kind of like shingles on a roof," Stout said.

Besides the loons, the group also is working with one pelican.

The oil cleanup was completed by Friday. The cargo ship, *Fortune Epoch*, left Monday for repairs in Tampa, Fla., Quirino said.

He said the Coast Guard and the U.S. Fish and Wildlife Service are investigating the spill. No criminal or civil charges have been filed yet.

<http://www.beaufortgazette.com/local_news/story/4260109p-4053133c.html>.

10. What technique does the author use to communicate the information on the injured birds?   Rd 2.2
   A. statements by concerned citizens   C. questions and answers
   B. interviews with experts   D. comparisons to past events

11. Which of the following is an inference that can be made based on the article?   Rd 1.8
   A. Tri-State Bird Rescue and Research plays an important role in wildlife preservation.
   B. The birds were harmed intentionally
   C. Because of the care they are receiving, all of the rescued birds will recover and be returned to the wild
   D. Cargo ships rarely have leaks.

12. Which of the following best describes the purpose of the article?   C 1.3
   A. to persuade   B. to analyze   C. to explain   D. to inform

13. Which of the following is a relevant topic of further research based on the article?   Rs 2.5
   A. the cargo ship's manufacturer   C. prevention of oil spills
   B. species of loons   D. birds of Georgia

14. Which of the following dictionary definitions of the word "rehabilitate" is correct as it is used in the article?   Rd 3.3
   A. To restore to good health or useful life, as through therapy and education.
   B. To restore to good condition, operation, or capacity.
   C. To reinstate the good name of.
   D. To restore the former rank, privileges, or rights of.

15. Which of the following best explains the credibility of those interviewed in the article?   Rs 2.2

    A.   They are concerned citizens who may not know much about the birds; therefore they are not very credible.

    B.   They are professionals who are rehabilitating the bird, so they are very credible.

    C.   They are witnesses of the oil spill, so they are somewhat credible.

    D.   They are employees of the faulty cargo ship manufacturer; therefore they are not credible.

16. What type of source is the article?   Rs 2.1

    A.   A secondary source because the author did not directly experience the event

    B.   A primary source because experts were interviewed

    C.   A secondary source because the author's perspective is biased.

    D.   A primary source because the author wrote the article shortly after the event

David's Dilemma

1 Rebecca sprawled on the chair by the living room window and looked out across the rain-soaked front yard. **2** The grey sogginess of the day matched her mood, and her head was filled with conflicting thoughts about so many things. **3** She wondered if she would ever get them sorted out. **4** She was watching for her older brother to get home from his part-time job. **5** She heard the back door open and heard both her father's and brother's voices.

6 She quickly sat up in the chair so she could see the door from the kitchen. **7** Trying her best to look nonchalant and grabbing the magazine she had been reading earlier, she waited for her brother to come into the living room. **8** She could hear low conversation and the sound of the refrigerator opening and closing.

9 In a minute, her brother came through the doorway alone and turned toward his bedroom.

10 "David," Becca called to him in a low voice. **11** "Come over here—I need to talk to you."

12 David sighed and crossed the room, standing in front of Becca. **13** "Now what? I wanna go take a shower."

14 "I need some information." **15** Becca looked at the kitchen door and then back at David with a different expression. **16** She lowered her voice a little, almost to a whisper, and let David know that she was going to say something particularly confidential. **17** She spoke hesitantly and carefully, "Tell me, do you know a guy at school named Alejandro?"

18 David nodded and look at her quizzically, "Yeah, sure."

19 "Do you like him?"

20 "He's OK, I guess. I don't really know him very well. He's a senior."

21 "I know." **22** Becca's face got red, and she looked flustered. **23** "Do other people at school like him?"

24 "I guess. Well, some do, and some don't. But he's a really good soccer player," David added. **25** "I heard that three or four colleges are trying to recruit him."

26 "And does Dad like him?"

27 "Who do I like"? Dad asked as he entered the room.

28 David hesitated, but Becca immediately spoke up. **29** "David was just telling me about one of your soccer players, Dad. His name is Alejandro."

30 Dad stiffened. **31** "Alejandro," he repeated. **32** "Yes, he is an extremely good soccer player." **33** He looked quickly at his daughter, Rebecca. **34** "You don't know him, do you?"

35 "Oh, I've only seen him a few times at the mall with the other guys."

36 "But, you don't know him—especially—do you?"

37 Rebecca didn't quite look at her dad. **38** "Oh, uh, we've just spoken a couple of times."

39 Her father just stood looking at her for what seemed like the longest time. **40** David saw something in his father's face which he couldn't understand. **41** He wondered and thought he recognized fear—an unadulterated, paralyzing fear.

17. Which of the following best explains Rebecca's internal conflict?   Rd 2.8
    A. She is worried that her brother will not approve of her dating Alejandro.
    B. She has feelings for Alejandro, but knows her father does not approve of him.
    C. She is concerned that Alejandro may have shoplifted from the mall.
    D. She wants to date Alejandro but fears he may be too busy with soccer.   Rd 2.2

18. Which word best describes the tone of the father as he discusses Alejandro with his daughter?
    A. nonchalant   B. light-hearted   C. condescending   D. concerned

19. What inference can be made about Alejandro based on the father's reaction to Rebecca's interest in him?   Rd 1.8
    A. Alejandro may be dangerous.
    B. Alejandro needs to concentrate only on playing soccer.
    C. Alejandro spends too much time at the mall.
    D. Alejandro does not get along with Rebecca's family.

20. Which sentence contains a misspelled word?   W 1.5
    A. sentence 5   B. sentence 14   C. sentence 36   D. sentence 41

21. Which of the following is the best way to revise sentence 7?

    A.   Rebecca, trying to look nonchalant and grabbing a magazine she had been reading earlier, waited for her brother to come into the living room.

    B.   She tried to look nonchalant, grabbed the magazine she had been reading earlier, and waited for her brother to come into the living room.

    C.   Grabbing the magazine she had been reading earlier, she tried to look nonchalant as she waited for her brother to come into the living room.

    D.   Correct as is

22. Which of the following words is closest in meaning to the word "quizzically" as it is used in the passage?

    A.   questioningly   B.   doubtfully   C.   hopefully   D.   forgetfully

23. Which of the following is the correct revision of sentence 27?

    A.   "Who do I like?" Dad asked as he entered the room.

    B.   "Who do I like," Dad asked as he entered the room.

    C.   "Who do I like? Dad asked as he entered the room.

    D.   Correct as is

24. Which sentence provides the most support the fact that Rebecca's father does not want her to date Alejandro?

    A.   sentence 34   B.   sentence 36   C.   sentence 40   D.   sentence 41

Thomas' Burden

Fleeing from the safety of the roadside forest, Thomas, bearing the unconscious monk in his arms, and somewhat faint from his own wounds, staggered in the direction of the chiming bell. He had but a short distance to go carrying the slightly built monk from the scene of combat to the tiny chapel where a lone friar was saying his prayers. Thomas hated to interrupt a holy man at one of his daily times of prayer, but he was afraid the monk he carried was seriously wounded. At the sound of Thomas' clattering armor and the footsteps approaching, the friar turned with a start and hastened toward the doorway. As he came closer, the dim light disclosed an elderly, but kind face lit by large brown eyes.

"Friar," gasped Thomas, "here is another holy man badly wounded for my sake. I beg you to use your skill with herbs to heal him. He stood beside me in battle and defended me as if I were a brother to him."

The friar motioned toward a doorway near the back of the chapel then turned and with a nimble gait led Thomas in that direction. They passed through the doorway and into the friar's own chambers. Thomas carried the injured monk as tenderly as he could and laid him down as gently as he could on the hermit's couch. The sight of blood soaking through the monk's robe caused Thomas to fear for the small man's life. Thomas' anxiety showed in his frantic glancing about the room.

"Son, you best step outside and let me tend to this wounded man," said the friar. "Go to the chapel and rest yourself. I will attend to your injuries when I see what need be done here. I think this brother is not wounded unto death."

Thomas went out falteringly, but obediently, as the monk faintly called his name. "Be not troubled," said the friar. "He does not know that he calls you. He is perhaps delirious." Collapsing onto a rough bench along the side wall of the chapel, Thomas slumped to one side and closed his eyes.

Alone with the monk, the friar turned his full attention to the long gash that went through the monk's robe and cut into the surprisingly delicate-looking shoulder. Gently probing to assess the wound, the friar looked more closely at the pale white flesh of the shoulder. On impulse, he turned the monk's head and pulled back the voluminous hood.

What he saw both surprised him and confirmed his suspicions. Long brown hair cascaded over the monk's delicate face. Carefully, so as not to cause pain to the wounded monk, the friar unfastened the large wooden buttons down the front of the monk's robe. As he drew back the sides of the robe, it revealed not a hearty monk but a slim person clothed in a loose nightgown-style garment.

The friar paused, looking with dismay at the frail body of a young woman.

25. Which statement best describes a connection or relationship between "David's Dilemma" and "Thomas' Burden"?   Rd 1.2
    A. Both concern a character's dilemma of whether to disclose another character's true nature.
    B. Both concern a love affair that is dangerous to one of the characters.
    C. Both concern characters who are trying to learn about themselves.
    D. Both focus on jealously between lovers.   Rd 1.2

26. Which word best describes David in "David's Dilemma" and the friar in "Thomas' Burden"?

    A. sentimental   B. conflicted   C. forceful   D. secretive

27. Which statement best compares the point of view used in "David's Dilemma" and "Thomas' Burden"?   Rd 2.6
    A. Both are written in first person.
    B. Both are written in second person.
    C. Both are written in third person.
    D. "David's Dilemma" is written in third person while "Thomas' Burden" is written in first person.

28. How do "David's Dilemma" and "Thomas' Burden" differ in style?   Rd 2.4
    A. "David's Dilemma" has more dialogue than does "Thomas' Burden."
    B. "David's Dilemma" has more formal language than does "Thomas' Burden."
    C. "David's Dilemma" has more action than does "Thomas' Burden."
    D. "David's Dilemma" has a more complex sentence structure than does "Thomas' Burden."

29. Which statement(s) best compare(s) the settings of "David's Dilemma" and "Thomas' Burden"?
    Rd 2.6
    A. Both take place in the past.
    B. Both take place in the future.
    C. "David's Dilemma" takes place in a family home from the past. "Thomas' Burden" takes place in the future.
    D. "David's Dilemma" takes place in a modern family home. "Thomas' Burden" takes place in a chapel from the past.

30. What is ironic about the injured monk's being a woman in "Thomas' Burden"?
    Rd 2.2
    A. She was not really a monk.
    B. She saved the like of a man during a time when women were believed to be the weaker gender.
    C. She tried to tell the monk she saved that she was a woman, but he didn't believe her.
    D. She disguised herself as a monk so that she could fight alongside the other monk.

31. How does the author's choice of narrator most affect the action in "Thomas' Burden?
    Rd 2.5
    A. The reader suspects the injured monk is a woman from the beginning.
    B. Like the friar, the reader is unsure if the injured monk will survive.
    C. Like the friar, the reader is surprised at the end to learn that the injured monk is a woman.
    D. The reader knows the thoughts of all the characters and knows that the injured monk is in love with the other monk.

Anna Sewell's *Black Beauty*: Chapter 1, "My Early Home"

The first place that I can well remember was a large pleasant meadow with a pond of clear water in it. Some shady trees leaned over it, and rushes and water-lilies grew at the deep end. Over the hedge on one side we looked into a plowed field, and on the other we looked over a gate at our master's house, which stood by the roadside; at the top of the meadow was a grove of fir trees, and at the bottom a running brook overhung by a steep bank.

While I was young I lived upon my mother's milk, as I could not eat grass. In the daytime I ran by her side, and at night I lay down close by her. When it was hot we used to stand by the pond in the shade of the trees, and when it was cold we had a nice warm shed near the grove.

As soon as I was old enough to eat grass my mother used to go out to work in the daytime, and come back in the evening.

There were six young colts in the meadow besides me; they were older than I was; some were nearly as large as grown-up horses. I used to run with them, and had great fun; we used to gallop all together round and round the field as hard as we could go. Sometimes we had rather rough play, for they would frequently bite and kick as well as gallop.

One day, when there was a good deal of kicking, my mother whinnied to me to come to her, and then she said:

"I wish you to pay attention to what I am going to say to you. The colts who live here are very good colts, but they are cart-horse colts, and of course they have not learned manners. You have been well-bred and well-born; your father has a great name in these parts, and your grandfather won the cup two years at the Newmarket races; your grandmother had the sweetest temper of any horse I ever knew, and I think you have never seen me kick or bite. I hope you will grow up gentle and good, and never learn bad ways; do your work with a good will, lift your feet up well when you trot, and never bite or kick even in play."

I have never forgotten my mother's advice; I knew she was a wise old horse, and our master thought a great deal of her. Her name was Duchess, but he often called her Pet.

Our master was a good, kind man. He gave us good food, good lodging, and kind words; he spoke as kindly to us as he did to his little children. We were all fond of him, and my mother loved him very much. When she saw him at the gate she would neigh with joy, and trot up to him. He would pat and stroke her and say, "Well, old Pet, and how is your little Darkie?" I was a dull black, so he called me Darkie; then he would give me a piece of bread, which was very good, and sometimes he brought a carrot for my mother. All the horses would come to him, but I think we were his favorites. My mother always took him to the town on a market day in a light gig.

32. Which word best describes the character of the master?   Rd 2.2

   A. strict   B. worrisome   C. kind-hearted   D. hard-working

33. What type of figurative language does the author use in the first paragraph of the excerpt of *Black Beauty*?   Rd 2.2

   A. metaphor   B. hyperbole   C. euphemism   D. imagery

34. What conclusion can the reader make about the life of the young horse called Darkie?   Rd 1.8

   A. It was carefree and fun.   C. He was malnourished.
   B. It was difficult.   D. He was too rambunctious.

Speech
Excerpt of Speech by Mark Twain in Praise of George Washington, Feb. 22, 1902

Did Washington's great value, then, lie in what he accomplished? No; that was only a minor value. His major value, his vast value, his immeasurable value to us and to the world and to future ages and peoples, lies in his permanent and sky-reaching conspicuousness as an influence.

We are made, brick by brick, of influences, patiently built up around the framework of our born dispositions. It is the sole process of construction; there is no other. Every man and woman and child is an influence; a daily and hourly influence which never ceases from work, and never ceases from affecting for good or evil the characters about it—some contributing gold-dust, some contributing trash-dust, but in either case helping on the building, and never stopping to rest. The shoemaker helps to build his two-dozen associates; the pickpocket helps to build his four-dozen associates; the village clergyman helps to build his five hundred associates; the renowned bank-robber's name and fame help to build his hundred associates and three-thousand persons whom he has never seen; the renowned philanthropist's labors and the benevolent millionaire's gifts to kindly works and generous outlays of money move a hundred-thousand persons whom they have never met and never will meet; and to the building of the character of every individual thus moved these movers have added a brick.

The unprincipled newspaper adds a baseness to a million decaying character-fabrics every day; the high-principled newspaper adds a daily betterment to the character-fabric of another million. The swiftly-enriched wrecker and robber of railway systems lowers the commercial morals of a whole nation for three generations.

A Washington, standing upon the world's utmost summit, eternally visible, eternally clothed in light, a serene, inspiring, heartening example and admonition, is an influence which raises the level of character in all receptive men and peoples, alien and domestic; and the term of its gracious work is not measurable by fleeting generations, but only by the lingering march of the centuries.

It was Washington's influence that made Lincoln and all other real patriots the Republic has known; it was Washington's influence that made the soldiers who saved the Union; and that influence will save us always, and bring us back to the fold when we stray.

And so, when a Washington is given us, or a Lincoln, or a Grant, what should we do? Knowing, as we do, that a conspicuous influence for good is worth more than a billion obscure ones, without doubt the logic of it is that we should highly value it, and make a vestal flame of it, and keep it briskly burning in every way we can—in the nursery, in the school, in the college, in the pulpit, in the newspaper —even in Congress, if such a thing were possible.

35. Which of the following best explains the author's bias?　　　　　　　　　　　Rd 1.4
    A. Twain is unbiased, objectively describing Washington as a president.
    B. Twain is biased against Washington and describes his shortcomings in detail.
    C. Twain is unbiased as he explains the lives of various presidents.
    D. Twain shows bias in favor of Washington and feels he was an excellent president.
    　　　　　　　　　　　　　　　　　　　　　　　　　　　　　　　　C 1.1

36. Which of the following would be the most effective way for Twain to have delivered his speech?

    A. to speak in a monotone and pace around　　　　C. to speak loudly and with feeling

    B. to speak softly and quickly　　　　　　　　　　D. to speak angrily to make his point

37. If you were giving a speech intended to persuade people that Washington was the most effective president we have had, which of the following would most likely serve as the best conclusion?
    A. As you can see, the various contributions made by Washington have made him our most effective president to date.
    B. Washington did the best with what he had.　　　　　　　　　　　　　C 1.5
    C. Washington messed up a lot, but he did pretty good for the most part.
    D. The United States has seen many good leaders, and many stand out as representatives of what a president should be.

38. Which of the following sources would probably provide the most accurate information on Washington as a president? Rd 2.2

    A.   recorded memories of citizens
    B.   political cartoons dedicated to his presidency
    C.   stories written about his life
    D.   historical books written about his life

39. Which of the following dictionary definitions of the word "baseness" is correct as it is used in the speech? Rd 3.3

    A.   Devoid of high values or ethics: *a base, degrading way of life.*
    B.   Containing inferior substances: *a base metal.*
    C.   Of low birth, rank, or position.
    D.   Short in stature.

40. Which source would provide information with the least amount of bias about Washington's presidency? Rd 2.2

    A.   biographies about Washington
    B.   memoirs written by Washington
    C.   opinions of current politicians
    D.   various speeches about Washington

41. In the passage, conspicuousness is to plainness as Rd 3.4

    A.   past is to history.
    B.   bright is to dull.
    C.   importance is to significance.
    D.   variation is to change.

42. Which of the following words is closest in meaning to the word "summit" as it is used in the passage? Rd 3.2

    A.   level   B.   mountain   C.   pitfall   D.   outrage

Greatest Fans

1 My friends Serena and Hogan are the greatest fans of a new band called Broken Glass.

2 Serena liked them when she first heard them. **3** But she became a really big fan when she saw them at the Tri-State Fair last summer. **4** When she realized Hogan was also a fan, the two of them spent hours researching the band on the Internet, emailing the fan club, and asking for ways to contact the band members.

5 Imagine their surprise when they found out some of the members are from our hometown. **6** Hogan was in shock when he found out his older brother knew two of the band members from the marching band.

7 Serena and Hogan were able to get in touch with the lead singer, and they begged the band to come play at the local hangout. **8** Lucky for us, they were successful!

9 Next month, Broken Glass is going to perform a big concert with most of the proceeds going to the local food bank. **10** The food bank is run from the church close to Serena's house.

11 As for Serena and Hogan, their picture will be in the paper, they will help host the concert, and they will get to go backstage with the band. **12** Hogan says he now has a whole new career plan; he wants to be a concert promoter.

43. Which sentence most effectively combines sentences 2 and 3? W 1.4

   A. Serena liked them when she first heard them, but she became a really big fan when she saw them at the Tri-State Fair last summer.

   B. Serena liked them when she first heard them: she became a really big fan when she saw them at the Tri-State Fair last summer.

   C. Serena liked them when she first heard them; she became a really big fan when she saw them at the Tri-State Fair last summer.

   D. Serena liked them when she first heard them, furthermore she became a really big fan when she saw them at the Tri-State Fair last summer.

44. Which sentence interrupts the logical flow of ideas? W 1.2

   A. sentence 3   B. sentence 8   C. sentence 10   D. sentence 12

45. Where is the most logical place to put sentence number 8? W 1.2

   A. immediately after sentence 9   C. immediately after sentence 11
   B. immediately after sentence 10   D. correct as is

46. Which word best describes the tone of the author? Rd 2.2

   A. bored   B. ecstatic   C. jealous   D. supportive

47. What was the author's main purpose for writing the passage? Rd 1.5

   A. To relate the actions of Serena and Hogan and the outcome.
   B. To describe the effects of music on teenagers.
   C. To explain how Serena and Hogan became friends.
   D. To encourage people to attend the upcoming concert.

48. What can the reader predict will be the outcome of the concert? Rd 1.8

   A. The concert will have to be cancelled because the band will decide to go on tour.
   B. The concert will bring Serena and Hogan together, and they will decide to start a band of their own.
   C. The concert will be a success, and it will bring in money for the food bank.
   D. The concert will be unsuccessful because few people like the band.

Flamingo Mania

1 What's pink and hangs out in your Grandma's yard or maybe even your own yard?

2 Yes, the all-American favorite — flamingoes.

3 Well, at least plastic ones.

4 The brightly colored lawn ornaments were first made in 1957 and have become a symbol of the entire decade.

5 They are sold in sets of two, and more than 20 million sets have been sold by the original manufacturer of lawn flamingoes.

6 Something about the birds manages to put a smile on people's faces, and putting a whole flock in someone's yard has become a popular practical joke. **7** In fact, one club used that trend as a fund raising project. **8** People could pay to have a friend's yard "flamingo-ed."

9 But the intended victims were not helpless. **10** They could buy "flamingo insurance," and even if a friend paid to have their yard flamingoed, the insurance policy prevented the disaster from taking place.

11 Aside from lawns, flamingoes and drawings of flamingoes show up in all sorts of places. **12** You can see flamingoes hanging in tropical themed restaurants and printed on Hawaiian-style shirts. **13** Souvenirs with flamingoes on them are a popular collector's item.

14 Although real flamingoes are extinct in the wild, they can be seen in bird sanctuaries, zoos, and resort hotel gardens.

15 But the plastic ones are everywhere!

49. Which of the following best explains the author's bias in the passage? Rd 1.4
    A. The author is unbiased, explaining the popularity of flamingoes.
    B. The author is biased in favor of flamingoes, believing everyone should own a pair of lawn flamingoes.
    C. The author is biased against flamingoes, believing lawn flamingoes are tacky.
    D. The author is unbiased, explaining the similarity between live flamingoes and lawn flamingoes.

50. Based on the passage, what can the reader conclude about lawn flamingoes? Rd 1.8
    A. They are swiftly losing popularity.
    B. They have been and will continue to be popular items.
    C. They have been viewed negatively, but are quickly becoming more popular.
    D. It is time to invest in a pair because they will soon become collector's items.

51. Which of the following best explains the purpose of the passage? Rd 1.5
    A. To encourage people to perchance lawn flamingoes
    B. To persuade people to donate money to zoos who breed flamingoes
    C. To encourage people to open tropical themed restaurants
    D. To explain the popularity of flamingoes

52. Which of the following definitions of the word "sanctuaries" is correct as it is used in the passage?

Rd 3.3

A. A sacred place, such as a church, temple, or mosque.

B. A sacred place, such as a church, in which fugitives formerly were immune to arrest.

C. A place of refuge or asylum.

D. A reserved area in which birds and other animals, especially wild animals, are protected from hunting or molestation.

53. Which of the following is the best revision of sentence 6?

W 1.4

A. Something about the pink birds manages to put a smile on people's faces, and putting a whole flock in someone's yard has become a popular practical joke.

B. Something about the fine-feathered friends manages to put a smile on people's faces, and putting a whole flock in someone's yard has become a popular practical joke.

C. Something about the pink, long-legged birds manages to put a smile on people's faces, and putting a whole flock in someone's yard has become a popular practical joke.

D. Something about the plastic birds manages to put a smile on people's faces, and putting a whole flock in someone's yard has become a popular practical joke.

54. If you were going to give a speech based on this passage, which of the following would be the most effective visual aid?

C 1.1

A. a lawn flamingo

B. a picture of a flamingo

C. a Hawaiian shirt

D. various souvenirs depicting flamingoes

55. What is the author's tone in the passage?

Rd 2.2

A. cynical

B. humorous

C. angry

D. nostalgic

EVALUATION CHART FOR SOUTH CAROLINA EOC DIAGNOSTIC TEST

Directions: On the following chart, circle the question numbers that you answered incorrectly, and evaluate the results. These questions are based on the South Carolina standards for reading and research. Then turn to the appropriate topics (listed by chapters), read the explanations, and complete the exercises. Review other chapters as needed. Finally, complete the practice test(s) to assess your progress and further prepare you for the South Carolina EOC Test.

*Note: Some question numbers may appear under multiple chapters because those questions require demonstration of multiple skills.

Chapters	Diagnostic Test Question
Chapter 1: Word Meanings	1, 4, 8, 14, 22, 39, 41, 42, 52
Chapter 2: Research and Resource Materials	13, 15, 16
Chapter 3: Presentations	12, 36, 37, 54
Chapter 4: Author's Purpose and Tone	2, 35, 47, 49, 51
Chapter 5: Inferences and Conclusions	3, 11, 19, 34, 48, 50
Chapter 6: Elements of Literature	27, 28, 29
Chapter 7: Literary Devices and Story Structure	5, 10, 17, 18, 25, 26, 30, 31, 32, 33, 38, 40, 46, 55
Chapter 8: Planning the Extended Response	
Chapter 9: Drafting the Extended Response	7, 24, 44, 45
Chapter 10: Revising the Extended Response	9, 43, 53
Chapter 11: Proofreading the Extended Response	6, 20, 21, 23

Chapter 1
Word Meanings

This chapter covers the following South Carolina end-of-course exam items:	
Reading 3.2	*Demonstrate the ability to use context analysis to determine the meanings of unfamiliar or multiple-meaning words.*
Reading 3.3	*Demonstrate the ability to use context analysis to use a general dictionary, a specialized dictionary, and a thesaurus.*
Reading 3.4	*Demonstrate the ability to use analogies, idioms, and words with precise connotations and denotations in a variety of oral, written, and graphic presentations.*

Words in every language are symbols for some object or idea. For example, look at the word "water." There is nothing about those letters, W-A-T-E-R, that are like real water. But reading the word brings to mind a clear, cold liquid. If you speak only English, the words *agua* and *l'eau* don't mean the same thing. To speakers of Spanish and French, however, those words do mean "water." Words convey meaning. So to learn new words in a language, you need to learn skills to decode what the letters are symbolizing or what the words mean. There are many methods for finding **word meaning**. The most basic method is what you are doing now. You are reading these words and putting them together to make sense of their meaning in this sentence. When we understand the *words*, we can understand the *ideas*, or *objects*, behind the words.

Usually, the first method for understanding word meaning is by using a good **dictionary** and **thesaurus**. The dictionary is a report on words and their uses. The amount of information in a good dictionary includes more than just correct spelling. It may contain a dozen or more kinds of information. The thesaurus is a dictionary of synonyms and antonyms. It is a treasure house for developing new word usage.

Another very important method is understanding **context clues**. **Context** refers to the words and ideas in the text surrounding a word. This text holds clues to the meaning of individual words. The context can also help you understand how the meaning of the word is being used according to the author's tone or purpose. This is called the **denotative** (apparent or surface) meaning or **connotative** (emotional) meaning of words. If you use a word without taking into account the emotional effect, you may send the wrong message to your audience.

The next method of studying word meaning is to understand both the **literal** (exact) and **figurative** (exaggerated) meanings of words. When the literal meaning doesn't make sense, we try alternative understandings. Figurative language is more picturesque and conveys meaning that is hard to convey in ordinary words. It is used in poetry, fiction, and everyday speech. Common figurative sayings are called **idioms**. You may have encountered idioms when you learned a new language. Usually, idioms can't be translated; they have to be learned, much like vocabulary words.

Becoming fluent in unlocking the meaning of unfamiliar words will add pleasure and profit to your reading and writing. Reading daily will develop and increase your vocabulary.

WORD MEANING

Instant Messenger™ mail, TV commercials, political speeches, and highway billboards have two things in common: They want to get your attention and send you a message. For the message to have meaning, you must *know* the words being used and *how* they are being used. The next few pages will list some of the strategies for developing an understanding of word meaning.

CONTEXT CLUES

One important method of finding the meaning of words is by using **context clues**. This means to look at the way words are used in combination with other words in their setting. Look at the words around an unknown word. Think about the meaning of these words or the idea of the whole sentence. Then, match the meaning of the unknown word to the meaning of the known text.

In the following examples, choose the word which best reflects the meaning of the bolded word.

1. Green algae remain **dormant** until rains revive them.

   A. dry   B. dead   C. small   D. inactive

2. Exercise that increases your heart and breathing rates for a sustained period of time is called **aerobic**.

   A. of long duration   C. requiring oxygen

   B. improving strength   D. strenuous

If the bolded words above are unfamiliar to you, there are several ways in which you can still determine their meaning. Using context clues is the most common strategy. For example, in question 1, the clause "until rains revive them" suggests that dormant is not a **dead** state but an **inactive** one, since the rains make the algae active again. In addition, the signal word "until" tells us that **dormant** is the opposite of **revive**. When two words are compared in this way, it is called a **contrast clue**.

For question 2, you may use a **definition clue**. The signal word "is" indicates that the definition of aerobic is described in the first part of the sentence. Since heart and breathing rates are *increased* and all organisms need oxygen to live, aerobic must mean "requiring oxygen."

Context clues help us determine the meaning of words from the way they are used in a sentence. The idea or message of the whole text becomes clearer if we use the correct meaning. By looking at and analyzing the phrases and signal words that come before or after a particular word, you can often figure out its meaning. Below you will find a list of the main types of context clues with their signal words.

Context Clues	Signal Words
Comparison	*also, like, resembling, too, both, than* Look for clues that indicate an unfamiliar word is similar to a familiar word or phrase. **Example:** The utility pole was *felled* by the accident like a tree for timber.
Contrast	*but, however, while, instead of, yet, unlike* Look for clues that indicate an unfamiliar word is opposite in meaning to a familiar word or phrase. **Example:** Stephanie is usually in a state of *composure* while her sister is mostly boisterous.
Definition or Restatement	*is, or, that is, in other words, which* Look for words that define the term or restate it in other words. **Example:** The principle's idea is to *circuit*—or move around—the campus weekly to make sure everything is okay.
Example	*or example, for instance, such as* Look for examples used in context that reveal the meaning of an unfamiliar word. **Example:** People use all sorts of *vehicles* such as cars, bicycles, airplanes, boats, and motorcycles.

Practice 1: Using Context Clues

Above each bolded word, write its meaning. Use context clues to help you.

1. Those who cannot afford **bail** cannot be freed on pre-trial release.

2. Hank said the ocean was very **tranquil;** I also thought the ocean was peaceful.

3. Sometimes strong **herbicides** are needed to eliminate weeds from the garden.

4. **Residues** such as ammonia even show up in grain sprayed with **pesticides**.

5. Since Brian disliked working for others, he decided to become an **entrepreneur**.

6. This word is **ambiguous**; it can have two meanings.

7. Jennifer wanted no **remuneration** in money or gifts; her reward was saving the pet.

8. He was a **fastidious** dresser, always very neat and particular about what he wore

9. After a **cursory** examination of only a minute or two, the doctor said he did not believe there was anything seriously wrong with the child.

10. Smoking too much is likely to have a **pernicious** effect on one's health; they're not called "cancer sticks" for nothing.

11. The bad odor from the leaking gas **permeated** the whole house.

Working with individual sentences is good practice. However, for a true practice of what you will be working with for classes and for any type of reading assessment, you will need to practice with longer passages of text.

Practice 2: Passage Practice

Read the following article. Then, answer the questions that follow.

What Is Ethics, Anyway?

Ethics is a concept we hear about, but few people today stop to think what it really means. However, philosophers and statesmen since the time of Plato have **contemplated** the definition and details of ethics, which is sometimes difficult to state. Clearly, ethics is not something invented by one person or even a society, but has some well-founded standards on which it is based.

Some people **equate** ethics with feelings. But being ethical is not simply following one's feelings. A criminal may "feel" robbing a person is okay, when really it is wrong and unethical to steal. Many people may identify ethics with religion, and it is true that most religions include high ethical standards and strong motivation for people to behave morally. But ethics cannot be confined only to religion, or only religious people could be ethical. There are even cases in which religious teaching and ethics clash: for example, some religions **inhibit** the rights of women, which opposes the ethical standard of basic justice.

Ethics also is not simply following laws or what is accepted by a society. The laws of civilized nations often **embody** ethical standards. However, unethical laws can exist. For example, laws have allowed slavery, which is unethical behavior as it takes the freedom of another human being. Therefor, laws and other conventions accepted by a society cannot be the measure for what is ethical. Doing "whatever society accepts" may be far outside the realm of ethics—Nazi Germany is an example of an ethically **debased** society.

What ethics really refers to is a system of people's moral standards and values. It's like a road map of qualities that people want to have to be "decent human beings." It is also the formal study of the standards of human behavior. Ethics relies on well-based standards of "right" (like honesty, compassion, and loyalty) and "wrong" (like stealing, murder, and fraud). Ethical standards **encompass** ideas such as respect for others, honesty, justice, doing good, and preventing harm.

1. In the context of this passage, what does the word **contemplated** mean?
   - A. thought about
   - B. looked at
   - C. taken apart
   - D. peered into

2. In the context of this passage, which of the following is closest in meaning to **equate**?
   - A. compare
   - B. multiply
   - C. balance
   - D. flatten

3. In this passage, which of the following is closest in meaning to the word **inhibit**?
   - A. lie about
   - B. live in
   - C. give to
   - D. hold back

4. Which dictionary definition of the word **debased** best applies to its use in the passage?
   - A. depraved
   - B. corrupt
   - C. impure
   - D. distorted

5. In this passage, which of the following is closest in meaning to the word **encompass**?
   - A. steer
   - B. include
   - C. begin
   - D. mean

CONNOTATIONS AND DENOTATIONS

One important part of word choice is knowing the difference between the **connotations** (emotional associations) and the **denotations** (dictionary meanings) of words. For example, the words *delicate* and *fragile* can both mean "easily broken." However, if you told a ballerina that her movements were *delicate*, the ballerina would probably thank you. But, if you told her that her movements were *fragile*, she would probably be offended. While both of these words **denote** "easily broken," the **connotation** of *delicate* is positive while that of *fragile* can be negative.

Now read the following sentence from O. Henry's short story, "The Last Leaf." Notice how the denotations and connotations of his words enrich the description of Greenwich Village:

> "In November, a cold, unseen stranger whom the doctors called Pneumonia, stalked about the colony, touching one here and there with his icy fingers."

O. Henry uses words like "cold," "stranger," "stalked," and "icy fingers" because of their strong connotations. The connotation of the four words together leads to an emotional reaction: they bring up the image or feeling of danger, the grave, or the angel of death.

At the same time, we must understand the denotations of words like "doctors" and "Pneumonia" to fully understand that the sentence is referring to a serious illness that medicine could name, but sometimes not cure. Today, pneumonia is rarely fatal.

Practice 3: Analyzing Passages for Connotation and Denotation

Read the description below of Ichabod Crane from "The Legend of Sleepy Hollow" by Washington Irving. In a small group or on your own, list 5–6 words with connotations that give a more vivid description of Ichabod Crane. Were there any words having only denotations? Discuss your findings with the class or your teacher.

Ichabod was a suitable figure for such a steed. He rode with short stirrups, which brought his knees nearly up to the pommel of the saddle; his sharp elbows stuck out like grasshoppers'; he carried his whip perpendicularly in his hand, like a scepter, and, as his horse jogged on, the motion of his arms was not unlike the flapping of a pair of wings. A small wool hat rested on the top of his nose, for so his scanty strip of forehead might be called; and the skirts of his black coat fluttered out almost to the horse's tail. Such was the appearance of Ichabod and his steed, as they shambled out of the gate of Hans Van Ripper, and it was altogether such an apparition as seldom to be met with in broad daylight.

Practice 4: Connotations and Denotations—A Last Look

A. Ads and Connotations: Look at the ads in your favorite magazine. We all try to ignore the advertisements. They are full of emotional appeals designed to make you want to spend your money on their products. For example, a famous ad reads, "We <u>want</u> to see you <u>smile</u>." For the word "want," the words *wish* or *need* could be used; they mean the same thing. However, *wish* has the connotation of something unlikely to happen, and *need* has the connotation of desperation. For the word "smile," the words *grin* or *smirk* could be used. These last two, while meaning the same facial movement, have negative connotations, and the company wanting you to feel totally comfortable, avoids using them. Look at several ads and note the words that are used to make a reader feel good about the product. Write words that could be used instead but have a negative connotation.

ANALOGIES

Analogies are a way of explaining or describing something unfamiliar or difficult to explain by comparing it with something familiar. You probably use analogies every day. Think about how often you have described something to a friend by using comparisons. A new rock band's style of music may be "like" another band that is well known. By using analogies, a writer or speaker gives the audience a concrete example and creates a mental picture of an object or idea. When you are writing (or speaking), try to think about analogies and how to use them to the best advantage to make your writing colorful and memorable.

Analogies are a type of figurative language and can be expressed as **similes** or **metaphors**. Similes are comparisons that use the words "like" or "as"; an example would be "Lisa's voice is like an angel's voice." Metaphors are direct comparisons that state something is something else. To express the same example as a metaphor, you might say "Lisa's voice is the voice of an angel." Although we may not literally know what an angel's voice sounds like, we have an idea in our mind that we will think of when someone compares Lisa's voice to an angel's voice.

Practice 5: Identifying Analogies

Read the following statements, and find the relationship between the words in the first part of each. Then choose the answer that shows the same relationship or a similar one. Write the letter of your choice on the answer line. Use your dictionary to look up the meanings of any unfamiliar words.

1. studying is to school as singing is to _____.
   A. playing   B. chorus   C. clapping   D. birds

2. dense is to sink as _____ is to float.
   A. raft   B. buoyant   C. Styrofoam   D. depth marker

3. grandmother is to granddaughter as ancestor is to _____.
   A. descendant   B. cousin   C. grandfather   D. parent

4. weak is to strong as _____ is to robust.
   A. muscular   B. energetic   C. body builder   D. frail

5. think is to cogitate as conclude is to _____.
   A. restrict   B. unfinished   C. deduce   D. immature

6. minor : *faux pas* :: serious : _____.
   A. blunder   B. insignificant   C. informal   D. dinky

7. spinning : dizzy :: relaxing : _____.
   A. excited   B. ready   C. sleepy   D. eating

8. burn : scar :: pierce : _____.
   A. ear   B. through   C. hole   D. nail

9. island : ocean :: mountain : _____.
   A. river   B. valley   C. cave   D. continent

10. dragonfly : eagle :: minnow : _____.
    A. tadpole   B. shark   C. algae   D. goldfish

LITERAL AND FIGURATIVE MEANINGS

One of the most important things to understand about word meaning is that a word or words can be used in different ways. An author may choose words to tell plain facts, or an author may choose words to give the text a double meaning or to add imagery (pictures in words).

Literal language is words used in their ordinary meaning without exaggeration or inventiveness. Dictionary definitions are written in literal terms. For example, "It is time to feed the *cats and dogs*." This phrase "cats and dogs" is used in a literal sense for the animals are hungry, and it is time for them to eat.

Figurative language departs from the ordinary meanings of words to emphasize ideas and emotions. Figurative language paints word pictures and allows us to "see" a point. For example: "It is raining *cats and dogs*!" Cats and dogs do not really fall from the sky like rain as this graphic illustrates. This expression is an **idiom**. An idiom is a common expression (in a particular language) that has a figurative or imaginative meaning. This sentence really means that the rain is heavy or hard. In this case, it would be difficult or impossible to decide the meaning of an unknown word from the surrounding text.

There are two ways to handle this situation. First, understand the author's purpose for writing a piece of text. If the text is a science book, an employee manual, or a government form, the text's purpose would be to inform. The language in those texts would most likely be literal or factual. Using context clues for these texts would benefit you in finding word meanings. If the text's purpose is to entertain or tell a story, however, context clues may not always work. These kinds of texts often use *idioms, similes, metaphors* and other *figures of speech* to convey ideas or emotions.

The second way to avoid confusion with the figurative use of words is to become familiar with different idiomatic phrases and with the different types of figurative language: metaphor, simile, personification, hyperbole, etc. A listing and explanation of these different types of figurative language devices may be found in Chapter 7 of this book.

Practice 6: Idioms

Read the sentences below, decide the meaning of the **bolded** words or phrases, and think about how you came up with those meanings. On your own paper, write an explanation of the meaning of each word or phrase and how you decided on this meaning.

1. The Nelsons go swimming **once in a blue moon.**

2. Filing tax forms is no one's **cup of tea**.

3. Eating octopus and squid is just **not my cup of tea.**

4. She's a **big cheese** in the Treasury Department, so you should listen to her.

5. Continuing in the **fast lane** of Hollywood society will cost him financially.

Here is an example of how to do a careful reading for context clues for the first three sentences. Compare the notes you made on those sentences with the following notes

---

READING NOTES:

1. The word "Nelsons" begins with a capital letter, so it must be a family name -- "go" is a verb meaning to move or travel -- "swimming" is known -- "once" is a count of some sort, usually a time -- "blue moon" is not known but the moon is often used to figure time.   I think that the swimming is a family activity that this family does not do very often. "once in a blue moon" sounds close to "once in a while," an idiom

2. "Filing" is a verb meaning putting paperwork in order -- "tax" is known to me, what you pay the government -- "forms" are documents or paperwork -- "no one" is nobody -- "cup of tea" -- normally means a drinking cup with hot liquid in it. I think that since most of the sentence is about bad stuff, taxes and paperwork, and nobody likes it so a cup of tea must be good. an idiom

3. "Eating octopus and squid" would be disgusting, and not at all pleasing to me, as a cup of tea certainly would. - an idiom

---

Do your notes follow this type of reading? You may go back and change anything you want to in your notes, and discuss with your class the meanings that you decided on for sentences 4 and 5. Then complete the next practice.

Practice 7:   Literal and Figurative Meanings

A. Read each of the following sentences. Using context clues and your own knowledge, decide and indicate if the underlined part is literal or figurative language. If you mark a phrase as figurative language, write the meaning on the line.

1. The spy set up a <u>red herring</u> to distract the police.

   ___literal OR ___figurative meaning _____

2. The new guy is making a lot of errors, but <u>his heart is in the right place</u>.

   ___literal OR ___figurative meaning _____

3. The extravagant pet food we get for my dog is <u>good for his heart</u>.

   ___literal OR ___figurative meaning _____

4. Seeing the puppies with their new owners <u>does my heart good</u>.

   ___literal OR ___figurative meaning _____

5. <u>Falling off a log</u> into dangerous mountain rivers can cause serious injuries

   ___literal OR ___figurative meaning _____

6. Fishing is as easy as <u>falling off a log</u>.

   ___literal OR ___figurative meaning _____

B. Read each of the following sentences and notice the figurative language. On your own paper, explain the figures of speech. The first one has been done as an example.

7. The view from our hotel window was as pretty as a picture.

   Pictures (photos or paintings) that people hang on walls are usually chosen because they are attractive, so the view from the hotel window was just as good as one of those types of pictures.

8. The noise from the classroom next door sounded like a herd of elephants.

9. Grandpa is as stubborn as a mule.

10. Chad went around the room introducing himself like a politician running for re-election.

11. My nephew is a real Bart Simpson.

12. The chrome on Jason's antique car was as shiny as a new dime.

DICTIONARY SKILLS

Dictionary - a reference book listing words in alphabetical order. For each word, a dictionary generally includes spelling, pronunciation, definitions, parts of speech, usage, etymology or word origin, and sometimes synonyms and antonyms. The kinds of information given in a dictionary are described in detail below.

Word Division	Each word is divided into a syllable or syllables. Each syllable is pronounced with a single sounding of the voice. For example, the word **swallow** is divided into two syllables, **swal** and **low**. In a dictionary, this is written as **swal·low**.
Principal parts	Each verb in a dictionary entry is immediately followed by the principal parts of that verb. For instance, the verb **see** is found in the different verb tenses as **saw, seen,** and **see′ ing**
Pronunciation	Each entry in a dictionary is followed by its pronunciation. For example, the word **radius** is pronounced **ray-dee-uhss** (**ra de us**). Consult a pronunciation guide in the in the front of the dictionary if you are unsure of how to pronounce a symbol. **(Example:** $\bar{e}$ **is ee)**
Plural form	Some words in a dictionary entry are also shown in their plural form. For example, the word **child** in the dictionary is immediately followed by the plural form, **children.**
Part of speech	Each dictionary entry also notes which part of speech the entry word is. Before the first definition or entry, the part of speech will appear in italics as an abbreviation. Here is a list of each part of speech and its abbreviation:

transitive verb = *vt.*   adjective = *adj.*

intransitive verb =*vi.*   preposition = *prep.*

noun = *n.*   conjunction = *conj.*

adverb = *adv.*   interjection = *interj.*

pronoun = *pron.*   article = *article*

Example: the word **holiness** is a noun, so the abbreviation *n.* appears after the word.

Definition	Each dictionary entry also contains a definition. A definition is the meaning of the entry word. **(Example: mascot - any person, animal, or thing supposed to bring good luck)** Sometimes there are several definitions listed for each entry word.
Etymology	The etymology (word origin) of each word is also part of each dictionary entry. Consult the etymology guide in the front of the dictionary to discover the meanings of the abbreviations. **(Example: OE means Old English, Fr means French, L means Latin, GR means Greek)**
Synonyms	Synonyms (words having similar meaning to the entry word) and antonyms (words having the opposite meaning to the entry word) are also commonly placed at the end of a dictionary entry. **(Example: raise - *v.* to cause to rise. SYN. See LIFT)**

The following is an example of a dictionary entry:

> **gris·ly** (griz′ lē) **adj.**[ME *grislich*] terrifying; horrible - SYN. See GHASTLY

From this definition, we know that the word **grisly** is divided into two syllables as gris·ly. We also know that **grisly** is an adjective. This word came from Middle English and has **ghastly** as a synonym.

Here is another dictionary entry:

> **cher·ry** (cher′ ē) **n., pl. -ries.** [OFr. *cerise*] 1. a small fleshy fruit containing a smooth, hard pit and ranging from yellow to very dark red   2. any of various trees (genus *Prunus)* of the rose family which bear this fruit

From this entry, we know that the word **cherry** is correctly divided as cher·ry. We also know that **cherry** is a noun and that the plural form is spelled **cherries**. The word is derived from Old French and does not have any synonyms or antonyms.

Practice 8:   Dictionary Skills

Read the following dictionary entries. Fill in the appropriate blanks with the correct answer.

1.

> **know** (nō) **vt. knew, known, know′ing** [ME *knowen*] 1. to have a clear perception or understanding of; to be sure or well-informed about (to *know* the truth) to be aware or cognizant of; have perceived or learned (to *know* that one is in control). SYN. See UNDERSTAND

A.	Word Division_____	D.	Pronunciation
B.	Part of Speech_____	E.	Verb Parts_____
C.	Etymology_____	F.	Synonym_____

2.

> **flur·ry** (flur′ ē) **n., pl, -ries** [unk] 1. a sudden, brief rush of wind; gust 2. a gust of rain or snow 3. a sudden confusion or commotion.

A.	Word Division_____	D.	Pronunciation
B.	Part of Speech_____	E.	Verb Parts_____
C.	Etymology_____	F.	Synonym_____

THESAURUS

Thesaurus - a book containing lists of synonyms and antonyms in alphabetical order. A thesaurus improves writing and one's knowledge of words.

Thesaurus Entry
88. HEIGHT

NOUNS

1. height, tip, stature, elevation

2. top, highest point, ceiling, zenith

3. hill, knoll, volcano, mountain

VERBS

4. heighten, elevate, raise, rear, erect

5. intensify, strengthen, increase, advance

6. command, rise above, crown, surmount

ADJECTIVES

7. high, towering, exalted, supreme

Antonyms: depth, descent

For Questions 1 – 3, circle the word that would best provide a synonym for the italicized word in each sentence below. Then answer questions 4–8.

1. With a *height* of 20,320 feet, Mt. McKinley is an impressive sight.   **stature   top   elevation**

2. The *high* skyscraper stood in the center of the city.   **exalted   supreme   towering**

3. The frequent thunder *heightened* our fears for Latasha's safety.   **intensified   erected   crowned**

4. T or F   **Increase** is the same part of speech as heighten.

5. T or F   A mountain is lower than a hill.

6. What part of speech is **height**? _____

7. What are the antonyms for **height**? _____

8. List the synonyms for **high**. _____

CHAPTER 1 REVIEW

A. Read each of the following statements, and choose the best meaning of the **bolded** word as used in the sentence.

1. Fort Moultrie on Sullivan's Island is a visible **remnant** of both the American Revolution and the Civil War.

   A. rubbish   B. stump   C. remainder   D. surplus

2. We were excited because Tanya is now **eligible** to play on the team.
   A. qualified   B. included   C. embraced   D. fit

3. The coach **intervened** to prevent a fight between the football players.
   A. hindered   B. came between   C. paused   D. interposed

4. Most mammals have strong **maternal** instincts to protect and take care of their young.
   A. nesting   B. fighting   C. fatherly   D. motherly

5. The **finale** of the concert was the best part of the show.
   A. opening   B. result   C. start   D. end

6. Can you **visualize** the day you will graduate from high school?
   A. picture   B. place   C. remember   D. plan

7. The University of South Carolina in Columbia has a $292.5 million **endowment** fund.
   A. talent   B. gift   C. ability   D. attributes

8. Bill Gates is perhaps the best known computer software **entrepreneur** in the United States and the world.
   A. rich man   B. schemer   C. spender   D. planner

B. Read the next passage, first for content. Then using context clues, answer the questions which follow. The following article offers information about squids and octopuses. Read the article and answer questions 9 through 17.

Shy Shadows: Octopus and Squid

As I watch, a shadow glides towards the ocean floor where it disappears into rocks which are pock-marked with holes and craters. I have had a close encounter with the world's first carnivorous predator. No, it is not the shark. My encounter has been with an octopus.

Luckily for me, the appetites of the two largest mollusks, octopus and squid, do not usually make them look at humans as dinner. These two prefer to dine on fish and crabs, being in the first active, or

hunting, family of animals. The predatory animals, the squid and the octopus, display unique behaviors and body systems.

Both of these marine animals are shy and quiet. When threatened, the octopus has been observed actually growing pale in color. This behavior provides an illusion of greater size and is a defensive action for the octopus. The octopus can also change colors to blend into the background around it. Another behavior or strategy that the octopus and the squid share is the ability to squirt a cloudy fluid which cuts down on the ability of possible attackers to see them.

The body feature that people think of when they think of an octopus or squid: the arms or tentacles. The octopus uses its arms also to move along the ocean floor as well as using a flow of water through its body to propel it along. It can take water into its body and then squirt the water out, propelling itself at a rapid pace. The squid differs only in that it does not use its arms to move. Instead, the squid stays suspended between the ocean floor and surface and moves only by the method of water propulsion. In fact, since the squid has no other means of movement, its body shape and muscles have become well suited to the water propulsion method, making it one of the fastest invertebrate (animal with no backbone) marine animals.

The squid is also one of the largest marine animals. There are theories that the old stories of sea monsters were spun by sailors who had seen giant squid. These squid can grow up to 70 feet (21.3 meters), and they have the largest eyes of any animal on earth. Oddly enough, no one has ever seen a living giant squid in its natural environment. Either it hides well, or the stories of sea monsters have a hold on even the most adventurous sea explorers. There are scientists now conducting new research off the coasts of New Zealand and Australia, trying to learn more about this intelligent behemoth of the deep.

Keeping an eye out for the marine creatures which do not turn down humans for lunch, I slowly head towards the rocks where the shadow has hidden. My time is running short, along with the air in my oxygen tanks. I must go back to my own world. Before I go, I catch a last glimpse of the creature, turned a reddish color to match the rocks behind it.

In numbers 9 –17, choose the answer which is closest in meaning to the **bolded** word in the sentences.

9. As predatory animals, the squid and the octopus display **unique** behaviors and body systems.
   A. varied   B. one of a kind   C. changeable   D. slimy and cold

10. This behavior provides an **illusion** of greater size and is a defensive action for the octopus.
    A. raw power   B. good excuse   C. safety net   D. false image

11. Instead, the squid stays **suspended** between the ocean floor and surface and moves only by the method of water propulsion.
    A. hung   B. twisted   C. bent   D. sewn

12. Instead, the squid stays suspended between the ocean floor and surface and moves only by the method of water **propulsion**.

    A. currents   B. power   C. propellers   D. buoyancy

13. The squid is also one of the largest **marine** animals.

    A. mammal   B. water   C. reptile   D. sea

14. There are scientists now **conducting** new research off the coasts of New Zealand and Australia, trying to learn more about this intelligent behemoth of the deep.

    A. speaking of   B. leaving   C. writing about   D. directing

15. How would the figurative phrase bolded in the sentence below be BEST written in a literal phrase?

    My time is running short, along with the air in my oxygen tanks.

    A. The time I have to breathe with the oxygen tanks is brief.
    B. My time is speeding away and taking the air with it.
    C. The time is too quick for me and my full oxygen tanks.
    D. My time is flying by and is using the air from my tanks.

16. How would the figurative phrase below be BEST written in a literal phrase?

    Keeping an eye out for the marine creatures which do not turn down humans for lunch, I slowly head towards the rocks where the shadow has hidden.

    A. Taking my goggles off of one eye   C. Being watchful for
    B. Injuring one eye   D. Using a special diving mask

17. In the following sentence, which replacement word would give the MOST positive, appropriate connotation to **encounter**?

    My **encounter** has been with an octopus.

    A. engagement   B. confrontation   C. brush   D. meeting

C. Each of the following sentences contains the word "bridge" used in a different sense or meaning. Other words or clues in the sentence tell you the type of specialized vocabulary it is related to. Underline the word(s) in the sentences that are the clues.

18. The dentist said I needed a bridge.

19. My violin needs repairs made to the bridge.

20. As the ship returned to the port, all of the officers gathered on the bridge and stood at attention.

21. "The bridge is broken" declared the doctors after examining the x-rays of my swollen nose.

D. Use the sample dictionary page to answer the questions that follow.

Sample Dictionary Page

dashboard - dassie

dash • board *n.* a panel under the windshield of the vehicle, containing indicator dials, compartments, and sometimes control instruments. [Scand. origin]

da • sheen *n.* a variety of the taro plant (sense 2). [origin unknown]

dash • er *n.* 1. one who dashes. 2. The plunger of a churn or ice cream freezer. 3. a spirited person

da • shi • ki *n.* a loose, brightly colored African tunic, usually worn by men. [Yoruba origin]

dash • ing *adj.* 1. audacious and gallant; spirited. 2. marked by showy elegance; splendid. - **da • shing • ly** *adv.*

dash • pot *n.* a piston-and-cylinder device used to reverse the motion of a machine.

das • sie *n.* the hyrax. [Afr. origin] dim. of das, badger [MDV]

---

22. What is the name for a brightly colored African tunic?

23. What is the adverb form of **dashing**?

24. What is the second definition for **dasher**?

25. Which word is of Scandinavian origin?

Chapter 2
Research and Resource Materials

This chapter covers the following South Carolina end-of-course exam items:	
Research 1.1	*Demonstrate the ability to ask questions to guide research inquiry.*
Research 1.2	*Demonstrate the ability to ask questions to investigate all aspects of a topic, including various viewpoints regarding it.*
Research 2.1	*Demonstrate the ability to distinguish between primary and secondary sources.*
Research 2.2	*Demonstrate the ability to evaluate the credibility of sources, including consideration of accuracy and bias.*
Research 2.4	*Demonstrate the ability to gather and evaluate information for its relevance to his or her research questions.*
Research 2.5	*Demonstrate the ability to refine a topic and ask additional questions based on the information that he or she has gathered.*

If you were thinking about getting running shoes, where would you buy them and how much would you pay? If you're a smart shopper, you would ask **key questions**, such as "Which store has the best selection?" and "Who might have a sale going on?" To answer these questions, you could browse through newspaper ads or scan the phone directory. Then you might call some stores near you to check prices and shoe availability. If you decided to shop at a mall, you might check the mall directory to find the shoe stores.

All of these activities are types of **research**: the study and investigation of some topic or field of knowledge. The ability to do research, and to choose and use **resource materials**, are essential life skills in today's society. Whether you are buying shoes, doing research in the library, or reading a schedule or map, you will face situations where you will need the right resources. Obtaining and using the information from these sources can help you answer questions or complete a task in school, at home, or on the job.

CHOOSING A TOPIC FOR RESEARCH

Sometimes a topic for research is obvious, as in the case of the new running shoes! Often, however, you will need to demonstrate that you can research a topic given to you, or you may have to **choose a topic** on your own. If you are choosing your own topic, the choices are almost endless. You will probably be given some guidelines as far as the general area of research you are to do. A good way to start your decision process is to think of a topic that you are truly interested in within the given guidelines.

Next, formulate your research question or questions. Based on your topic and your answers to "what I know" and "what I want to know," research questions help determine exactly what you will investigate. Here are some examples:

Topic:	ancient art of scrimshaw	hot peppers
What I know:	carvings in ivory; no longer done because ivory is protected	spices up food; can aid digestion; popular in certain cultures
What I want to know:	is anyone still doing it? what are the most creative & valuable examples?	how many kinds of spicy peppers are there? how else are they used?
Research question:	how did scrimshaw get started, and why did it end?	are hot peppers good for health? what are all their uses?

SOURCES FOR RESEARCH INFORMATION

Once you have chosen a topic and are ready to start researching, you will need to decide which sources to search. In addition to traditional resources such as books, periodicals, reference materials, and others, there are also sources like workplace, consumer, and public documents. Some of these resources contain **primary sources** (firsthand accounts of an event), and some are mostly made up of **secondary sources** (written about the event from a distance of time and place). When reading the material, you will need to choose the sources which have the best descriptions or current statistics for your topic. There are more options for finding informational material today than ever before. That is why the media says that we are living in the "Information Age."

TYPES OF RESOURCE MATERIALS

In this part of the chapter, you'll learn about the common structures and elements of important resource materials. You'll also practice answering questions about these resources. The following is a list of common primary and secondary sources.

Primary Sources	Secondary Sources
Public Speaking	Encyclopedia
Letters	Journals & Magazines
Diaries	Newspapers
Private Journals	Computer Software
Eyewitness Accounts	Internet

PRIMARY SOURCES

A **primary source** provides firsthand evidence about the event in question. Often, this is a document that was actually written at the time of the event, or shortly thereafter. Primary sources have the advantage of presenting a rendering of the events as a person actually experienced them, or, in the case of documents, providing data that was written down at the time the event occurred. This is an important advantage because stories become distorted as they are retold, and memories deteriorate overtime. For these reasons, historians usually prefer to work with primary source information. However, one must be careful to recognize that primary sources may reflect the point of view of a particular person or group. Because of this, they may not give all sides of the story. Examples of primary sources include: memoirs, public speeches, meeting minutes, journals or diaries, letters, applications, transcripts, notes, travel documents, land deeds, birth certificates, death certificates, marriage certificates and prison records.

SECONDARY SOURCES

Secondary sources present material secondhand or provide commentary or opinions on events, but the authors have not directly experienced those events. These resources include writing such as reviews, biographies, literary criticism, and so on. For example, let's say you are writing about the benefits of regular exercise. Your primary sources might include firsthand observations about your own exercise routine or that of others. You might also conduct an interview about exercise with your gym teacher or the school nurse. Secondary sources could be anything that someone else has written about the topic, such as recommendations from doctors, books about exercising, and reports of studies that attest to its advantages.

Practice 1: Primary and Secondary Sources

A. Determine which of these sources is a primary source and which is a secondary source.

1. *A Pocket Guide to Shakespeare's Plays*, K. McLeish & S. Unwin, editors (1998)   ____ P ____ S

2. *Memoirs of a Mountain Biker*, by D. Larrow (2003)   ____ P ____ S

3. "Top 10 Reading List for Young Adults," by T. Ratcher (Sep. 2004 issue)   ____ P ____ S

4. *The Age of Chivalry and Legends of Charlemagne* (1993)   ____ P ____ S

5. *My Little Town: 1915–1940*, by I. Jacobsen (1948)   ____ P ____ S

B. Become a Historical Figure: Using research, create a journal from any time period. Write it in your voice. Describe things and events fully so that anyone can read and understand what you are writing.

C. **Write a Letter to an Ancestor:** Research an important historical event that happened in your lifetime. Write a letter to a family member who lived before you, such as a great grandparent. Be sure to describe new technology in a way your audience will be able to understand. Remember, someone who lived in the 1800s will not know about airplanes, computers, or microwaves.

D. **Speaker of the House:** Write and deliver a speech to your family suggesting a change in policy. Write as if you are speaking to a public gathering or government officials. For example, deliver a speech encouraging your lawmakers (parents) to increase minimum wage (allowance).

FINDING AND EVALUATING RESEARCH SOURCES

Research should not be scary! We all do research: When you compare colleges or technical schools you may attend, you are conducting research. Using your topic and your research questions, you can list some **key words** that will guide your research efforts. Then, access research sources available from many places, including **libraries**, **book stores**, and **internet** sites. In some cases, people also do **field research**, meaning that they make firsthand observations or conduct interviews about a topic.

Have you ever used the internet and typed a single key word into a **search engine** (a site that enables searches of the World Wide Web)? If so, you know that there are so many Web sites on the internet that a single key word turns up an enormous and jumbled array of possible pages to view. If this is the case for your research topic, try narrowing your search by entering several of the key words at once, simply separated by a space. In that way, sites that contain *all* the key words will come up first.

COMPUTER RESEARCH

THE INTERNET

So much information is available on the internet today that it has changed the way we do research. If you are finishing a research paper and you have not yet gone "online," you have not exhausted the tools available to you. The ability to best find and use Web sites is a vital skill in this rapidly growing world of internet access. Whether you are looking for the best price for your spring break travel, finding out the details of a job you are applying for, or writing a paper for class, the internet is a valuable resource if used wisely and efficiently.

Using the internet can challenge your research skills. First, you must access various **search engines** such as Google, Yahoo, or Lycos to find the best Web sites about your topic. Then, you must **validate** the material, checking the site for its credibility or the material for accuracy. Next, you must decide how best to use the material and if it is an **appropriate** source for your topic. Finally, you need the skill of **safe research** on the World Wide Web.

VALIDATION: CHECKING SOURCES

Why should you bother with validating sources? After all, if you can find material on a Web site, it must be OK, right? No, not always. Many Web sites are created by students and ordinary citizens, who may believe what they have posted is true, but are mistaken in that belief: "Let the searcher beware!" Researchers protect their work by screening the material they find for quality and accuracy.

1. Find two or more sources that agree with the information you wish to use.

2. Read material carefully, watching for bias or particularly strong opinion expressed in it (also see Chapter 4 in this book for more details about bias).

3. Look at the URL (Uniform Resource Locator, otherwise known as the Web address) for the source of the material, which is usually an organization or individual. If the organization is an educational, government, or professional center, the material is probably valid.

4. Look for "links" within the text of a Web site; these are an indication of a serious, validated work (they're like footnotes in a book). Go to some of the linked sites to check the validity of the sources, as well as to find additional material.

5. Look at the homepage of the source for other related works by the author of the site. The more the author has published on a topic, the more trustworthy the material.

6. Check the date on the material. Obviously if your topic is on a current event, the more recent the date, the better the information. Also keep in mind that recent data and theories are valuable for any topic.

7. If you are using informal sources, such as chat rooms, for clustering or sharing ideas, again, the information needs to be confirmed by two or more other sources before it is validated.

Some sites on the internet have been validated already. These are listed in **database sites**. The organization which creates the database checks the material to ensure both accuracy and relevancy. Many databases are offered through educational organizations and are free to all. One example is *thinkquest.com,* a site that indexes award-winning, student-created Web sites. The site covers many topics and many levels of study. One word of caution: **Plagiarism** or copying directly from a source is a serious offense; be sure to always cite your internet sources. If you want to use a reproduction of material, as on this page, get written permission from the Web site owner to use it.

RESEARCHING ON THE INTERNET

The use of the internet, without special "safe" servers is basically unregulated and unguarded. This situation brings up concerns over credibility, safety, and privacy issues. The following is an informal listing of ways to make your internet use as safe and positive as possible. For more about safety, contact your internet provider.

1. Develop a "healthy distrust" of much of what you read on the Web. Databases are usually OK, but chat rooms and personal Web sites are open to all sorts of deceptions and second rate information, causing frustrating detours for you.

2. Always use a very different name to identify yourself on the internet and understand that others are doing the same as a safeguard or as a false identity. The exception to this is when you must provide your correct name or student identification to use library resources.

3. Understand that some sites have built-in roadblocks; there is no way for you to exit the site. Should you run into this trap, disconnect from your internet server, and then sign on again. You will also want to alert your teacher or the Webmaster about the problem.

4. Watch out for any online site or person asking you personal questions. This is a dangerous site. Do not respond to those questions and exit that site.

5. Use a **pop-up blocker** (usually provided as an option by your internet provider) to stop advertising from coming up constantly during your internet searches. If you do use such a blocker, be aware that some sites use pop-up technology to offer material that you will want to see, so learn how to turn off the blocker selectively.

Practice 2: Internet Activities

Follow the instructions for each step of this activity.

1. Choose one of the following controversial issues as a topic.

   • The causes of global warming

   • The effects of radiating food

   • The use of aluminum bats in Little League

   • Pro athletes using steroids

   • Television in schools

   • The protection of animal rights

   • The protection of human rights

   Do a search for your chosen topic on the internet, using key words and synonyms. Use three different options: search engines, databases, and chat rooms. Notice which options give you the best results.

2. Print two Web pages, each on a separate sheet of paper. Print one which contains mostly unsupported opinion and print another which relies on well-supported facts.

3. After printing, check to see that the URL is printed on the pages *before you leave the site*. You will need that URL for your "Works Cited" page or bibliography and for citing direct quotations. Any information taken off the internet must be acknowledged in one of several formats. Ask the teacher which documentation style is required for research citations. The most common are the MLA and APA styles of citing works, which are found in books about writing research papers.

4. Exchange printouts with others in the group. Discuss which are best for research and why.

CHOOSING THE RIGHT RESOURCE MATERIAL

In the first part of this chapter, you learned about important **resource materials**. Then, you practiced answering questions about them. Now is a good time to learn to choose the best, most relevant resource material for your needs.

Let's say that you are doing a report on cowhands. Several sources may give some information about cowhands, but only a few sources will give you enough material for a report. For example, a **dictionary** will give you a definition of cowhand. A **bibliography** might list some books about cowhands. The **library catalog** can help you locate the books about cowhands if you have any in your library. You might even locate a **map** of states where cowhands live. However, only one or two reference sources may provide enough information for a report, depending on the length and complexity that are required. Most likely this information will come from longer articles in an **encyclopedia** (in book form or in **computer software**), from **books** or **magazines/journals,** or from educational sites on the **internet**.

Based on the above example, you can see that choosing the right reference source means: 1) Clearly defining your own research needs, 2) Being familiar with different resources and their strengths, and 3) Being able to use each form of resource material effectively.

INTEGRATING RESEARCH SOURCES

Finding and reading research materials is like putting together a jigsaw puzzle, but the pieces for this kind of puzzle come from different boxes. As you find **research materials** for a paper, you must decide if the pieces of information from different sources are the information that you need, and then you have to fit those pieces together as a whole, complete statement. This is called **synthesizing** information.

Whatever you decide to do with the direction of the paper, you need to be aware of how your information is blending and fitting together to form a logical, well-supported statement. Once your research is done, you have to create your report. If you are choosing the form for the **presentation of your report**, remember, you have many options besides a written report.

Suppose that you are assigned to write a report about coded communication used throughout history. You then narrow your topic to the Native American code talkers who helped the United States triumph in WWII. The following pages provide several different sources of information to read regarding this topic.

Article "Native American professor tells real story of code talkers"

Table of Contents from *The Comanche Code Talkers of World War II*

Article "The secret is out on WWII Navajo Code talkers"

Key word search on "code talkers" from the internet.

Excerpts from the *Navajo Code Talkers' Dictionary*

Review all of the resources provided, and read the articles for understanding. Think about where else you could find information about this topic. Also, think about how you would paraphrase and summarize this information as you combine it with facts from other sources. Complete the practice section that follows.

Document 1: Article from *Bozeman Daily Chronicle*

Native American Professor Tells Real Story of Code Talkers; Sets History Straight

By Gail Schontzler, Chronicle Staff Writer, January 22, 2004

Hollywood did a poor job telling the story of Indian code talkers in the movie *Windtalkers*, says a Native American studies professor from Montana State University. Walter Fleming, associate professor and author of *The Complete Idiot's Guide to Native American History,* joked that the movie put an "Indian-deprived" actor, Nicholas Cage, and his "angst" at the forefront.

The history of Indian code talkers in war is more complex and interesting, he told a crowd of 50 people Tuesday at the Bozeman Public Library. His talk, "10 Things About Native Americans I Learned While Looking Up Something Else," was sponsored by the American Association of University Women.

Not all code talkers were Navajo, said Fleming, a member of the Kickapoo Kansas tribe who grew up on the Crow reservation in Montana. Choctaw, Comanche, Sioux and Crow soldiers also used their languages to help the U.S. Army communicate secretly and thwart enemy spying, he said. The first to do so were eight Choctaw Indians, who helped the Allies outmaneuver the Germans in the Argonne.

Document 2: *The Comanche Code Talkers of World War II* **- Table of Contents**

The Comanche Code Talkers of World War II
By William C. Meadows
Table of Contents

Document 3: Article from *The Chicago Tribune*

The secret is out on WWII Navajo Code talkers

By Bill Papich, *Chicago Tribune*, March 17, 2000

GALLUP, NM - During World War II, they spoke the Navajo language as a code to confound Japanese eavesdropping on American military communications. Today, Hollywood and the country's second largest toy company listen to them. When the surviving Navajo code talkers meet once a month in this railroad and ranching town bordering the Navajo Nation, they talk about their newly found fame.

Two major motion pictures about the Navajo code talkers are in the works, and last month toymaker Hasbro Inc.™ introduced Navajo Code Talker GI Joe™, the company's first doll to speak a Native American language. "All of a sudden, the code talkers are starting to be known all over the world," says Frank Thompson, 79, who was among the 400 to 450 Navajo Indians entering the Marines from 1942 to 1944 who were trained as code talkers.

Navajo is not a written language. That frustrated the Japanese who never broke the code and never captured a Navajo code talker. Until 1968, existence of the code talkers was classified. The Pentagon was unsure whether the Navajo language might be needed in another war.

The importance of the Navajo language represented a turnaround for the code talkers, most of whom attended government schools on the Navajo Reservation. When they went to school students were punished if they spoke in Navajo, a practice that continued into the 1950s. Teddy Draper Jr., whose father was among the code talkers, credits them with starting a revival of the Navajo tongue.

The Beach at Normandy on D-Day
June 6, 1944

"They had been beating us down, and then they use our language to win the war," the younger Draper said. "In 1968, within months of declassification of the Navajo code, the Navajo people started pushing for their history, their culture and their language in the schools."

Document 4: Selections from Internet Key Word Search on "Code Talkers"

Web Sites

1. Navajo **Code Talkers** in World War II - fact sheet about the involvement of code talkers in WWII and information about the **code talker** dictionary

    Category: **Code Talkers** > Navajo

2. Navajo **Code Talkers**, The - includes articles about how Navajo Language assisted the military forces to defeat the enemy and pictures of the commemorative medallions awarded to code talkers

    Category: **Code Talkers** > Navajo

3. Navajo **Code Talkers** - Web site of U.S. Senator Jeff Bingaman of New Mexico, who introduced the "Honoring the Navajo **Code Talkers** Act" signed into law on December 22, 2000

    Category: **Code Talkers** > Navajo

4. The **Code Talkers** - featuring news, upcoming gigs, photos, message boards, and more about the band, The Code Talkers

    Category: Rock and Pop Artists

5. Canku Ota: **Code Talkers** – brief but detailed histories of the Choctaw, Comanche, and Navajo **code talkers**

    Category: **Codes** and Ciphers > **Code Talkers**

6. **Code Talkers**, America's Secret Weapon - discusses the use of Native Americans languages as secret **codes**

    Category: **Codes** and Ciphers > **Code Talkers**

Document 5 - Excerpts from *Navajo Code Talkers' Dictionary*

REVISED AS OF 15 JUNE 1945 (DECLASSIFIED UNDER DEPARTMENT OF DEFENSE DIRECTIVE 5200.9)
Department of the Navy – Naval Historical Center, Washington, DC

ORGANIZATIONS	NAVAJO WORD	LITERAL TRANSLATION
CORPS	DIN-NEH-IH	CLAN
PLATOON	HAS-CLISH-NIH	MUD
SQUAD	DEBEH-LI-ZINI	BLACK SHEEP
NAMES OF COUNTRIES		
AMERICA	NE-HE-MAH	OUR MOTHER
BRITAIN	TOH-TA	BETWEEN WATERS
GERMANY	BESH-BE-CHA-HE	IRON HAT
ITALY	DOH-HA-CHI-YALI-TCHI	STUTTER
JAPAN	BEH-NA-ALI-TSOSIE	SLANT EYE
RUSSIA	SILA-GOL-CHI-IH	RED ARMY
NAMES OF AIRPLANES		
DIVE BOMBER	GINI	CHICKEN HAWK
TORPEDO PLANE	TAS-CHIZZIE	SWALLOW
OBSV. PLANE	NE-AS-JAH	OWL
FIGHTER PLANE	DA-HE-TIH-HI	HUMMING BIRD
BOMBER PLANE	JAY-SHO	BUZZARD
PATROL PLANE	GA-GIH	CROW
TRANSPORT	ATSAH	EAGLE
NAMES OF SHIPS		
SHIPS	TOH-DINEH-IH	SEA FORCE
BATTLESHIP	LO-TSO	WHALE
AIRCRAFT	TSIDI-MOFFA-YE-HI	BIRD CARRIER
SUBMARINE	BESH-LO	IRON FISH
DESTROYER	CA-LO	SHARK
TRANSPORT	DINEH-NAY-YE-HI	MAN CARRIER
CRUISER	LO-TSO-YAZZIE	SMALL WHALE

Practice 3: Synthesizing and Evaluating Information

Choose the best answer for questions 1 – 6. Write your response to question 7 on your own paper.

1. Why could the Japanese not decipher code talkers' messages, spoken in Navajo and other tongues?

    A. Code talkers utilized a secret radio frequency for transmitting the coded messages.

    B. There are sounds and inflections used in Navajo that do not exist in the Japanese language.

    C. The languages are not written, and regular vocabulary was used for military designations.

    D. As several languages were used, the Japanese never knew which one they were hearing.

2. Which of the following would be the BEST topic sentence for a report on "Code Talkers?"

    A. Native American code talkers were a vital ingredient toward America's victory in WWII.

    B. World War II marked a turning point for the acceptance of Native American languages.

    C. Navajo, Comanche, Choctaw, Sioux and Crow soldiers all served as code talkers in WWII.

    D. There are many resources available to research the code talkers and their role in WWII.

3. Which of the following Web sites discusses a law passed to honor the code talkers?

    A. the one that includes a fact sheet and code talker dictionary
    B. America's Secret Weapon
    C. the one with pictures of commemorative medallions
    D. Senator Jeff Bingaman's site

4. Based on the *Navajo Code Talkers' Dictionary*, what kinds of words were substituted for military terms, which did not exist in Native American languages?

    A. closest words in pronunciation in Navajo to the meaning in English
    B. words for natural things that approximate the meaning of the English words
    C. words with absolutely no connection to make the code unbreakable
    D. easiest words to pronounce for clear code transmission over the radio

5. Suppose you are going to write an outline of your report on the topic of Native American code talkers. Which of the following is the BEST list of main topics for your outline?

    A. the use of code talkers during wars, acceptance of Native American languages as a result, new popularity through film and toys
    B. unique qualities of Native American languages, other codes used during WWII, what happened to code talkers after the war
    C. importance of code talkers in WWWII, why the code was so effective, results of Native American soldiers participating in this way
    D. explanation of code used during WWII, why the Japanese could not decipher it, eventual declassification of the code

6. Based on all the documents, which of the following statements BEST expresses the role of code talkers during WWII?

    A. Enlisted Native Americans soldiers could only serve as code talkers.
    B. There were not enough code talkers, or the war would have ended sooner.
    C. Surviving Native American code talkers keep up their skills and teach them to soldiers today.
    D. Native American solders were a small percentage of the U.S. force but played a pivotal part.

REFINING THE RESEARCH TOPIC

Once you have begun to investigate different sources for a topic, you may choose to keep heading in the same direction with your **thesis** (main statement) or to change direction entirely for the thesis. This process is called **extending ideas**.

EXTENDING IDEAS: ASKING ADDITIONAL QUESTIONS

When reading material for a research idea, you may find other ideas and questions to explore. Asking questions as you read materials is an important part of research. Those questions can help you focus your ideas or guide you to the next steps you need to take. Research is similar to following a map; you can start at one place and travel in a straight line holding to one idea, or you can take off in new directions pursuing new ideas.

After you have read material like that provided about code talkers, it is time to think beyond the information you've found. In this case, it's the history and effects of the code talkers' role in WWII. What other ideas or topics could also be related?

To **extend** or stretch an idea, you may ask yourself more questions about the reading or look for several key words from the reading. For example:

"How did the involvement of the code talkers in WWII affect goals important to the tribes?"

Possible answers: helped focus attention on the value of their native languages, stopped reformists from trying to eradicate these languages, showed patriotism of Native Americans, reinforced the warrior traditions of the tribes, and so on.

Now, think for a moment about where to find information about these related topics. Start with the materials already used. 1) Search for other works by an author who wrote some of the material you used. 2) Look for suggested readings in the materials you used. 3) Use the bibliographies found in your sources.

There will probably be information and statistics in government documents, newspaper articles, history books, and Web searches with different key words, such as *tribes*, *Native American history*, *military history*, *Native American languages*, and so on. The possibilities for extending the information for an idea to other topics are vast.

Practice 4: Extending Ideas from Information

Use the research material on "code talkers" from the preceding pages to answer the following questions on a separate sheet of paper.

1. What are some possible ways to gather primary source information related to the topic?

2. The information provided earlier in the chapter includes a key word search on "code talkers." After reading the various information in the chapter, think of at least six other possible search terms that you could use to expand and extend your research on this topic.

3. In September 2004, President George W. Bush made the following statements in an executive memorandum issued by the White House.

    "The White House will work with tribal governments in a manner that cultivates mutual respect and fosters greater understanding to reinforce these principles of government-to-government relationship and support for tribal sovereignty and self-determination."

Based on this information, what questions can you think of to extend your research?

4. While working on this research topic, a group of students brainstormed the following list. Rate the ideas for their relevance to the original topic "code talkers and their role in WWII." Use the following scale: 1 = very related to the topic 2 = somewhat related to the topic 3 = not really related to the topic.

    Native American influence on U.S. government today_____

    education on Indian reservations _____

    number of Native American soldiers_____

    importance of maintaining one's native language_____

    history of various American Indian tribes_____

ranks and duties of Native Americans serving in WWII _____

comparison of languages of various American Indian tribes_____

other contributions of Native Americans to U.S. history_____

5. Choose one of the ideas in question 4 above and explain what information about it you would hope to find, and how that would be related to the original topic.

CHAPTER 2 REVIEW

A. Read the passage that follows. Then answer the questions below.

Soaring with the Eagles!

Have you ever yearned to fly? No, not by flapping your wings and jumping off the roof but by acquiring a pilot's license! Learning to fly can be very exciting, and you need to be just 16 years old to be a student pilot, and 17 to get a pilot certificate—which is the real Federal Aviation Administration (FAA) term for a pilot's license. However, be prepared: You need to consider the time and expense involved.

First, learning to fly a plane is expensive. The most common method by which people learn is to train part-time at a local small airport or flight school. Training can run anywhere from $3,000 to $6,000, depended on your location. While most training programs allow you to pay over time, it's still a good idea to think ahead about whether this is an amount you can invest.

Second, getting a pilot's license requires plenty of time. In addition to studying for written and oral exams, there is a minimum requirement of 40 hours of flight time. Lessons last about three hours, beginning with ground instruction and flight preparation, including the flight itself, and ending with post flight instruction. Most students log close to twice the minimum hours in order to feel comfortable about passing their final check ride. It's possible to complete pilot's training as a part-time student in about four to six months, but only if you devote the required time.

Other requirements include passing a medical examination and being able to read, speak and understand English. Whether you just want to fly recreationally or pursue aviation as a career, you need to begin by getting a private pilot's license, which allows you to pilot single-engine planes. If you're still interested in this fun but demanding pastime, there are plenty of books and FAA handbooks that can help you prepare. So, read up, save up, and get ready to take to the skies!

1. This passage would be most helpful for a student research project on

    A.   hobbies that are expensive.   C.   the flight patterns of eagles.

    B.   requirements for a pilot's license.   D.   pursuing a career with an airline.

2. Where would be the BEST place to do further research about obtaining a pilot's license?

    A.   The South Carolina air traffic controller's handbook.

    B.   The book *Around the World in 80 Days*.

    C.   The FAA Web site "Education & Training" pages.

    D.   Flight simulation software, such as FlitePro.

B. Read all of the following informational materials, and answer the questions that follow.

List of Informational Materials on Overstuffed Backpacks

Article: Ben T. Down (2001) "Weighted Danger"

Internet key word search: "+backpacks +health"

Line graph: "Estimated Cases of Back Pain from Backpacks in SC 1980–2000"

Excerpt of speech: Speech given at Central County High School's orientation by Principal J. C. Powell, 8-26-03

Weighted Danger

There are many things to consider as you are shopping for back-to-school supplies—other than your favorite brand of snacks that is. One of the newest alerts being sent out, along with that school supply list that you are clutching in your sweaty palm, is the warning about oversized and then overstuffed backpacks. Manufacturers are making the packs bigger, and Hey! everyone knows that bigger is better, right?

Well, in this case, not. Both parents and teachers have noted the increase in back and neck strain caused by carrying a load that would bring a grown water buffalo to its hairy knees. Kids are struggling through hallways banging into each other and their empty lockers. (What? You thought that's where the books would go? So uncool!) The backpacks are, on average, about twenty pounds, twenty percent or more of the weight of many school kids. That is a serious load.

So, when you go out looking for the perfect way to lug all those books around, don't ask your big sister to shoulder the weight. Look for a smaller backpack or a book case on wheels. It's smarter...

Key Word Search: "+Backpacks+health"

- **Science World: Back Whack.(weight of backpacks) (Brief Article)**

  Ever feel like you're carrying the weight of the world on your shoulders? Blame it on your backpack!
  URL: http://www.findarticles,com/ m1590/ 5_56/57534966/p1/article.jhtml
  Last modified 8-Jun-2003 - page size 10895 bytes - in English [Translate]

- **Weigh the Risks of Backpacks**

  Parent Home. Activities. Ages and Grades. Parenting. School Help. Special Needs. Entertainment. Family Finance. Message Boards. What Works. Expert...
  URL: http://myschoolonline.com/article/0, 1120,44-2931,00.html
  Last modified 3-Apr-2002 - page size 41146 bytes - in English [Translate]

- **John's Journal Online - Teens at the Chiropractor; sound funny**

  November 2000. Teens at the Chiropractor; sound funny? By Shelley. Teens these past few years have been showing up more at doctors offices where...
  URL: http://jajhs.kana.k12.wv.us/jahome/paper/archive/2000/november2000/backaches_capito.html
  Last modified 5-Dec-2000 - page size 6721 bytes - in English [Translate]

• **CNN - Back Pain - Children**

More children suffering from back pain, study says - February 20,1999.
URL: http://www.cnn.com/HEALTH/9902/20/teen. back.pain/
Last modified 8-Apr-2001 English [Translate]

Line Graph

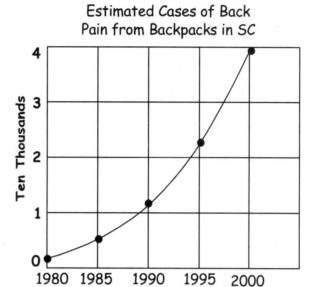

Estimated Cases of Back
Pain from Backpacks in SC

Excerpt of Speech Given at

Central County High School's Orientation–August 26, 2003

by J.C. Powell, Principal

"The latest information that our school has from the state administration is that chronic back pain is on the increase in the student population because of overstuffed back-packs. Now I have heard students say that school in general can be a pain, but this trend of back pain is no laughing matter.

What can this administration and student populations do to make sure that our students are healthy in mind and body? In the new handbook, you will find an outline of changing policies. One is that students will be allowed more time between classes to visit and use their lockers for storing books throughout the day. Teachers will be scheduling time in their classes for some "homework" to be done at school. Also, our curriculum staff is looking for smaller books and more options to have materials on the internet. These changes are all designed to stop the increase of back injuries at school.

These changes will not work without the participation of each and everyone of you. I am challenging you to use your lockers! Use the internet! Do homework at school! When we all change our habits from the old to the new, this entire student body will be healthier for it."

3. Which of the following is the BEST example of a new direction that this research could take?

    A.   benefits of prayer in school

    B.   debate over high-energy drinks

    C.   safety benefits of clear backpacks

    D.   debate over in-line skates for hallways

4. If you are using the previous materials to write a two page report for health class, which of the following would be the best and most appropriate topic?

    A.   the reasons that students should be issued laptops and books on CD-ROM

    B.   students need to be aware of the back-injury dangers caused by heavy, overloaded backpacks

    C.   the history and design of bookbags and backpacks

    D.   the need for a new time schedule at this high school

5. Based on the materials, which of the following is the BEST list of main topics for an outline on this topic?

    A.   heavy backpacks can cause pain, kids have too many books, some solutions need to be found

    B.   smaller backpacks are healthier, more kids are seeing chiropractors, schools need to allow on-campus homework time

    C.   heavy books should be left at school, larger lockers are needed, schools should order paperbacks

    D.   schedules should allow more time between classes, homework can be done in a study period, parents should be aware of weight their kids carry

6. Which of the following is the BEST example of a new direction that this research could take?

    A.   Kids have too much homework these days

    B.   Teachers should try carrying backpacks

    C.   Alternatives to carrying a heavy load of books

    D.   Tracking of reported back injuries among kids

Chapter 3
Presentations

As you read in Chapter 2, you will often do research to create a report. Many times, the report will be in written form, but sometimes you will be required or allowed to do other types of presentations. This chapter focuses on **analyzing presentations.** It also covers an additional research skill, **understanding an interview**, and the speaking and listening skills needed for effective interviewing.

PRESENTING INFORMATION

Sometimes you will be asked to present information in a way other than essays and written research reports. Speaking, like writing, is a way to convey information to others and can serve the same purposes as different types of essays: to **inform**, to **persuade**, to **entertain**, and so on. You may be required to give an oral report in class, to present to a club or organization, or to make a speech to a group of people.

On the South Carolina End-of-Course Exam for English, you will be required to analyze an oral presentation. Oral presentations can vary in **purpose, organization, rhetorical devices** used, and **audio-visuals** that accompany what you say.

In making the decision about how to analyze presentations, you will want to take into consideration the **type of information** you are reading and the **audience** for this information. Is the information complex, perhaps with a great deal of numbers and statistics? Or perhaps the information is primarily description; a presentation that is **visual,** either completely visual or at least partly visual, will help the audience to better understand by seeing pictures or graphics of what is presented. Where does the presentation take place? Who is the audience: perhaps classmates, adults, or club members?

There are a great number of ways to present information visually. **Posters** might be the first thing you think of, but there are others to consider. **Demonstrations** might be appropriate for some topics. **Videos** are popular and may be the best medium in some cases. A **PowerPoint™ slide show** or a **Web site** might be a good method for some information that is a combination of text (written word) and visual information. Finally, think back to elementary school — a **diorama** is still an appropriate method to present some information; a diorama is like a miniature museum display, able to present a wide variety of information.

PREPARING A PRESENTATION

As you begin reading the presentation, you will want to consider its **purpose**, the **intended audience**, and **place and time** it is given.

DETERMINE YOUR PURPOSE

One of the first things to think about is the purpose of an oral presentation. Like essays, oral presentations can have any of the purposes below, or a combination of two or more.

inform	An informative or descriptive speech presents a new subject or new information about a familiar subject. You can find some of the same types of supporting detail that you would in an expository essay, such as concrete examples, vivid description, and instructions (if applicable). *Example*: "The Sonar Language of Whales."
analyze	A presentation that analyzes a topic examines it methodically by separating it into parts and studying the relationships between them. *Example*: "Fast Publishing: How Daily Newspapers are Written, Printed, and Distributed."
explain	An explanatory speech helps people to understand a topic by defining it and giving reasons behind it. *Example*: "The History and Rising Popularity of Extreme Sports."
persuade	A persuasive presentation is meant to change attitudes or behavior of the audience, or to convince them that your point of view is the best. *Example*: "Our Community's Public Library Needs to Expand"

compare and contrast	A presentation that compares and contrasts topics discusses the similarities and differences between them. Sometimes the main focus may be mainly to compare or mainly to contrast. Comparing and contrasting also can be effectively used in conjunction with other purposes, such as helping to persuade, for example, by emphasizing one thing being better than another. *Example:* "Why Electronic Mail Has Become More Popular than Traditional Mail"
entertain	An entertaining presentation primarily captures and holds the attention of the audience. Often incorporating narrative presentation, speeches that entertain usually also have another purpose (such as to inform or to persuade). *Example*: "A Funny Thing Happened to Me on the Way to the Monster Truck Rally"

In addition to informational (expository) and persuasive speeches, you might have to analyze a narrative (story) or a descriptive presentation, respond verbally to literature you read, and use interview techniques to gather information. All of these are specific applications of speaking skills.

ANALYZE YOUR AUDIENCE

In analyzing a presentation, the goal is to know that the audience believes the speaker is knowledgeable about the topic and well prepared to speak about it. For example, if the speaker is the superintendent speaking to your school's PTSA, you can assume the audience will be made up of teachers, parents who want to be involved, and students who take a leadership role, such as being part of the student government.

Audiences vary greatly; but to analyze an oral presentation, identifying the audience is a key factor in evaluating the success of the presentation. For example, based on the topic and the occasion, oral presentations can be addressed to your peers, teachers, parents, church or community members, citizens, doctors, and lawyers too, to name a few.

Practice 1: Consider Purpose and Audience

A. Read the following scenario: You are president of the drama club at school, which is planning some big productions that everyone is excited about. To purchase the needed costumes the club wants, it will need to raise some additional funds. As president, you need to make sure the money is raised or costumes obtained somehow so that the plays can be staged.

For each of the audiences below, determine what your purpose for speaking would be. Also note what assumptions you can make about the audience. Use your own paper if you need more room.

Purpose:	Audience:	Assumptions:
_____	club members	_____
_____	costume shop	_____
_____	local civic club that supports the arts	_____

The Naturalization Process

1   U.S. citizenship is a lifetime benefit bestowed upon an individual who is born in the United States. It can also be acquired through a process called Naturalization. Naturalization is the way immigrants become citizens of the United States. If you were not born a citizen, you can become one through the process of naturalization.

2   As a citizen, you have unique rights and privileges, some of which include voting, having a U.S. passport, the U.S. government's protection when abroad, and the right to petition for green cards (permanent residency) for your children and immediate family. As a U.S. citizen, you cannot be deported or lose your citizenship even if you commit a crime or choose to live elsewhere in the world, unless you misrepresented yourself to get citizenship or were ineligible at the time.

3   Becoming a citizen through naturalization is not an easy decision for some. Giving up one's homeland citizenship, a national identity, the place of one's birth, friends, and remaining family, can be painful. Becoming a citizen also means you are ready to fight for America and defend the Constitution of the United States, no matter what. "I pledge allegiance to the flag of the United States of America and to the republic for which it stands..." are not words to be taken lightly.

1. Which of the following questions would be an avenue of further research suggested by the information in this speech?

    A.   What is the process for becoming a citizen?
    B.   Who are some famous naturalized citizens?
    C.   What are the requirements for becoming a citizen in Mexico?
    D.   Should non-citizens be allowed to get a driver's license?

2. To improve the effectiveness of this presentation, which prop or visual aid could Angela use when giving this speech?

    A.   an American flag
    B.   a map of the United States
    C.   an application for citizenship on a PowerPoint™ presentation
    D.   Angela's baby picture

3. What is the purpose of Angela's presentation?

    A.   to entertain
    B.   to analyze
    C.   to compare and contrast
    D.   to inform

4. Which of the following should Angela assume about her audience?

    A.   Each person in her audience is already a citizen.
    B.   Most of her audience has little or no knowledge of the naturalization process.
    C.   The audience will not want to ask questions.
    D.   The audience will want Angela's autograph after the presentation.

ORGANIZING THE ORAL PRESENTATION

Making an outline can help your understanding of a presentation. A brief outline works best, one that provides the **major points** to discuss and the **key words or phrases**

Keep in mind that, much like an essay, a well developed oral presentation has a **beginning**, **middle**, and **end**. The points made also need to be **supported**. Speakers use a variety of evidence as support, including the list below on the left. It's also important to remember that a good presentation **captures and keeps the attention** of the audience. Effective ways to gain and keep interest include those in the list below on the right. In the next section, you will learn about rhetorical devices that can improve the effectiveness of a presentation.

Types of Supporting Evidence	Techniques to Capture Audience Attention
• facts, statistics	• tell a brief, related narrative
• authoritative or expert opinions	• cite surprising or little-known facts
• appropriate examples	• utilize humor, if appropriate
• definitions	• use a relevant and interesting quote
• logic	• incorporate audio-visual aids
• emotional appeals	• imagery and figurative language

Presentations can be organized in several ways. Making a brief outline of the presentation will help you analyze the content and answer questions. Here is an example of an outline of a presentation.

- A **topical** presentation outline has a list of the main ideas presented, with transitions and key words/phrases included with each point. It works well especially for expository presentations.

The Demise of the Dinosaurs

I. opening: imagine land, water, and air filled with mighty creature (describe); suddenly they're gone

II. Why did dinosaurs become extinct? many theories

   A. Main 2 "serious" theories - both supported by iridium findings (rare element from outer space or earth's core)

      1. asteroid theory

         a. Alvarez brothers & clay testing

         b. Hildebrand & Yucatan impact site

      2. volcano theory

         a. resulting acid rain, greenhouse effect

   B. Other theories - tectonic shifts, temperature changes, mammals eating dino eggs, methane, exhaustion of food supplies

III. conclusion: seems it must have been a combination of things; several articles I read support this idea

   A. excerpt from Museum of Natural History article

- **Chronological** organization works well for narrative presentations. A chronological outline can also be especially helpful for understanding sequence of events.
- A **cause-effect** focus can be very effective for persuasive speeches. The outline can show the problem or cause first, followed by the solution or effect.
- **Comparison-contrast** organization is useful for both informative and persuasive presentations. The outline can focus on the topics being compared and/or contrasted either point-by-point or one side at a time.

Now that you have outlined the main points and the general organization of the presentation, you will want to identify some techniques and language that can strengthen the presentation.

RHETORICAL DEVICES

Later in this book, in Chapter 6, you will read about literary devices used in literature. Spoken presentations can use similar techniques, called **rhetorical devices**, to make them interesting and to help the speaker move an audience to a desired feeling or action. Here are a few of the rhetorical devices that speakers can use. Each includes an example from a famous speaker who used it. You can also review "Figurative Language on Pages 115 – 117 for other devices that can be used in a presentation.

anaphora   a series of sentences or phrases begun with the same word or group of words to build tension or emphasize a point.
Example: "We shall not flag or fail. We shall go on to the end. We shall fight in France, we shall fight on the seas and oceans, we shall fight with growing confidence and growing strength in the air, we shall defend our island, whatever the cost may be, we shall fight on the beaches, we shall fight on the landing grounds, we shall fight in the fields and in the streets, we shall fight in the hills. We shall never surrender."

– Winston Churchill

asyndeton   listing items, one after another, without placing conjunctions between them. Reading the list without pause gives a dramatic tone to the list.
Example: "Music is a moral law. It gives soul to the universe, wings to the mind, flight to the imagination, a charm to sadness, and life to everything." – Plato (427 BC – 347 BC)

metonymy   is a form of metaphor. It uses one part of an object to stand in for the whole. It's a very common rhetorical device in English.
Example: "Beneath the rule of men entirely great, the pen is mightier than the sword." – Edward Lytton

metaphor   a direct comparison of two unlike things without using "like" or as"
Example: All the world's a stage, And all the men and women merely players."   – William Shakespeare, *As You Like It*

rhetorical question	asking a question without expecting an answer, often because the answer should be obvious

Example: Men of England! You wish to kill me because I am a Frenchman. Am I not punished enough in not having been born an Englishman?"

– Voltaire

simile	comparison using "like" or "as"

Example: Are creeds such simple things like the clothes which a man can change at will and put on at will?"   – Mahatma Gandhi

Practice 2: Speech Organization and Rhetorical Devices

Below are the opening paragraphs of a speech given by Sojourner Truth in 1851 at the Women's Convention in Akron, Ohio. A former slave, she had gained her freedom prior to the Civil War. Read the speech and answer questions 1 – 6.

Ain't I A Woman?

Well, children, where there is so much racket there must be something out of kilter. I think that 'twixt the negroes of the South and the women at the North, all talking about rights, the white men will be in a fix pretty soon. But what's all this here talking about?

That man over there says that women need to be helped into carriages, and lifted over ditches, and to have the best place everywhere. Nobody ever helps me into carriages, or over mud-puddles, or gives me any best place! And ain't I a woman? Look at me! Look at my arm! I have ploughed and planted, and gathered into barns, and no man could head me! And ain't I a woman? I could work as much and eat as much as a man—when I could get it—and bear the lash as well! And ain't I a woman? I have borne thirteen children, and seen most all sold off to slavery, and when I cried out with my mother's grief, none but Jesus heard me! And ain't I a woman?

1. Why do you think Sojourner Truth used the device of rhetorical questions in her speech?
   A. She uses them as a refrain, to emphasize her points and give her speech structure.
   B. She wants the crowd to answer her questions so that they are actively involved with the speech.
   C. She needs to reinforce the idea that she is, indeed, a woman.
   D. They act as an overriding metaphor that shapes her speech.

2. What is the main point Sojourner Truth is trying to get across in this part of her speech?
   A. Slavery should be abolished.   C. Black men should be equal to white men.
   B. Women should have the same rights as   D. She is a woman.
      men.

3. Based on the language in Sojourner Truth's speech, how would you expect her to have delivered this speech?
   A. sedately, standing in one place
   B. only addressing the men in the audience
   C. with flair and an occasional curse to prove her point
   D. with energy and movement

4. Identify the purpose Sojourner Truth has when she addresses "that man over there . . ."
   A. venting her anger about what that particular man said to her earlier.
   B. trying to make him change his mind about what he said to her.
   C. using him to represent the hypocritical ideas of a larger group against which she is arguing.
   D. making him up because she was at a women's convention and there were no men there.

5. For supporting evidence in her presentation, Sojourner Truth mainly uses
   A. statistics.   C. examples.
   B. logic.   D. expert opinion.

6. In her speech, Sojourner Truth starts her sentences with similar groups of words or phrases. This rhetorical device is called
   A. metonymy.   C. rhetorical question.
   B. anaphora.   D. asyndeton.

A STRONG INTRODUCTION AND CONCLUSION

A very important part of an effective oral presentation is a strong **introduction**. The speaker must grab the **attention** of the audience with an interesting fact, a humorous remark, or a strong example. This is also the time the presenter introduces the **topic and its major points**. Basically, the speaker needs to give the audience a very brief outline of what will be said. As all professional or experienced speakers know, the way a presentation is laid out is something like this:

Introduction   "Tell them what you're going to tell them."

Body   "Tell them what you want to tell them."

Conclusion   "Tell them what you told them."

It seems repetitious, but **repetition** is important in an oral presentation. Unlike readers looking at an essay, an audience listening to a presenter cannot go back and read major points to refresh themselves. They also do not know where the speaker is in the course of the presentation, so the speaker needs to tell them along the way. For example, the speaker needs to say things such as, "The first of my three points is..."

As in an essay, the introduction of a speech also serves as the place to focus on the importance or relevance of the topic and to present a **thesis**. A presenter should not say, "I want to talk to you about recycling today." Rather, the speaker should tell the audience something about the purpose, such as, "I'm here to talk about recycling because the city is considering a new recycling center, and I'll give you reasons why we should support that plan."

The **body** of a speech, like the body of an essay, will contain the supporting detail. The presenter should include **appropriate examples**, **vivid description**, and **concrete details**. Another way to keep the attention of the audience is to involve them somehow, such as by asking questions (whether you expect answers or not), having them do activities as you speak (such as, "Write down the number of items you recycle"), or engaging more of their senses by using audio-visual aids.

Finally, the **conclusion** serves as a way to wrap up. The presenter uses it to accomplish the following:

- let the audience know the presentation is coming to a close

- summarize major points

- if it is a persuasive speech, it strengthens the appeal

- if not persuasive, the presenter should leave the audience with something to think about or a memorable idea

- thank the audience for listening

- ask the audience if there are any questions (if the time and format allow)

Practice 3: A Strong Introduction, Body, and Conclusion

For career day at your school, several parents and community members have volunteered to give presentations about their careers. This is part of a presentation that Mr. Chen is writing to present at career day. Read this draft and answer questions 1 – 6.

Good morning. Thank you for inviting me to come and speak at your school. Today I plan to talk to you about my career as a financial advisor. Although I do not work with many current students at this school, I have worked with some of your parents and their colleagues, as well as some graduates of this school. People come to see me when they are ready to begin investing their money in stocks, bonds, and mutual funds. I also have clients with fully developed portfolios who come to me for advice in diversifying, consolidating, or investing additional funds.

To give you an idea of what I do, imagine that you have $100. If you put this in a savings account in a bank, it will earn a fixed percent interest, and at the end of a year, you may have $102. That's pretty good, but I can help you do better. I can recommend certain investments that could leave you with $150 after a year. That sounds better than a savings account, doesn't it? Well, it does and it doesn't. Although you have the chance of earning more money, there is risk involved. What I mean by that is that you may actually lose money and only have $90 left at the end of a year.

1. In rewriting the first paragraph of his speech, what should Mr. Chen do to increase the chances that students will understand what he has to say?

    A.   Remind himself to speak slowly and clearly.

    B.   Define some of the more complicated vocabulary words he uses.

    C.   Add specific details about the portfolios of some former students with whom he has worked.

    D.   Add the names of the students with whose parents he has worked.

2. In the second paragraph of the speech, Mr. Chen tries to interest the students in what he has to say by

    A.   talking about banks.

    B.   giving good advice about savings accounts.

    C.   describing a situation they can relate to.

    D.   throwing out some numbers.

3. What would you select as the BEST sentence Mr. Chen could add and why?

    A.   *This is why I spend my days doing research, asking questions, and trying to find the safest ways to invest money with the highest returns—meaning that after a year, you end up with more.* Add this sentence because it is a relevant, logical statement.

    B.   *The most famous person I've worked with this year is Mrs. Crane, the editor of our local paper, who came to me in dire need of diversification.* Add this sentence because it uses the bandwagon approach.

    C.   *Last month I had a client who doubled an investment by buying some pharmaceuticals stock I recommended.* Add this sentence because it's a glittering generality.

    D.   *If you think you might like to be a financial analyst, take a statistics course, and put in some extra time the next time you have to do a research paper—research is a big part of this job.* Add this sentence because it is a personal tie-in.

4. Which conclusion would be the most effective and appropriate way for Mr. Chen to end his speech?

    A.   Finally, if any of you are interested in learning more about the work of a financial advisor, please come visit me at my office.

    B.   I can answer questions now if you'll come up here with me and talk into the mike.

    C.   In conclusion, when you realize that along with helping other people make financial gains, you also get some tips to help yourself, I think you'll agree that going into the financial sector is a very wise idea indeed.

    D.   I'd really like to relate more stories about how I've helped people make financial gains by investing their money wisely, but it looks like we've run out of time.

5. Which sentence best introduces the main topic of the presentation?

    A.   Thank you for inviting me to come and speak at your school.

    B.   I can recommend certain investments that could leave you with $150 after a year.

    C.   People come to me when they are ready to begin investing their money in stocks, bonds, and mutual funds.

    D.   Today I plan to talk with you about my career as a financial advisor.

6. The purpose of Mr. Chen's presentation is to
   - A. analyze.
   - B. explain.
   - C. entertain.
   - D. persuade.

CONDUCTING AN INTERVIEW

In preparing a presentation, a speaker will often gather information through research in libraries, on the internet, and through other resources. Remember that a presenter can also do original research, which includes **conducting interviews**. This form of research is included here because of the speaking and listening skills involved in this activity.

BEFORE THE INTERVIEW

- Who should be interviewed? In doing an interview as part of research, the presenter wants to be sure the person chosen is an **expert** on the topic for researching. For example, if writing about sports teams in a school, a speaker could interview any of the coaches or players.

- When preparing to do the interview, the presenter should make a **list of questions** that will be asked.

- Then, the presenter needs to contact the person to be interviewed, and **schedule a time and place** to meet. Remember that a speaker can also conduct interviews over the telephone. If the presenter does not know the person to be interviewed, bring along a parent or other adult.

- The presenter should ask the person if he can **record the interview** so the facts are clear. Usually people do not object. Then, the speaker should be sure he has a fresh cassette tape, an extra tape just in case, and a tape recorder that works properly. The presenter should still **take notes** to help remember important points and to have in case anything goes wrong with the recording.

DURING THE INTERVIEW

- The presenter should start by asking about the person's background and his or her expertise in the subject area that will be addressed in the presentation.

- As the person answers questions, the presenter should listen carefully and take notes. Often, things come up that may need to be pursued further. If this happens, the interviewer should not interrupt the interviewee, but rather jot a note in the margin on a note pad. That way, the presenter can come back to that point later.

- The presenter should allow the person to talk, but if he or she begins to ramble or get off track, the interviewer should politely steer the conversation back to what is needed to find out.

AFTER THE INTERVIEW

- The speaker should thank the person interviewed for taking time and sharing information. After the presentation, the presenter might also write a thank-you note that includes how the presentation went.

- If the speaker used a tape recorder, he should listen to the tape, and write down important points and interesting quotes. They can be incorporated into the rest of the research information, as long as the source is cited.

Practice 4: Interviews

Read this interview carefully. Then answer the questions that follow.

> *Matt Werner is doing research for a report in his high school English class. His subject is fitness for teens. He interviewed two classmates who shared what they gained from their new fitness program. Matt interviewed Tiffany Kimball and Scott Blaine in the school cafeteria after the 3 pm dismissal bell.*

Matt: I know you two want to get home, so I'll be brief.

Tiffany: Good. In fact, I'm going to my ballet lesson at 4 pm today.

Matt: Tiffany, why did you pick ballet for a fitness program?

Tiffany: I always admired ballet dancers. They looked so fit and trim. I also see the beauty and art in this form of dance.

Matt: What about you, Scott? What do you do for better health and fitness?

Scott: For me, it's swimming. One day I saw a picture of myself with my big belly. My favorite foods were doughnuts, hamburgers, French fries, and pizza. At 5"7", I was almost as wide as I was tall. I even had high blood pressure.

Tiffany: I was a little overweight too, and I lacked energy to finish chores and homework.

Matt: What changes have you seen from ballet?

Tiffany: Luckily, I have the right body type. So, I felt like I was born for ballet. Now, I'm much stronger. I don't slouch when I sit. I feel more beautiful. I have more confidence.

Matt: Scott, has swimming been good for you?

Scott: Sure has. My swim teacher was in the Olympics. He is terrific. I swim three times each week at the YMCA. I've already dropped 5 pounds, and I switched to a low-carb diet. I'm getting ready for my first competition with guys my age. Exercise for me was getting chips and cheese from the kitchen during the commercials.

Matt: What advice would you give to other teenagers looking for a fitness program?

Scott: Check out one of the fitness centers in your neighborhood. Talk to a physical education teacher or your counselor about fitness programs in your area.

Tiffany: Even twenty minutes of fast walking every day can improve your health. I have a friend that goes horseback riding for two hours every other day. Her upper body is stronger, and she lost weight.

Scott: Running, handball, biking, and weight lifting are also good exercises.

Matt: Thank you both for your time.

1. Why did Matt choose Tiffany and Scott for his research?

    A. They are friends from school.

    B. They are knowledgeable about the topic.

    C. They have some free time after school.

    D. They enjoy being interviewed.

2. What could help Matt improve his interview?
   A. Do an interview over the telephone
   B. Interview either Tiffany or Scott but not both
   C. Record the interview on tape for later review
   D. Offer some money to Tiffany and Scott for the time involved

3. If Matt were to continue this interview, which of the following questions would be most appropriate?
   A. Among your classmates, who is most in need of a total fitness program?
   B. How long will you continue your fitness program?
   C. Which food is the most difficult to give up on your fitness program?
   D. Why did you choose to engage in a fitness program?

4. Which of the following interviewees provides the most details in the interview?
   A. Matt
   B. Tiffany and Scott
   C. Tiffany
   D. Scott

CHAPTER 3 REVIEW

Read the following questions about presentations. Then choose the best answer for each of them.

1. If you have been asked to make a short report about overloaded backpacks to a faculty committee at your school, which of the following is the best choice for presentation?
   A. a ten-page, detailed research paper
   B. a display with pictures of students with overloaded backpacks
   C. a ten minute oral report with a single page summarized handout
   D. a home video made by you and your friends that dramatizes the dangers and consequences of heavy backpacks and the resulting injuries

2. Read the list of topics that follows. Imagine that you are listening to a presentation on each topic. Decide the BEST purpose for each presentation (remember that some may serve two or more purposes), and place a checkmark in the appropriate space or spaces. Justify your answers.

	inform	analyze	explain	persuade	compare & contrast	entertain
Generic and store-brand products are just as good as the more expensive name brands.						
There are many different types of palm trees in the world. Most are native to a specific region.						
Television used to be free, thanks to commercials. Now that everyone pays for cable or satellite, there should be no more commercials on TV.						
Solar power is a clean, efficient alternative energy source that can be set up to work much like a rechargeable battery to run electric functions.						

Read the following selections from presentations and an interview. Then answer the questions about each one.

Patrick Henry's Speech - "Liberty or Death!"

...Mr. President, it is natural to man to indulge in the illusions of hope. We are apt to shut our eyes against a painful truth, and listen to the song of that siren, till she transforms us into beasts. Is this the part of wise men, engaged in a great and arduous struggle for liberty? Are we disposed to be of the number of those who, having eyes, see not, and having ear, hear not, the things which so nearly concern their temporal salvation?

For my part, whatever anguish of spirit it may cost, I am willing to know the whole truth, to know the worst, and to provide for it. I have but one lamp by which my feet are guided; and that is the lamp of experience. I know of no way of judging of the future but by the past. And judging by the past, I wish to know what there has been in the conduct of the British ministry for the last ten years, to justify those hopes with which gentlemen have been pleased to solace themselves and the House?...

We have held the subject up in every light of which it is capable; but it has been all in vain. Shall we resort to entreaty and humble supplication? What terms shall we find which have not been already exhausted? Let us not, I beseech you, sir, deceive ourselves longer.

Sir, we have done everything that could be done to aver the storm which is now coming on. We have petitioned; we have remonstrated; we have supplicated; we have prostrated ourselves before the throne, and have implored its interposition to arrest the tyrannical hands of the ministry and Parliament.

Our petitions have been slighted; our remonstrances have produced additional violence and insult; our supplications have been disregarded; and we have been spurned, with contempt, from the foot of the throne. In vain, after these things, may we indulge the fond hope of peace and reconciliation. There is no longer any room for hope.

If we wish to be free — if we mean to preserve inviolate those inestimable privileges for which we have been so long contending — if we mean not basely to abandon the noble struggle in which we have been so long engaged, and which we have pledged ourselves never to abandon until the glorious object of our contest shall be obtained, we must fight! I repeat it, sir, we must fight! An appeal to arms and to the God of Hosts is all that is left us!...

Is life so dear, or peace so sweet, as to be purchased at the price of chains and slavery? Forbid it, Almighty God! I know not what course others may take; but as for me, give me liberty or give me death!

– March 23, 1775

3. The purpose of Patrick Henry's presentation is to
   A. inform
   B. entertain
   C. persuade
   D. explain

4. The audience for Patrick Henry's presentation is the
   A. British Parliament
   B. representatives of the 13 colonies
   C. United Nations
   D. King of England

5. What is the main point of Patrick Henry's speech?

A. a call to fight against Great Britain

B. acceptance of British authority over the 13 colonies

C. a continued hope for peace in North America

D. debate the issues between the 13 colonies and Great Britain

6. Which rhetorical device does Patrick Henry use in the fourth paragraph of his speech?

A. metonymy   C. metaphor

B. asyndeton   D. anaphora

Jesse Jackson - "The Rainbow Coalition," 1984 Democratic National Convention

...We leave this place looking for the sunny side because there's a brighter side somewhere. I'm more convinced than ever that we can win. We will vault up the rough side of the mountain. We can win. I just want young America to do me one favor, just one favor. Exercise the right to dream. You must face reality — that which is. But then dream of a reality that ought to be — that must be. Live beyond the pain of reality with the dream of a bright tomorrow. Use hope and imagination as weapons of survival and progress. Use love to motivate you and obligate you to serve the human family.

Young America, dream. Choose the human race over the nuclear race. Bury the weapons and don't burn the people. Dream -- dream of a new value system. Teachers who teach for life and not just for a living; teach because they can't help it. Dream of lawyers more concerned about justice than a judgeship. Dream of doctors more concerned about public health than personal wealth. Dream of preachers and priests who will prophesy and not just profiteer. Preach and dream!

Our time has come. Our time has come. Suffering breeds character. Character breeds faith. In the end, faith will not disappoint. Our time has come. Our faith, hope, and dreams will prevail. Our time has come. Weeping has endured for nights, but now joy cometh in the morning. Our time has come. No grave can hold our body down. Our time has come. No lie can live forever. Our time has come. We must leave racial battle ground and come to economic common ground and moral higher ground. America, our time has come. We come from disgrace to amazing grace. Our time has come. Give me your tired, give me your poor, your huddled masses who yearn to breathe free and come November, there will be a change because our time has come.

7. Which sentence best summarizes the main point of Mr. Jackson's presentation?

A. Suffering breeds character.

B. You must face reality — that which is.

C. Our time has come.

D. We are often reminded that we live in a great nation.

8. Which of the following groups is the audience for this presentation?

A. middle-aged adults   C. preachers

B. the human race   D. youth

9. Read the second paragraph of this presentation again. What rhetorical device does Jackson use most effectively?

    A. rhetorical question

    B. anaphora

    C. metaphor

    D. metonymy

10. Which type of evidence does Jackson use to support his presentation?

    A. logic and emotional appeals

    B. facts and logic

    C. opinions and definitions

    D. emotional appeals and statistics

Read this student interview. Then answer the questions that follow.

> Shandra Jones is writing an article for her high school newspaper on Patriots Point in Mount Pleasant, South Carolina. As part of the research for her article, she interviewed fellow junior Eric Coleman who is considering a career in the United States Navy.

Shandra: Eric, when did you visit Patriots Point?

Eric: During spring break, my parents, my brother, and I stayed in Charleston. I'm joining the navy and wanted to see real naval vessels. One day we decided to see Patriots Point. It's near Charleston.

Shandra: Whoa, Eric. You're getting ahead of me. I just asked when you were there! Okay, so you want to join the navy, and you like ships.

Eric: Yeah, I've never been on a real ship. I've just read about them.

Shandra: So, what kind of ships did you see?

Eric: We saw an aircraft carrier, a submarine, and a Coast Guard cutter.

Shandra: Which one impressed you the most?

Eric: The *USS Yorktown*. It's huge, 888 feet long, and could house a crew of 3400 officers and enlisted men. This carrier could also keep 90 planes in its hangars. The *Yorktown* earned 11 battle stars.

Shandra: Slow down again, Eric. I can't write that fast. That's quite a ship!

Eric: We got to tour the *Yorktown* too. There were several floors of control rooms, offices, and bunkers. I saw a huge bakery and mess hall too.

Shandra: Did you see any planes?

Eric: Definitely. The massive flight deck still had some planes. I also saw an F4F-3 Wildcat Fighter plane and a B-25 Mitchell Medium Bomber in the hangar bays.

Shandra: What about the submarine?

Eric: We saw the *Clamagore*, which served our country from 1945 to 1981. Ten torpedoes were on this ship. Living spaces were very small and narrow.

Shandra: Eric, you said you toured a Coast Guard cutter.

Eric: That was the *Ingham*. It was involved in many battles in World War II and sunk a German U boat. Later the *Ingham* served off of the Vietnam coast with 336 men on board.

Shandra: Would you recommend that students visit Patriots Point?

Eric: Absolutely. In fact, we're going back next year. I missed seeing the Laffey, a World War II destroyer and the Vietnam Base Camp. There's a lot of living history at Patriots Point.

Shandra: Thanks for answering my questions, Eric.

Eric: Sure. No problem.

11. Shandra seems to have a difficult time writing down Eric's answers. Which of the following ideas would help Shandra the most?
    A. Ask Eric to repeat every answer carefully.
    B. Ask Eric to pause until she writes down each answer to her questions.
    C. Tell Eric to write down his answers to her questions.
    D. Bring a tape recorder, and use it to record the interview.

12. For her article, Shandra wants to interview another person about Patriots Point. Which of the following persons would provide the most information?
    A. a visitor to Patriots Point
    B. a tour guide at Patriots Point
    C. a World War II naval historian
    D. a retired naval veteran

13. To complete her research on Patriots Point, which of the following questions would most likely need to be answered?
    A. How did the Laffey contribute to naval successes in World War II?
    B. Why did the United States need a navy in World War II?
    C. Where is Patriots Point in South Carolina?
    D. What snack do visitors like the most at Patriots Point?

14. What would be the best title for Shandra's article on Patriots Point?
    A. The Role of the *USS Yorktown* in World War II
    B. The Ships of Patriots Point
    C. The History of World War II
    D. Great Naval Battles of World War II

15. Which of the following words best describes the tone of this interview?
    A. critical
    B. nostalgic
    C. objective
    D. subjective

Chapter 4
Author's Purpose and Tone

This chapter covers the following South Carolina end-of-course exam items:	
Reading 1.4	*Demonstrate the ability to evaluate the clarity and accuracy of information as indicators of author's bias.*
Reading 1.5	*Demonstrate the ability to define the purpose of a variety of communication formats such as poetry, drama, fiction, essays, business letters, memos, instructions, policy statements, user manuals, lab reports, and Web sites.*

When you read, you need to be able to tell whether the text is a balanced and accurate account that aims to explain or inform, or whether it is slanted in an attempt to persuade you toward the author's point of view. Evaluating **clarity** and **accuracy** of information can help you recognize an author's **bias**, which is important in fully understanding what you read.

Authors write for many different reasons. Whether you are compiling a shopping list, writing e-mail, or creating an outline for an essay, you have a distinct reason each time you write. As you learned in the last chapter, the **purpose** or reason for writing and presenting can be to inform, to analyze, to persuade, to entertain, and so on, or a combination of more than one of these. In this chapter, you will learn additional, more specific purposes for writing.

The English I End of Course Exam will require you to demonstrate an ability to analyze different types of informational materials and literature. This skill will be valuable to you at school, in the workplace, and even in your leisure time. Some of the materials you will learn to evaluate include examples of the following:

fiction	business letters
poetry	memos
drama	instructions
essays	policy statements
Web sites	manuals

AUTHOR'S PURPOSE

A first step in analyzing texts is to ask yourself questions about the **author's purpose** or motivation for writing a selection, as well as how the author uses **tone** to communicate a feeling or an attitude in the writing. The questions below will help get you started in the process of analysis.

1. What is the author's **purpose** or motivation for writing the text?

2. Does the author use an obvious **tone** or display a certain attitude when referring to the topic?

Every author writes for a specific purpose. Authors usually want to create a particular response in their readers. You can infer the author's purpose or motivation from the way an author writes. The motivation which moves a writer to put pen to paper (or fingers to keyboard) is very similar to the purpose. For example, one reporter writes a required article about laws for conserving water. Another reporter writes an opinion-based article to persuade others to conserve water. The first reporter is motivated by the assignment to inform (purpose), and the second reporter is motivated by a desire to persuade (purpose) others to agree with the personal belief in civic duty.

Reporter - may write to inform, describe an event, or relate an experience	 	**Literary author - may write to entertain, to create a mood, or to describe feelings**

See if you can determine the author's purpose in writing the two paragraphs below.

1. Animals are different from other organisms in that they are many-celled and cannot make their own food. They must take in food to get the energy for life processes. They respond to their environment, grow, and reproduce. Animals are divided into two main groups: vertebrates and invertebrates.

2. One warm fall evening, our son Tom went out to the garage to feed the cat. Suddenly we heard him yell out, "A rat! A Texas-sized rat!" His older brother Joey walked out to investigate and reported back, "Sure enough, Mom. It *is* a rat!" Finally, Barb and I left the safety of the house to look at this "rat." When the plump, furry critter turned around to see us gawking, we realized that it was a 'possum . . . a fat 'possum.

possum

Both paragraphs discuss animals, but they do so in very different ways. Paragraph 1 provides basic information about the classification of animals and their biological processes. The author is writing in an objective tone. There are few descriptive words, no dialogue, and no action. This paragraph would fit well in a science textbook. The author's purpose is **to inform**.

Paragraph 2, on the other hand, describes characters, action, and events with expressive words and interesting dialogue. It is part of a brief story of a surprising and funny event. Perhaps you would find it in a book of short stories. The author's purpose is purely **to entertain**.

The ability to determine the author's purpose in writing a text can greatly enhance reading comprehension. Become familiar with the following list so that you may better understand why an author writes.

Author's Purpose		
Purpose	**Definition**	**Sample Title**
To analyze	To examine methodically	"Inner Workings of Cuckoo Clocks"
To inform	To present facts and details	"Ocean Fishes"
To explain	To help people understand	"How Daylight Savings Time Began"
To persuade	To urge action on an issue	"Raise Penalties for Polluters"
To compare/contrast	To show similarities/differences	"Advantages of Digital Cameras"
To entertain	To amuse or offer enjoyment	"That Time I Slipped in the Mud"
To instruct	To teach concepts and facts	"Tips for Healthy Living"
To create suspense	To convey uncertainty	"Will Tom Win the Race?"
To motivate	To encourage to act	"You Can Survive!"
To cause doubt	To be skeptical	"Are Adults Responsible?"
To describe an event	To narrate	"9-11: USA Under Fire!"
To teach a lesson	To furnish knowledge	"Mastering Exponents"
To introduce a character	To describe a person's traits	"First Look at Captain Nemo"
To create a mood	To establish atmosphere	"Gloom in the House of Usher"
To relate an adventure	To tell an exciting story	"Lost in a Cave"
To share a personal experience	To tell about an event in your life	"The Time I Learned to Share"
To describe feelings	To communicate emotions through words	"When My Dog Died"

Remember, it is rarely enough to sum up the author's purpose in one word: "The author's purpose is to _____." Try to make the statement about the author's purpose specific to the passage. For example, the passages on the previous page would have responses for the author's purpose like the ones shown below:

Passage 1. The author's purpose is to inform readers about certain animal characteristics.

Passage 2. The author's purpose is to entertain readers with the family members' different reactions to an unexpected visitor.

Practice 5: Author's Purpose

Based on the list of author's purposes, identify the author's purpose for the following reading passages. Then, discuss your choices with your class or the instructor.

1.   The fire crackled musically. From it swelled light smoke. Overhead the foliage moved softly. The leaves, with their faces turned toward the blaze, were colored shifting hues of silver, often edged with red. Far off to the right, through a window in the forest, could be seen a handful of stars lying, like glittering pebbles, on the black level of the night.
          – Stephen Crane, *Red Badge of Courage*

    A.   to describe an event during the war   C.   to persuade that war is destructive

    B.   to create a mood of momentary peace   D.   to teach a lesson about nature

2.   Columbus' own successful voyage in 1492 prompted a papal bull dividing the globe between rivals Spain and Portugal. But the Portuguese protested that the pope's line left them too little Atlantic sea room for their voyages to India. The line was shifted 270 leagues westward in 1494 by the Treaty of Tordesillas. Thus, wittingly or not, the Portuguese gained Brazil and gave their language to more than half the people of South America.

    A.   to inform people how maps are created

    B.   to describe feelings about different papal bulls

    C.   to relate an adventure off the Atlantic coasts of South America

    D.   to inform readers about one effect of Columbus's voyage

3.   There is still a great deal of controversy about the future of the space program. While some people believe it is a waste of much needed funds, others point to the great scientific and technological advances that have resulted from the exploration of space. Supporters of the program most frequently cite the wide uses of microprocessors as one of the major contributions to space-related research.

    A.   to inform readers about viewpoints regarding the space program

    B.   to describe the feelings of people who defend the space program

    C.   to inform readers about the way microprocessors work

    D.   to relate an adventure about future planetary space travel

4.   Hand grippers can help give your arms those bulging biceps you're after, but only if they offer enough resistance. If you can squeeze them repeatedly for one to two minutes, and your hands don't get tired, they're too weak for you. You can keep buying stronger ones or make something at home that can do the same job.

    A.   to instruct about the correct use of hand grippers

    B.   to persuade people to buy the right kind of hand gripper

    C.   to describe an event while using hand grippers

    D.   to instruct how to make homemade hand grippers

**Nonamé Delivery Co.
Manual: Time Clock**

1. Find your card.
2. Guide the card, lower end first, into the slot on top of the clock.
3. Wait to hear the click. Then pull the card out.
4. Replace your card in the rack.
5. NEVER clock another employee in or out.

5. What is the purpose for this time clock sheet?

A. to entertain people as they chat when they arrive at work
B. to describe an event in the workday of a typical employee
C. to persuade employees to keep their time cards in order
D. to instruct employees about how to use the time clock

Amazing Achievements

Around the world are many amazing achievements in architecture which are distinctly different and can never be built in the same way. One such structure is the Taj Mahal in India. The Emperor Shah Jahan built this magnificent monument in memory of his wife. Constructed of pure white marble, this building took 20,000 workers 20 years to

finish. Sadly, the emperor executed the architect of this structure, so he could never design a more beautiful one.

A similar fate awaited the architect of the impressive St. Basil's Cathedral in Moscow, Russia. Ivan the Terrible ordered this vividly painted church to be built from precious stones. After this structure was completed, he had the architect blinded, so no one could duplicate this masterpiece.

Even more astonishing was the task of building the Great Pyramid of Egypt over 4,500 years ago. It contains enough stone to construct a 10-foot high wall around Spain. For 30 years, over 4,000 men hauled stones weighing 16.5 tons each. Nearly 2,300,000 stone blocks were needed to build the Great Pyramid.

6. **Constructed Response.** Use your own paper for your response.

What is the author's main purpose in writing this passage? Give a reason with details from the passage for your answer.

Practice 6: Author's Purpose—Activities for Understanding

Working in a group or on your own, review six articles from newspapers or magazines. Using the list of authors' purposes from this section, identify the author's purpose in each selection, and show evidence which supports your responses. Exchange your passages with a classmate to see if he/she identifies the same purpose and supporting evidence for it. Then, discuss your findings with the class or with your teacher.

AUTHOR'S TONE AND ATTITUDE

A tone of voice can be evident in a piece of writing just as tone is evident in a voice when someone is speaking aloud. While growing up, you have probably heard a parent or other adult say, "Don't use that tone of voice with me!" And you have probably responded, "What tone?!" **Tone** is the feeling or **attitude** that underlies words. You know that the same words can be said in many different tones. Just think of the many different ways you can say "Yes" or "Hey." In writing, tone is the way a writer uses words to present a certain attitude or feeling to the reader.

A writer can use the same type of words to convey very different attitudes. Read the following two letters and notice the similar language yet the different attitudes and tones.

To Whom It May Concern:

I am very displeased with the service I have received from Acme, Inc. In fact, it would be more accurate to say the "disservice" which I have received from your company. On three separate occasions (May 11, 14, and 15), I have dialed your so-called "Helpline" and been left on hold for over twenty minutes. You may find it hard to believe, but I have much better ways of spending my time than listening to sleep-inducing music while I'm waiting for your service personnel. Therefore, I am writing this letter so that you may waste your time contacting me at the phone number below. If I do not hear from a representative by the end of this week, I will cease doing business with your company.

Sincerely,

Cindy Ewing (1-800-IAM-FEDUP)

Dear Ms. Ewing,

Please accept our apology for the inconvenience you suffered because of our Helpline. In general, we try to respond to customers within 45 seconds of their call. At times, the volume of calls we receive prevents us from doing that. I am sending this letter to let you know that I have asked one of our representatives to call you this afternoon. If you have not received that call by the time you receive this letter, please use the number below to reach me directly, and we will solve your problem immediately. Thank you for working with Acme, Inc., and we look forward to serving you in the future.

Sincerely,

Zhong Li Customer Service Director (1-800-LET-USHELP)

The authors of both letters use formal language to express their ideas. However, the tone which each author uses is very different.

In Example 1, the author is clearly frustrated about being left on hold. She states directly that she is "displeased with the service" she has received. She adds a slightly sarcastic twist in the second sentence by calling the company's service "disservice." The author states her problem and uses stronger sarcasm in the sentence which begins this way, "You may find it hard to believe..." The last sentence is called an **ultimatum**, that is, a challenge for someone to do something or else suffer certain consequences. This shows that the author is ready to take serious action. Therefore, the author's attitude could be described as angry, sarcastic, or serious. However, **frustrated** is the most accurate description of the author's tone.

The author of the second letter is responding to a frustrated customer. The author wants to solve the customer's problem and make her feel better so that she will still be a customer. He begins his letter by apologizing. He tries to offer an explanation without making excuses. He states the action he has taken and gives the customer direct access to his phone. This action shows that he, too, is serious about solving her problem. The tone of his letter may be called **apologetic**, expressing sorrow for his part in doing something wrong.

The next two letters are examples of the same type of communication. Can you identify the tone of each letter?

Dear Customer,

We miss your business! Our records indicate that you have used our car repair services in the past, but we haven't heard from you lately. Even if you have purchased a new automobile, we can serve you by providing routine maintenance for your vehicle. We now employ five certified mechanics with a total of over 75 years of experience. Each of our mechanics also has specialized training from various auto manufacturers. We hope you are enjoying good, reliable service from your vehicle; but if not, we can help!

Your friendly mechanics,
Acme Auto Care Center

P. S. Don't forget, we offer discounts on towing services!

To Acme Auto Care

Yes, you are missing my business and will continue to miss my business. After the last repair trip my auto made to your garage, I can guarantee that I will never bring another vehicle to your shop. Not only did you unnecessarily replace parts and charge me a huge amount, your "expert" certified mechanics let my car slip off the overhead lift rack causing thousands of dollars of damage to my car. Even though your insurance company paid for those repairs (at another garage!), my car never has been, and never will be, the same.

I have warned everyone I know to stay away from your garage. I demand that you remove my name from your customer mailing list.

Your ex-customer,
Mrs. Mary Smith

The first letter's tone is optimistic, and the second letter has an angry tone.

Below is a partial list of tones authors use to give (or not give) their writing emotion and tone. Define and learn the ones you do not know.

Some Tones Used by Authors				
angry	stiff	dramatic	optimistic	sad
anxious	relaxed	fearful	pessimistic	tragic
rude	hysterical	flippant	humorous	satirical
merry	expectant	lofty	threatening	serious
frustrated	apologetic	sarcastic	sympathetic	objective

Practice 7: Author's Tone

Based on the list of types of tone, identify the author's tone for the following passages. Then, discuss your answers with your class or instructor.

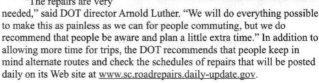

Storms Hit Coast Again

Read up-to-the-minute coverage of the latest weather

FULL STORY

Weekend Movies Promise to Entertain

See the latest movie listings, times, prices, and trailers on our Entertainment page

FULL STORY

Panthers Ready for a New Season

Get all the details about trades, starting lineups, the injury list, and more on our Sports page

FULL STORY

● Heath Scene

● Fashion Page

● Calendar of Howardville Events

Road Repairs Just Ahead

The Department of Transportation announced today that there would be extensive shutdowns over the next three to five months so that repairs could be made to the approximately 24 railroad crossings city-wide. The repairs will be completed outside of rush hour traffic as often as possible, but motorists should expect significant delays.

The DOT explains that over the years there has been a great deal of damage where railroad tracks cross roads. This is due to the expansion and contraction of different building materials occurring at different rates.

"The repairs are very needed," said DOT director Arnold Luther. "We will do everything possible to make this as painless as we can for people commuting, but we do recommend that people be aware and plan a little extra time." In addition to allowing more time for trips, the DOT recommends that people keep in mind alternate routes and check the schedules of repairs that will be posted daily on its Web site at www.sc.roadrepairs.daily-update.gov.

A joint effort of the railroad system and the highways administration, the repairs will be funded partially through transportation taxes with the remainder coming from railway and DOT budgets. FULL STORY

All contents © 2004 Daily News

1. What is the author's tone in the main article on this Web site?

    A. critical   B. optimistic   C. fearful   D. serious

"In the Eye of the Shark" editorial by B. A. Wares

Here's a new idea: Put yourself into a shark's skin. Do
you dare to enter the world where they must glide alone and
hungry? Imagine you feel the emptiness of a creature for
whom there is no free lunch, no supermarket, and no way to
beg for even a single fish scale. You are that animal. You cast
your gaze through the waters: the waters that grow dimmer
and lose oxygen every day. You, as the shark, don't realize that
it is pollution from some very profitable corporations that is
suffocating and blinding you. You only know hunger and
want. Now you feel the tugs and swishes in the water which
signal food, life. You move with silent purpose towards the food. You feel the weight of
the water moving against your skin as the food bobs in front of your eyes. Your eyes see
little through the murky water, little but the food you must have to live, and the urge to
live is stronger than the pull of tides. Now the moment is here, and you open your mouth
to grasp the food that comes from your place in the ocean; as a meat-eater your place is to
eat the weak and misshapen. Your eyes must close against the struggling food. You see
even less than before. There are flashes of pain as you hold on to food that will sustain
your life. The ache of hunger is gone, and you move to deeper, clearer water.

Listen people: Fearing and condemning sharks won't change their needs or their
natures. We, as intelligent beings, must simply take our chances or stay out of the water.

2. What tone does the author use in this passage?

    A. calm   B. threatening   C. cynical   D. persuasive

"The Man He Killed" Thomas Hardy (1840 – 1928)

"Had he and I but met
By some old ancient inn,
We should have sat us down to wet
Right many a nipperkin!

"But ranged as infantry,
And staring face to face,
I shot at him as he at me,
And killed him in his place.

"I shot him dead because –
Because he was my foe,
Just so: my foe of course he was;
That's clear enough; although

"He thought he'd 'list, perhaps,
Off-hand like – just as I –
Was out of work – had sold his traps –
No other reason why.

"Yes; quaint and curious war is!
You shoot a fellow down
You'd treat if met where any bar is,
Or help to half-a-crown."

3. What tone does the author use in this poem?
    A. rude   B. anxious   C. regretful   D. happy

Lady Warriors: Victory with Honor

Last night's basketball game was a thriller like none this town has ever seen! The final score was 16-15, with the Warriors victorious over the Lions at the end, but the score does not speak of the excitement and yes, even the heartache of the battle. The two teams, both in the championship match for the first time in their history, fought almost tooth and nail. Yet a spirit of true athletic goodwill sped the teams and their coaches to a cleanly fought contest of plays made—and risks taken. The Warriors had three girls who were injured in the game, only to return playing even more fearlessly. The Warriors led the game in steals and in rebounding. The Lions kept the game close and led in the number of outside shots. The lead was traded five times in the closing minutes, bringing encouraging shouts from both sections of fans. At the sound of the last buzzer, both benches emptied for congratulations. Could there be a rematch next year? Those of us who could not leave the stands, not even for pizza, are hoping so.

4. What is the tone of this passage?
    A. pessimistic   B. relaxed   C. rude   D. excited

AUTHOR'S BIAS

When you are reading a passage in which the author's purpose is to present a certain opinion or bias indirectly, it is important to notice the way the author says something or the language he/she uses. Also notice if the author is presenting only one point of view as if it were the truth.

Tips for Recognizing an Author's Bias

1. **Identify the opinion or viewpoint on the issue.** It will generally appear near the beginning of the selection, but it may also appear at the end as a conclusion. It may not be stated directly, but may be apparent through the focus of ideas in the selection.

2. **Read the supporting reasons or evidence for the opinion or bias.**

3. **Listen to the tone that is being used in the passage.**

   Hint 1: The tone is **objective** when the passage is written with no emotion and with facts presenting both sides fairly.

   Hint 2: The tone is **biased** when the passage is written with positive emotion or passion directed at one side of the topic or issue while the other side of the issue is being ignored or is expressed with negative terms.

4. **Notice the language used.** For example, in a political speech, the speaker's belief or opinion will be presented in glowing terms with connections that make most people want to agree; words such as freedom, rights, liberty, equality, fairness, honor, community, family, justice, courage, etc. The opponent's side of the issue will be ignored or the language will be negative: irresponsibility instead of freedom, wants instead of rights, chaos instead of liberty, anarchy instead of equality, weakness instead of fairness, ego instead of honor, and so on.

Read the following passage, first for content, and then read it again for author's attitude.

> At least 4,500 non-native animals and plants have established populations in the US, and approximately 15% have become invasive, harming natives. And the invasions are accelerating. "The amount of both passenger and commercial cargo traffic has increased by about 100% in the past decade and people and cargo bring things in with them, . . ." said Dan Glickman, US Secretary of Agriculture. Although regulators have made advances in stopping invasive species at the border, "A whole host of plants that have become invasive pests are still for sale in nurseries," observes Janet Marinelli, director of publishing at the Brooklyn Botanic Garden. By choosing not to buy such invasive plants or products made from threatened species, we may help turn back the species-ravaging tide.

– Allison Sloan, *The Green Guide*

Despite statistics and titled authorities written into this report, the author conveys an inferred attitude or bias. The report is not objective. You may have noticed the word labels used by the author and their negative connections: *invasive* (battle), *invasions* (aggression), *stopping at border* (illegal entry), *invasive, threatened* (in peril), and *species-ravaging* (violent).

Other words that are less biased which might be used in the passage are *overly fertile, successful transplants, blocking entry, adaptive transplants, fertile, difficult-to-manage.*

Read the passage below with these milder terms replacing the more biased ones (the direct quotes are not changed).

> At least 4,500 non-native animals and plants have established populations in the US, and approximately 15% have become **overly fertile**, harming natives. And the **successful transplants** are accelerating. "The amount of both passenger and commercial cargo traffic has increased by about 100% in the past decade and people and cargo bring things in with them..." said Dan Glickman, US Secretary of Agriculture. Although regulators have made advances in **blocking adaptive transplanted** species before **entering US soil**, "A whole host of plants that have become invasive pests are still for sale in nurseries," observes Janet Marinelli, director of publishing at the Brooklyn Botanic Garden. By choosing not to buy **such fertile** plants or products made from **less fertile** species, we may help turn back the more **difficult-to-manage species**.
>
> **Paraphrased** – Allison Sloan, *The Green Guide*

Does reading this reworded passage give you a different feeling than the original? While the author of the original passage has a valid concern and evidence to back up her opinion, she also uses biased language in the passage to persuade other people to be concerned about this issue.

The author has used one other tactic within the text to lead readers to follow the bias of the passage. Did you see it? It is her use of the pronoun "we" in the last sentence of the passage. The passage is well written for the purpose of communicating an attitude: First comes the statistics, slanted language, authorities in agreement, and last comes the pronoun "we" that brings the reader into the group of people who agree with the author's feelings or opinion.

Practice 8: Recognizing Objectivity or Bias

Read each of the following selections. Decide whether the passage is written with **objectivity** or with **bias**. On your own paper, write a brief explanation of your choice, using at least one example from the text.

1. ### Excerpt from *Letters From New York* by Lydia Maria Child, (1843)

    That the present condition of women in society is the result of physical force, is obvious enough; whosoever doubts it, let her reflect why she is afraid to go in the evening without the protection of a man. What constitutes the danger of aggression? Superior physical strength, uncontrolled by the moral sentiments. If physical strength were in complete subjection to moral influence, there would be no need of outward protection. That animal instinct and brute force now govern the world, is painfully apparent in the condition of women everywhere; from the Morduan Tartars, whose ceremony of marriage consists in placing the bride on a mat, and consigning her to the bridegroom, with the words, "Here, wolf, take thy lamb,"—to the German remark, that "stiff ale, stinging tobacco, and a girl in her smart dress, are the best things."

2. ### Chairs

    The piece of furniture known as the chair has had an unique history. It has, above all other furniture items, been a public symbol of power and prestige in many cultures. A monarch did not lay down upon a throne but always sat upright on "the seat of power" to rule the realm. Even today in the Western culture, to "chair a committee" means you are in authority over others. A top business position is labeled "chairperson." Take a glimpse into the offices at your place of business or even in your family's house. Who in your company or in your home has the largest or most comfortable chair? Think about it. Power and prestige.

3.
Excerpt from *To Make Laws* by James H. Hutson

There can be no question that Congress is more efficient than it was in its early days. Legislative business in both houses can now be conducted effectively; many weapons of obstruction that the rules once permitted have been eliminated. It is in the nature of a partisan body that some members will object to the manner in which the rules and procedures are applied. Congress would not be Congress—indeed, democracy would be in danger—if there were not complaints about how the institution was being run. But the long view yields the conclusion that, although Congress might conduct its business better in the future, it is operating more effectively now than it did in the past.

4.
Say Yes to Animal Rights! - Excerpt from *Coalition for Animal Awareness* Pamphlet

Please learn with me how we are exploiting animals on this earth of ours. Over 20 million cats and dogs are euthanized in the United States each year. Millions of animals undergo cruel treatment in unsanitary research laboratories. They are caged, addicted to drugs, and sometimes killed and dissected in these laboratories.

Animals that perform in circuses, television, movies, and even zoos often suffer neglect, boredom, and harsh abuse at the hands of their trainers. Foxes, beaver, and mink caught in traps for their fur suffer a slow, painful death. Over six billion pigs, chickens, and cows become food for millions of consumers. Racing greyhounds are often euthanized once they can no longer compete, and only a few find homes through greyhound rescue organizations.

We must end this exploitation and cruelty to our animal friends today. Writing emotional letters of protest to your representatives can make a significant difference. You can set the best example by eating vegetables and fruit instead of meat. Everyone should encourage pet adoptions. Spread the word that buying animal furs is wrong.

CHAPTER 4 REVIEW

A. Read the following passages carefully. For each one, write the **author's purpose.** Also, write the **tone** which BEST describes the passage. You may refer to the lists of purposes and tones found in this chapter. Then write out an **explanation of your response** and how this influences your answers about the passage's purpose and tone.

1.
Radio Ad

Announcer: Grace Chisolm, the well-known newscaster, has this to say about the Cheetah XR-71:

Grace Chisholm: "It drives like a sea breeze. I can definitely tell this car is going to redefine the future of the automotive industry."

Announcer: Like Ms. Chisholm, we at Sunrise Motors believe this sports car looks better, rides better, and drives better than anything else in its class.

2.

The Balm From Gilead

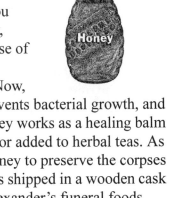

Can you name the material that can be used as an antiseptic salve, a treatment for stomach ulcers, an embalming fluid, and a great tasting topping for your morning toast? No such thing, you say? Be ready to be surprised. The answer is honey! The sticky, sweet, super-saturated sugar is all those things and more. The use of honey through the ages has met both medicinal and nutritional needs. Many cultures have used honey as a balm for wounds. Now, scientists have proven that the high level of sugar in honey prevents bacterial growth, and the fluid has moisturizing properties that promote healing. Honey works as a healing balm also for stomach ulcers when eaten by itself, with some foods, or added to herbal teas. As for embalming, the Greeks, Romans, and Egyptians all used honey to preserve the corpses of their revered dead. Alexander the Great's body, it is said, was shipped in a wooden cask filled with honey to his home in Greece for burial. Some of Alexander's funeral foods were most likely prepared with honey to sweeten and to thicken them. So, tomorrow morning take a jar of sourwood honey (my favorite, though there are many other types) and pour the golden drops of bee-ripened nectar on your biscuit or into your tea. You'll see that honey is truly one of the sweetest surprises on earth.

3.

Excerpt from *Official Report to the Government on Grand Canyon Exploration*

….and the geologist, in the light of the past history of the earth, makes prophecy of a time when this desolate land of Titanic rocks shall become a valley of many valleys, and yet again the sea will invade the land, and the coral animals build their reefs in the infini-tesimal laboratories of life, and lowly beings shall weave nacre-lined shrouds for them-selves, and the shrouds shall remain entombed in the bottom of the sea, when the people shall be changed, by the chemistry of life into new forms; monsters of the deep shall live and die, and their bones be buried in the coral sands. Then other mountains and other hills shall be washed into the Colorado Sea... Thus ever the land and sea are changing; new lands are born, and with advancing periods are found; new complexities of life evolved…

John Wesley Powell, June 16, 1874

4.

Excerpt from "Clarissa's Speech" in *Shams* by John S. Draper

"I stand as firm as the rock of Gibraltar on the right that women have to shape the thoughts, socially and politically, of the world. They can make our country better and purer, just as they appreciate their own rights. I am in favor of women's rights—in their rights to rise up in the majesty of the nature their Creator gave them and emancipate them-selves from the foolish fashions and sentiments of the age. When they do rise, they will be more respected by all mankind than all the rulers of the earth from Adam down to the present day."

5.

The Moon

Through space exploration, scientists have constructed a history of the moon dating back to its infancy. Rocks collected from the lunar highlands date about 4.0 to 4.3 billion years old. It's believed the solar system formed about 4.6 billion years ago. The first few million years of the moon's existence were so violent that few traces of this period remain. As a molten outer layer gradually cooled and solidified into different kinds of rock, the moon was bombarded by huge asteroids and smaller objects. Some of the asteroids were the size of small states like Rhode Island or Delaware, and their collisions with the moon created huge basins hundreds of kilometers across

The catastrophic bombardment died away about 4 billion years ago, leaving the lunar highlands covered with huge overlapping craters and a deep layer of shattered and broken rock. Heat produced by the decay of radioactive elements began to melt the inside of the moon at depths of about 200 kilometers (124 miles) below its surface. Then, from about 3.8 to 3.1 billion years ago, great floods of lava rose from inside the moon and poured over its surface, filling in the large impact basins to form the dark parts of the moon called maria or seas. Explorations show that there has been no significant volcanic activity on the moon for more than 3 billion years.

B. Read the following passage carefully, and answer the questions that follow.

Mr. Sanchez Makes His Rounds

It was midnight. Mr. Sanchez always made a final round of the barn at night to check that all was in order. He was later than usual tonight, and he shuffled more than walked, struggling to keep his eyes open. It was hard enough to see through the moonless gloom. For a moment, it seemed all was well. Horses stood in their stalls in quiet, unfathomable submission to the winter cold, dreaming, perhaps, of grassy fields. Then, "Aw, not brought in, tonight?" Mr. Sanchez thought, as he glimpsed two small equine shadows standing patiently at the pasture gate next to the barn's outer row of stalls. "Not doing their job," he mumbled, picking up one of the lead ropes always, it seemed, within reach. He made his way through the side passage out of the barn and towards the gate. He only needed one rope for the ponies. He knew that little Fantasia would stick like hoofed devotion to Midnight's side on the way back to their shared stall.

Mr. Sanchez opened the gate a little. "C'mon, big girl, let's go home," he coaxed. His gentle words had hardly passed his lips when they blended in the night air with unearthly screeches, snarls, and growls. A black, shapeless streak hurtled towards the small group from nowhere and everywhere at once as horrible screams and grunts wrenched themselves from some unnameable throat. In an instant, the world was full of black mane, hooves, tails, legs, screams, and terror. Mr. Sanchez had no sense of his body, which had turned to jelly and had lost all connection with the earth beneath it. He was falling.

A stall! The thought pierced the fog of his panic. Ten paces away. He had no memory of covering the distance. Somehow he half dove, half flew over the stall door, and there he was, on his back, on a floor of wood shavings and dirt, eye-level with a set of palomino hooves. At his entrance, Sunshine, having almost panicked during the preceding moments of chaos outside her stall, had started nervously, and then calmed down. She snorted, regarding her owner from this new perspective with some interest. Mr. Sanchez looked back at her. She seemed to be wondering if, after all the upsetting commotion of moments ago, this clumsily delivered package at her feet was supposed to be her comic relief. After a minute, though, all interest waned, and she lipped up a clump of alfalfa from under her hanging grain bucket. Her ears relaxed back into their contented position, and life went on.

Mr. Sanchez pulled himself up against the stall door. A pig, he thought; it must have been a wild pig. Where in tarnation had that monster come from? For that matter, where in tarnation have the ponies disappeared to? He had work to do, he could see, but that could wait. When the coast was clear—*very* clear—he would call the sheriff and report the menace. But for now, he patted Sunshine. Her warm strength and simple contentment gave him confidence. Still rattled from his fright, he was in no hurry to leave.

Open-ended responses. Use your own paper to write your response.

6. What is the author's main purpose or motivation for writing this passage? Give a reason with details from the passage for your response.

7. What is the author's purpose in not mentioning the word "pig" until the end of the story? Use details from the story to support your response.

8. What is the author's attitude towards the main characters in the story? What was the author's attitude toward the character of the horse, Sunshine? Give specific details from the story to support your response.

Chapter 5
Inferences and Conclusions

This chapter covers the following South Carolina end-of-course exam items:	
Reading 1.8	*Demonstrate the ability to draw conclusions and make inferences.*

Whenever you read, you are applying your previous knowledge and experiences to figure out what a text is really saying. You can understand what you read more deeply by applying what you already know to it. This type of understanding comes from developing **inferences and conclusions.**

We make inferences often in our daily lives. For example, if you observe your football coach jumping for joy after an interception, you might infer that your team gained a chance to score a touchdown. Even though no words are spoken, the actions speak for themselves.

If you were to make an inference based on the photo about how this dog would react if you walked up to pet it, what could you infer? An **inference** is an educated guess based on information already given. The dog is playfully rolling on the ground and wagging its tail, so if you infer that the dog is friendly and decide to pet it, you would be making a prediction that you are safe. A **prediction** is a statement about future events using information already given.  Your **conclusion** (decision) to greet the dog and the logical outcome (consequence or result) would probably be positive. It would be a generalization to assume that all dogs are friendly. Remember that not all generalizations are accurate.

In this chapter, you will learn how to make **inferences,** and how to draw **conclusions**. These skills are important for improving your reading comprehension and literary analysis. When you take the English I End of Course Exam, you may need to answer questions that directly ask you to demonstrate these skills. These skills are also necessary to make other interpretations and evaluations of fiction and non-fiction writing.

INFERENCES

Making **inferences** is making connections between the various pieces of information given in the text, or reading appropriately between the lines. The ability to make suitable inferences is an important skill for a reader to develop. Many writers don't tell you everything but rely on you making reasonable inferences. The passage below has a topic that must be inferred. Notice how the details contribute to the inference.

> These storms occur over land and are the most violent of all atmospheric disturbances. They are highly localized and, therefore, do not affect large areas at one time. The actual path of destruction of these storms is rarely more than 100 yards in width. They take the form of a rotating column of air that extends down to the land from a thundercloud. They happen most frequently in the Midwestern states and in the southeastern part of the United States.

Can you infer the topic of this passage? If you decided that the author was describing **tornadoes**, you were right. The facts and details provided all of the clues. Such information included the following:

- storms occurring over land
- the violence and localized nature of the storms
- a narrow path of destruction
- a rotating column of air
- storms common in the Midwest and the Southeast

You could also draw other inferences about the selection. For example, you could infer that tornadoes cause great damage to people and property. The passage also suggests that since tornadoes emerge from thunderclouds, they occur during unstable weather such as thunderstorms.

Now reread the selection. Write two other inferences you could make about the information.

Look at the following newspaper ad and answer the questions.

Want Ad:

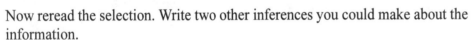

Energetic person to work at Ourtown Memorial Stadium. You'll see every home game. Some sales experience helpful, but not necessary. Uniform provided. Apply at Gate 6 Concession Stand, 2401 East Gridlock Freeway.

1. The person who takes this job will probably work as a **(a)** football player; **(b)** water boy; **(c)** hot dog vender.

2. What two details tell you what kind of job this is?

You should be able to infer that the job opening is for a hot dog vender. Information concerning selling and mention of concession stand are the bases for the inference. The mention of the stadium and uniform apply equally well to jobs as football player and water boy.

Practice 1: Inferences

Read the following passage. Choose the best inference for each question.

Why Is There So Much Fighting in Northern Ireland?

Conflict has been a way of life for centuries in Ireland, the island off the western shore of England. The Anglo-Normans first invaded the island in 1167, and there has been unrest ever since. To understand this or any ongoing conflict, it is important to learn about its history.

Ireland tried to get free from British rule for many years. There were many uprisings especially in the 18th and 19th centuries. All this time, the Irish people fought a common enemy: the British invaders. But by the end of the 19th century, the Irish began fighting among themselves. They started to disagree about having home rule (become an independent nation). In the North (which was now industrialized and where many Protestants lived), the "Unionists" wanted to be united with Britain. After all, it was good for business. They were also afraid that independence would bring influence from Rome, the seat of Catholicism, because Ireland's capital was Dublin (in the South, mainly a farming area where many Catholics lived).

In 1912 Ireland finally became independent on paper. However, the first world war put everything on hold. By the end of the war, no real steps had been taken. So the Irish Republican Army (IRA) was formed and started to attack the occupying British. In 1920, Britain set up a parliament in Ireland. They thought this would make it seem as though Ireland had its own government. Meanwhile it would help the British control Ireland. The Unionists accepted this. But the Nationalists were determined to gain real independence.

Finally, an Irish Free State was established in 1921. This step officially divided Ireland's 32 counties. The 26 counties in the South became the Republic of Ireland. The remaining 6 counties in the North were now called Northern Ireland. Of course, this did not mean everyone was happy or that all Irish citizens lived where their views were accepted.

There was much discrimination against Catholics in Northern Ireland. As a result, civil rights protests began in the 1960s. People there were inspired by the civil rights movement in the United States. But in Northern Ireland, the movement became ever more violent. A crucial moment came during the infamous Battle of Bogside (a Catholic section of Londonderry) in 1969. To stop this two-day riot, the Irish Prime Minister asked for military help from Britain. British force was again brought in, and British troops remain in Northern Ireland to this day.

Over the years, many more horrible clashes have happened. An example is Bloody Sunday in 1972, when British troops killed more than a dozen protesters, claiming they were fired on first. Many solutions also have been tried. One example is the Belfast Agreement of 1999 that tried to transition troops out of Northern Ireland, but unsuccessfully. There always seems to be some part of the treaties that favors one side or the other. Still, everyone continues trying to find a way to stop the fighting.

The BBC-Belfast reported at the end of 2004 that most citizens just want to get on with their lives. People were asked how they feel about the Protestant-Catholic problem. Responses showed that most people do not see the other side as the enemy. For example, 9 out of 10 people do not care whether their doctor is Protestant or Catholic. Over 90 percent would consider selling their home to someone from the other tradition. Many peace projects have started, and the governments continue to negotiate. Everyone hopes that one day both sides will find the perfect balance to put an end to the fighting in Northern Ireland.

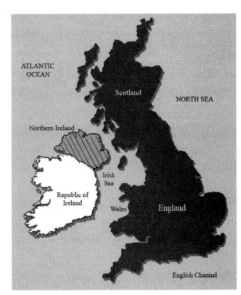

1. Based on the passage, we can infer that

    A. ordinary citizens can get along for the most part.
    B. there are fewer Catholics than Protestants in Ireland.
    C. the 1969 arrival of British troops was helpful.
    D. the IRA should keep peace in Ireland.

2. The passage suggests that

    A. military force is greatly needed in Ireland.
    B. conflicts are based on both politics and religion.
    C. dividing the country helped to decrease the fighting.
    D. the IRA accomplished what it set out to do.

3. Which of the following has most likely happened?

    A. Many Irish citizens have moved to England to escape the fighting.
    B. All Catholics eventually left Northern Ireland and went to live elsewhere.
    C. Political leaders are no longer trusted, so none of the peace proposals can work.
    D. Religious beliefs have become associated in many ways with political views.

Practice 2: More Inferences

Clip at least two passages from newspapers or magazines. Read each one carefully. What inferences can you make from the information in each passage? Cite *facts* or *details* to support your inferences. Exchange passages with another student and make inferences from their passages. Compare your inferences to the inferences made by your partner. Discuss any differences between the inferences you each made.

CONCLUSIONS

Drawing a conclusion is a common type of inference skill. When you draw a conclusion, you form a judgment or opinion based on the details in a passage as well as your personal knowledge and experience. S. I. Hayakawa, a famous professor of *semantics* (the study of meaning in language), once said that conclusions are "statements about the unknown made on the basis of the known." To draw conclusions, use all the facts and clues present in the passage with your previous knowledge and experience. When a conclusion is logically based on the facts and details provided, then it is a **valid conclusion**.

Read the following passage. Check the conclusion that can be drawn from this passage.

Hayley has studied all week for her algebra test. She spent three hours every night working on the review exercises in her textbook. Last night she could not sleep very well because she was afraid she would sleep through her alarm.

_____ 1. Hayley will pass her test.

_____ 2. Hayley is nervous about her algebra test.

_____ 3. Hayley gets nervous before big tests.

Here is an explanation of the answers:

The statement for (1) is not a conclusion, but is a prediction. Something could happen to Hayley on the way to the test that would prevent her from taking it; therefore, she would not pass. She might also fall asleep during the test, since she didn't sleep well the night before.

The statement for (2) is a conclusion. We can conclude Hayley is nervous about her test since she studied for long hours and could not sleep well the night before.

The statement for (3) is a not a conclusion, but rather a generalization. The passage is only speaking of an algebra test. There is no evidence to indicate that she gets nervous before all big tests.

For further practice, read the following paragraph, and then answer the question.

At a signal from the captain, the propeller had been disengaged and the fins placed vertically; then the *Nautilus* had shot up at a terrifying speed, like a balloon being carried into the atmosphere. It cut through the water with a loud quivering noise. We could see nothing. In four minutes we had covered the four leagues between us and the surface, and after leaping into the air like a flying fish, we came hurtling back down onto the water, making it splash up to a prodigious height.

– Jules Verne, *20,000 Leagues Under the Sea*

Based on this paragraph, we can conclude that the *Nautilus*

   A.   was descending into the ocean.
   B.   was a flying fish named by the captain.
   C.   rose out of the ocean with great force.
   D.   raced across the ground at amazing speeds.

To choose the best answer for this question, you should read the paragraph carefully, paying special attention to the facts and details. Next, narrow your choices to responses that contain stated information from the paragraph. You also should eliminate responses that do not contain facts or details from the passage.

Following this process of logic, you will disregard A. Rather than descending, the author says the Nautilus "shot up" and leapt "into the air like a flying fish." B would be eliminated because the passage does not mention the captain naming the *Nautilus* after a flying fish. The *Nautilus* is compared to a flying fish, but this is different from the B response. Choice D is not appropriate because the *Nautilus* "cut through the water." Therefore, the best answer is C. The facts and details about cutting through water and covering "four leagues," lead us to the conclusion: the *Nautilus* "shot up" and rose out of the ocean with great force.

Practice 3: Conclusions

A. Drawing Conclusions Reread the passage, "Why There is so Much Fighting in Northern Ireland" on pages 85 – 86. Choose the best answer for the question below. Then, cite the evidence to support your answer.

1.   Which is the most likely conclusion a person can draw?

   A.   Only a leader who does not side with either religion can unite Ireland.

   B.   Ireland is a part of the British Isles, so Britain should remain in control of it.

   C.   Areas of Ireland should be set aside for Protestants and others for Catholics.

   D.   Ending British occupation of Northern Ireland is a first step toward peace.

B. Reading for Conclusions. Read the following passages. Check only the valid conclusions from the choices given after each passage. Then, cite the evidence to support each answer.

Sleeping

   Some people think they don't move at all while they sleep. They believe that they go to bed and never change position. Not true. Studies show that everybody makes at least eight to twelve major posture shifts a night. Insomniacs may double or triple that.

Which is a valid conclusion? Explain the evidence for your choice.

_____ 1. Insomniacs shift positions less often than regular sleepers.

_____ 2. Insomniacs shift positions more often than regular sleepers.

Flight

   When Orville Wright made the first powered airplane flight in 1903 at speeds of 50 kilometers (31 miles) per hour, the significance of his achievement was barely recognized. Yet in little more than half a century following that historic event at Kitty Hawk, astronauts succeeded in orbiting Earth at speeds measured in thousands of miles per hour and set foot on the moon.

Which is a valid conclusion? Explain the evidence for your choice

_____ 3. Orville Wright was widely praised for the first powered airplane flight in 1903.

_____ 4. Orville Wright was a pioneer of the Space Age.

Excerpt from *Tartuffe*, by Jean Baptiste Poquelin Molière

The characters in this scene are Orgon and his daughter, Mariane.

ORGON: What say you of—Tartuffe?

MARIANE: Who? I?

ORGON: Yes, you. Look to it how you answer.

MARIANE: Why! I'll say of him—anything you please.

ORGON: Well spoken. A good girl. Say then, my daughter,
That all his person shines with noble merit,
That he has won your heart, and you would like
To have him, by my choice, become your husband. Eh?

MARIANE: Eh?

ORGON: What say you?

MARIANE: Please, what did you say?

ORGON: What?

MARIANE: Surely I mistook you, sir?

ORGON: How now?

Portrait of Molière

MARIANE: Who is it, father, you would have me say
Has won my heart, and I would like to have
Become my husband, by your choice?

ORGON: Tartuffe.

MARIANE: But, father, I protest it isn't true!
Why should you make me tell this dreadful lie?

ORGON: Because I mean to have it be the truth.
Let this suffice for you: I've settled it.

Which is a valid conclusion? Explain the evidence for your choice

_____5. Mariane does not wish to marry Tartuffe.

_____6. Orgon and his daughter are both hard of hearing.

C. Passage Practice. Read several passages from newspapers and magazines. What conclusions can you draw from the information? Cite facts or details to support your conclusions. Share your passages and conclusions with other students. Is there agreement about the conclusions?

D. Create Riddles. Cut pictures of people, places, or objects from magazines or newspapers. Each student writes the name of each item in the corner of the picture. Exchange your pictures around the room. Then each person writes a riddle of five clues for each picture. The students in the class number their papers. Then students take turns reading each riddle, and everyone writes the answers on paper. The student solving the most riddles wins a prize.

E. Riddle Game. The instructor makes a list of familiar objects for several class teams. Each student must clearly describe one of the objects to his or her team without naming it. If the team guesses the object in three minutes, it receives a point. The team with the greatest points wins.

F. Popular Games. Practice drawing conclusions by playing *Clue*™ (board or video version), ***Where in the World is Carmen Sandiego?***™, or ***Cranium***™. These games are available at retail stores. Another good game for practicing this skill is charades.

Tips for Answering Questions About Inferences and Conclusions
1. Read the passage twice.
2. Read the question and answer choices.
3. Choose your answer based on the stated facts or clues in the passage.

CHAPTER 5 REVIEW

Read the following passages, and answer the questions after each.

Can Snakebites be Healthy?

Bill Haast, an 85-year-old Floridian, has developed a reputation as a man with an acquired immunity to snakes. Playing with a cobra is an everyday activity with Mr. Haast, who has been bitten no fewer than 162 times by venomous snakes.

He began his experimentation with snake venom in 1948 by injecting himself with small amounts of rattlesnake venom. Over the years, he has built up the dosage. He believes the snake venom has kept him healthy. He has not once been sick since he began injecting himself with venom.

He had his near death experiences, though. In 1958, Haast was bitten by a blue krait, an Asian snake which has venom many times more poisonous than a cobra's. It has been known to kill elephants. During his ordeal, Haast realized that something as powerful as venom must have something useful for medicine.

In the late 1970s, Haast produced a drug called PROven which mirrored the effects produced by his own immunity to snake bites. The drug has been used to treat rheumatoid arthritis and multiple sclerosis. Over 7,000 patients have been treated with this high-demand drug.

He recently purchased a house for snake-keeping in Southwestern Florida. Daily he collects venom from over 400 snakes and sells it to laboratories. His own blood is so full of antibodies that it is used as an antidote for victims of snake bites.

1. Based on this passage, what is likely to happen if Bill is bitten again by a poisonous snake?

2. Which of the following conclusions can be drawn from the passage?

   A.   Bill Haast has unique powers.

   B.   Other people could build immunity in half the time.

   C.   Very few people support Bill's lifestyle.

   D.   Bill Haast is not afraid of snake bites.

Healing Waters Flow in South Carolina

The Healing Springs supply water is said to have medicinal—even miraculous—powers. The water comes from an artesian well. Native Americans always considered the waters to have healing powers and would bathe in them when ill or injured. Legends about the springs date back to the 1770s. According to those legends, four severely wounded soldiers from a British garrison were left at Healing Springs. Two other healthy soldiers were also left to care for the wounded until they died. The story goes that several months later, all six men rejoined their ranks in Charleston! So if you're in need of some recuperation, stop at Healing Springs, just three miles north of Blackville, SC. Admission is free; open daily from dawn to dusk.

Visit God's Acre

An area of land near Blackville, South Carolina, is listed on the books as owned by "God, Almighty." Known informally as God's Acre, the area is home to the famous Healing Springs, an artesian well thought to possess healing qualities. The springs are open for all to sample the water and take some when they leave. Many residents of South Carolina, Georgia, and some from farther away stop to fill jugs with the mineral water. There are many other attractions nearby as well. Those include Barnwell State Park, Thoroughbred Country, and the South Carolina Heritage Corridor. Make a day or even a week of it, and visit all the attractions!

3. From the information offered, what can we conclude that Healing Springs offers for visitors?

4. Based on these articles, who do you think is the intended audience?

The Hermit's Hut

Thomas, bearing the unconscious monk in his arms, and somewhat faint from his own wounds, staggered in the direction of the chiming bell. He had but a short distance to go from the scene of combat to the tiny chapel where a hermit was saying his prayers. At the sound of Thomas' clattering footsteps, the hermit turned with a start and hastened toward him disclosing a kindly face lit by large brown eyes.

"Brother," gasped Thomas, "here is a holy man badly wounded for my sake. I beg you to use your skill with herbs to heal him."

The hermit responded quickly and led them into his chambers. Thomas carried the monk with tenderness and laid him down on the hermit's couch.

"I best be alone with him," said the hermit. "Go outside and wait till I come to you. I think the brother is not wounded unto death."

Thomas went out obediently as the good monk faintly called his name. "Be not troubled," said the hermit. "He does not know that he calls you. He is delirious."

Alone with the monk, the hermit began to look at the wound. The hermit looked at the soft white flesh of the shoulder with surprise. Then on impulse, he removed the hood and confirmed his thought. Long hair cascaded over the monk's delicate face. The hermit paused, looking at her frail body in dismay.

5.   Why did Thomas help the monk?

6.   Why did Thomas think the hermit could help the monk?

7.   How did Thomas feel about the monk?

8.   What about the identity of the monk surprised the hermit?

9.   What inference can you draw from this passage about the wounded monk?
   A.   The monk was desperate to fight in the war.
   B.   The monk had tried to enter the war before.
   C.   The monk wanted to fight beside Thomas and was willing to die for him.
   D.   The monk will probably die.

From an Editorial

In the early 1990s, the town of Hilton Head, South Carolina, was already famous for its adult recreation but had little space dedicated to kids. The former mayor was set against using public funds to build parks when they could be used for golf courses and marinas that catered to wealthy visitors and residents.

Fortunately, a great deal has changed in the last few years. Since adopting the 1995 Recreation and Open Spaces Plan, Hilton Head has developed about half a dozen new public parks. The spaces vary in amenities, including nature walks, sports fields, pet areas, and boardwalks. They are great for youngsters from throughout the area, but also cater to adults who love the outdoors. The parks also open up opportunities for community gatherings such as festivals.

The population of Hilton Head has grown, including the number of families with children. It stands to reason that green areas and recreation opportunities accompany that growth. The current town officials should be applauded for their vision and action.

Keep it up; we're thrilled with the results!

10. From the editor's point of view, which word best describes the attitude of the former mayor?
    A. greedy   B. indifferent   C. adventurous   D. professional

11. What does the writer claim are the reasons why parks are good for the community?

Harry Houdini

In the summer of 1912, a man was chained and then nailed into a wooden box. The box was bound with rope and steel cables and lowered into the East River. Minutes passed as the audience waited to see what would happen. Fearing for the man's life, many gasped for breath themselves. Suddenly, the man emerged from the water, unharmed and freed from his chains. His name was Harry Houdini.

Houdini spent a lifetime performing escapes that left his audiences astonished and clamoring for more. Dangling upside down from a crane, he could wrestle himself out of a straightjacket in minutes. He could be handcuffed and lowered into a steel drum secured with padlocks and filled with water. Three minutes later, he would emerge alive and well.

How did Houdini accomplish his feats? Besides being a master of illusion, he also possessed two unique talents. His body was flexible and muscular which allowed him to untie knots with his fingers and teeth. He also trained himself to hold his breath under water for up to four minutes. Besides that, he could pick apart any lock or chain in the world. In fact, he often showed people from his audience that he could open locks they brought to him. In this way, he proved that the ones he picked were not fake. In 1901, he was handcuffed to a pillar by police who would return in an hour to free him. He escaped before they left the room. In 1903, German police accused him of cheating and encouraging criminals. He escaped in the courtroom and won the case.

Mark each of the following conclusions or inferences as *valid* or *invalid*.

12. Houdini didn't use good sense in his performances.   Valid   Invalid

13. Houdini had a death wish.   Valid   Invalid

14. Houdini developed some of his skills through practice.   Valid   Invalid

15. Houdini didn't have a fear of death.   Valid   Invalid

16. Houdini's father was an escape artist.   Valid   Invalid

17. Houdini was a master escape artist and entertainer.   Valid   Invalid

18. Houdini's physical skills were critical to his success.   Valid   Invalid

19. What conclusion can you draw about Houdini's lock-picking skills?
    A.   Houdini learned to pick locks by watching thieves steal from banks.
    B.   As a magician, Houdini knew how to trick his audience into believing he could pick locks.
    C.   Houdini mastered the art of picking locks by using intelligence and speed.
    D.   Houdini's lock-picking skills always allowed him to escape the police.

20. What do Houdini's daring feats suggest about his attitude toward death?

Chapter 6
Elements of Literature

This chapter covers the following South Carolina end-of-course exam items:	
Reading 2.3	*Demonstrate the ability to compare and contrast universal literary themes as they are developed in works in a variety of genres.*
Reading 2.4	*Demonstrate the ability to compare authors' styles on the basis of such elements as word choice and sentence structure (syntax).*
Reading 2.6	*Demonstrate the ability to use a knowledge of internal structures to compare selections from works in a variety of genres.*

The **elements** of literature include **genres** (types of literature) and the development of **characters**, **plot**, **setting**, and **theme**. Authors develop distinctive **writing styles** by using elements in different ways. In addition, authors' individual styles also come from how they use words, sentences, and other structures available to them in their writing.

Understanding a work of literature can help deepen your appreciation of it. Once you understand individual works of literature, you can also begin to see the patterns that group them into genres or unite them with universal themes. By analyzing literature, you can also discover insights into the human experience that may enrich your life. To **analyze** something means to take small parts of a whole and study the parts for understanding. The analysis of literature is much like the study of the human body. To understand how the human body works, you would study the brain, heart, lungs, muscles, and other organs. Then, you would study how these organs work together as a whole system. How the human body works is easier to understand with that type of study.

LITERARY GENRES

Just as a heart is a heart because of what it does, not because of whose body it is in, literary **genres** (types of literature) aren't always determined by author, subject, or setting (time and place). Written works are grouped in genres according to certain structures and technical characteristics they share. Authors have used some of these types of literature for thousands of years while others are more recent inventions. The following is a list with definitions and examples of some common literary genres.

LITERARY NONFICTION

Nonfiction is writing which is meant to be true or factual. It is written to teach or to inform you. **Functional nonfiction** includes materials such as manuals, "how-to" books, and scientific explanations. **Literary nonfiction** presents factual information as well, but uses elements that are traditionally used by fiction writers, such as characterization, plot and setting development, inclusion of theme, and others that you'll read about in this chapter and the next.

General NonFiction

Biography   the story of a person's life written by someone else. Examples include John Kennedy's *Profiles in Courage* and Alfred Kroeber's *Ishi, Last of His Tribe.*

Autobiography   the story of a person's life written by that person. Two examples are Beryl Markham's *West with the Night*, about life in Africa and the life of a pilot, and *Anne Frank: Diary of a Young Girl,* a firsthand account of a Jewish family trying to hide from Hitler's soldiers.

Essays   analytical or interpretive writing about a topic. Examples include a series of essays by Sir Francis Bacon, reflecting his ideas about topics such as truth, marriage, superstition, friendship, and many more. Henry David Thoreau wrote the famous essay, "On the Duty of Civil Disobedience," offering his thoughts about the role of government and the responsibility of citizens to oppose unjust laws.

FICTION

Fiction is narrative writing, which means telling a story. To create fiction, writers draw on imagination rather than recount actual events. The term fiction is most often used to describe novels and short stories. Fiction can be short but powerful, as in Shirley Jackson's "The Lottery," or it can be long and full of adventure as in Alexandre Dumas' *Three Musketeers.*

Novel   any long, fictional story usually written in prose, not poetry. Two examples are James F. Cooper's *The Last of the Mohicans* and Stephen King's *Carrie.*

Short Story   tells a complete story in just 500 to 15,000 words. Most often, the story has a clear beginning, middle, and end. It reveals the characters' personalities through actions and thoughts. Examples include Eudora Welty's "A Worn Path," John Steinbeck's "The Chrysanthemums," and Richard Connell's "The Most Dangerous Game."

POETRY

Poetry is literature that strongly conveys emotion, uses vivid description and figurative language, and is usually written in lines and stanzas. Unlike **prose**, which follows standard grammar rules including sentence and paragraph structure, poetry can be much-more free-form, though some types of poetry follow complex systems of rhythm and meter. Also, rhythm and sometimes rhyme often make poetry different from prose. John Milton called poetry "simple, sensuous, impassioned language." The sound effects of poetry are heard best when the poems are read aloud. Examples: "Psalm 51," Maya Angelou's "And Still I Rise," and Robert Frost's "The Road Less Traveled."

DRAMA

Drama is a story told in action and **dialogue** (conversation) between actors who perform as characters. Dramas, or plays, can be written in prose (Example: *Death of a Salesman* by Arthur Miller) and poetry (Example: *Othello* by William Shakespeare). They may be read as books, but they are intended for performance on the stage. There are many kinds of dramatic literature from comedy to tragedy. Drama contains some elements that are found in no other type of literature, such as scenery and props instead of narration to convey setting, and devices such as **soliloquy** (pronounced so-li-la-kwee), which is when a character speaks aloud to no one in particular to reveal inner thoughts.

Practice 1: Literary Genres

Read the following passages. Circle the genre of literature for each passage, and then explain why you chose your answer.

The First Woman

Once there was a beautiful woman who lived in a pleasant valley on the earth. The rest of the world was filled with rocks and mountains. In this valley, summer was the ruling season, and honey and fruit were always available. Her only companions were the dove and the doe. She was the reigning spirit of this world, and nothing ever grew old or died.

One morning the woman followed a scarlet butterfly to a remote waterfall where the butterfly disappeared. Realizing she was lost, the woman fell asleep from exhaustion. When she woke, a being like herself stooped down and lifted her off the ground. Clothed in a robe of clouds, the man being told her he saw her as he traveled across the sky.

Because he rescued her, the man being had broken the command of the Great Spirit. He would remain on earth and share her companionship. For many moons, they lived happily in the valley. The woman bore a child. Sad because he broke the law, the man sought the guidance and forgiveness of the Great Spirit. The Great Spirit took pity on the man and the woman. He opened up many more valleys and plains for the future inhabitants, but because of the broken command, the Great Spirit caused the man and woman to labor for their food. They would also suffer from cold, grow old, and die when their heads became as white as the feathers of swans.

1. short story   nonfiction   autobiography   myth

2. Why did you choose this answer?

Excerpt from an Old Folk Song

Work, work, my boy, be not afraid;
 Look labor boldly in the face;

Take up the hammer or the spade,
 And blush not for your humble place.

There's glory in the shuttle's song;
 There's triumph in the anvil's stroke;

There's merit in the brave and strong,
 Who dig the mine or fell the oak.

– Eliza Cook (1879)

3. poem   essay   novel

4. Why did you choose this answer?

The First Confrontation

After we had conversed, he stated to me that he was completely undone; he had not been able in a long time to take any Indians; he knew not which way to turn, and his men had well begun to experience hunger and fatigue. I told him of Castillo and Dorantes, who were behind, ten leagues off, with a multitude that conducted us. He thereupon sent three cavalry to them, with fifty of the Indians who accompanied him. The Negro returned to guide them, while I remained. I asked the Christians to give me a certificate of the year, month, and day I arrived there, and of the manner of my coming, which they accordingly did. From this river to the town of the Christians, named San Miguel, within the government of the province called New Galicia, are thirty leagues.

From the *Relation of Alvar Nunez Cabeza de Vaca*, March 1536

5. short story   autobiography   drama

6. Why did you choose this answer?

Excerpt from George Bernard Shaw's *Pygmalion*

Higgins bursts in. He is, as the parlor-maid has said, in a state.

HIGGINS: Look here, mother: here's a confounded thing!

MRS. HIGGINS: Yes, dear. Good morning. [*He checks his impatience and kisses her, whilst the parlor-maid goes out*]. What is it?

HIGGINS: Eliza's bolted.

MRS. HIGGINS: [*calmly continuing her writing*] You must have frightened her.

HIGGINS: Frightened her! Nonsense! She was left last night, as usual, to turn out the lights and all that; and instead of going to bed she changed her clothes and went right off: her bed wasn't slept in. She came in a cab for her things before seven this morning; and that fool Mrs. Pearce let her have them without telling me a word about it. What am I to do?

MRS. HIGGINS: Do without, I'm afraid, Henry. The girl has a perfect right to leave if she chooses.

7. drama   biography   short story

8. Why did you choose this answer?

Practice 2: Folder Free-for-all

With a partner or on your own, use your literature book and other books and periodicals your instructor suggests; look for one example of each type of literature listed in this section. Find an example of as many genres as you can from this chapter. Include the title, author, and a 2 – 3 sentence description of the literary work. Write down your results, and save them in a folder for later reference.

AUTHOR'S STYLE

Authors develop different **styles** using literary elements, words, sentences, and other structures. Sometimes, an author's style can become like a signature, immediately recognizable as that author's work. For example, many readers of mystery novels are familiar with the gruff narration of detective Philip Marlowe, the protagonist in a series of mysteries (including *The Big Sleep*, *The Lady in the Lake*, and *The Long Goodbye*) by author Raymond Chandler.

Now, look back at the selections in Practice 1: "Literary Genes" on Pages 97 – 99. Notice how each writer has used a different style to help convey the story. In "The First Woman," the author tells the story as one would tell a fairy tale, using simple sentences and relatively simple vocabulary, so that anyone can understand it. The events are told in order to clearly relate the tale, as the events are the most important aspect. The second selection, from an old folk song, uses strong, direct language and simple structure to convey the theme of taking pride in one's work. Next, "The First Confrontation" is written in a formal style with detailed descriptions, in the way someone trying to record actual events might do. Finally, the excerpt from *Pygmalion* has a conversational style appropriate for the dialogue taking place, and the words and sentence structure used help depict the characters' background, education, and emotional state.

Practice 3: Author's Style

Read the following selections, and answer the questions that follow.

A.   On the window sill sat a formidable black cat. The feline fixed me with such a menacing stare that I felt gooseflesh crawl up my arms. I had never been particularly afraid of the creatures, but looking at this glowering specimen—which seemed ready to pounce without warning, all its muscles taut and twitching beneath its lustrous ebony fur—I now understood what superstitious people saw in them!

B.   Chasing the mice
     'Til none dare come near.
     You never think twice,
     Just bask in their fear.

     A spring and pounce—
     Now I can't bear to see
     That poor little mouse,
     Oh, how mean cats can be!

1. Both passages are about a cat. Comparing the two, decide which answer BEST describes what else is similar about them?

    A.   Both describe a very friendly cat.   C.   Both talk about the cat's beauty.
    B.   Both authors dislike something   D.   Both authors want to run away from the cat.
         about the cat.

2. Explain why you chose this answer, citing how the author's words contribute to your choice.

3. In selection A, which phrase is the BEST indicator of how the author feels at the moment?

    A.   "The feline fixed me with such a menacing stare"
    B.   "I felt gooseflesh crawl up my arms"
    C.   "I had never been particularly afraid of the creatures"
    D.   "I now understood what superstitious people saw in them"

4. In selection B, some of the author's style is determined by devices used. Which statement BEST describes this dependency?

    A.   The sentence structure needs to accommodate the rhyming pattern.
    B.   The lines and stanzas are determined by the sequence of events.
    C.   Vocabulary used must be simple because the poem is a short one.
    D.   Sentences are limited, as they can only be as long as a single line.

LITERARY CHARACTERS

In literary works, **characters** (the people who appear in the work) must tell each other and the reader about their ideas and feelings. The way that characters in a story **interact** (behave) with each other is a big part of telling the story. Through their words and actions, the story comes alive.

There are different types of characters in a story. There are the **main characters** who are the most important characters to the story, and there are **minor characters** who may have a connection to the main characters or may be complete strangers to the main character. They are in the story because they have some connection to the plot.

AUTHOR'S USE OF CHARACTERS

Development of characters is one of the tools that authors use to create a literary work, and every character serves some purpose. Sometimes a character serves a very specific purpose or plot function. Some purposes may be immediately obvious—a person who delivers a telegram or a police officer investigating a crime, for instance. The main character has to get the telegram from someone, so the delivery person comes into and out of the plot. If a private investigator needs to get reliable information about a crime from someone, having a friend who is a police detective is a convenient way for the character to get the facts. Below are some common functions a character can serve.

CHARACTER ROLES

Narrator the person telling a story. In *Huckleberry Finn*, the narrator is Huck, and he is a main character. In Maya Angelou's *I Know Why the Caged Bird Sings*, the narrator is a young girl who is the main character. Often, the narrator will be a character, but in many cases, the narrator is an outside, unknown character.

Protagonist the main character(s). Jim and Huck are the main characters in *Huckleberry Finn.* In Shakespeare's famous play named for its main characters, Romeo and Juliet are the protagonists. The protagonist is not always a hero or even a likeable character. For example, Shrek, the ogre in the movie of the same name, is not likeable in the beginning of the movie and certainly does not act like a hero.

Antagonist an opponent, rival, or obstacle to the protagonist. The antagonists in Hemingway's *Old Man and the Sea* are the sharks. The Southern laws and culture are the enemy for Huck and Jim in *Huckleberry Finn.*

Foil a character who is the opposite of another character, often the main character. The use of a foil helps emphasize a character's attributes. A character and a foil give the reader something to compare in order to understand the character more clearly. For example, if the main character is very cautious and fully thinks through everything before taking action, then the author might create a friend who is a foil—someone who is reckless and who reacts instead of thinking everything through.

CHARACTERIZATION

Characterization is the process by which a writer develops a character. Sometimes a character is described directly to the reader, and sometimes the reader has to gather clues about a character based on the actions and reactions of other characters.

The main trait of a dog is its loyalty to its master. Like that example, the traits, or features, of characters show what you can expect of their behavior: silly, serious, loyal, kind, rude, educated, street-smart, etc. To create vivid characters, the author develops them in the following five ways:

CHARACTER TRAITS

Description an author can tell how characters look, dress, and what their ages are, just as you might describe a friend of yours to someone. In Eudora Welty's short story "A Worn Path," the narrator begins by describing the main character Phoenix Jackson, as an old, small Negro woman in plain but neat clothing.

Narration the telling of the story through a speaker. The speaker could be one of the characters or could be an unknown observer. The speaker will tell how other characters feel or think or will describe how they act. In Stephen Crane's *The Red Badge of Courage*, there is an unknown narrator who is limited to telling the story through the eyes of a young soldier. (You can read more about **point of view** in the next chapter.)

Dialogue is conversation between two or more people. People in literature speak to each other as people in real life do. In *Huckleberry Finn,* Mark Twain shows the character traits of Huck and Jim in the talks they share while they float down the Mississippi River, including the dialect they use when speaking.

Dialect is used to portray a character's cultural and regional heritage by illustrating his manner of speaking. Twain is famous for his use of the Southern dialect in his novels and short stories.

Actions sometimes the actions of a character speak louder than words to show the character's true self. For example, Saruman the White, the head wizard in J.R.R. Tolkien's *The Lord of the Rings*, is the protector of the inhabitants of Middle Earth and Gandalf the Grey's mentor. He should protect Gandalf but betrays him for the power that Sauron, the evil antagonist in the story, promises. He hides his lies behind his robe and staff.

Practice 4: Characters and Characterization

Read the following passage for content. Then, answer the questions.

One of the most inspiring "rags to riches" stories is absolutely true. A boy child was born a slave in 1856. As a slave, he wasn't allowed to go to school. After the Civil War, the one dream that the boy had was to get an education. In 1872, Booker Taliafero Washington journeyed to the Hampton Institute in Virginia. The young man had neither money nor references, but he had a clear desire to learn and to help others learn. Luckily, he had come to the right place since the Institute trained black teachers.

Booker T. Washington was a successful student and was quickly employed as a teacher. When a black college, the Tuskegee Institute, was built in Alabama, he became its first president. Washington proved to be a true leader and a man of vision. He was a handsome man and kept himself healthy and physically fit. He spoke well to individuals and large groups. He was able to translate his vision for the college into words so that he was able to raise a great deal of money for the Institute's growth. One of the people he convinced to help was Andrew Carnegie. Carnegie was a man who had also risen from poverty to become successful. Carnegie visited the college and helped fund many of Washington's ideas. Washington was also good at recruiting other leaders in education. George Washington Carver, a botanist, was one such person who came to the Institute.

Booker T. Washington was the first black man to dine at the White House. President Teddy Roosevelt invited him. The two men shared many views, including the need for healthy physical activity, the value of books and knowledge, and the power of morality.

In his time, Booker T. Washington was a great leader for his people, encouraging them to learn skills to become economically equal with the white race. He did, however, believe in the system or philosophy of the races being kept separate. He was called "The Great Accommodator." Other black leaders grew impatient seeing the slow change within the United States, and they urged stronger measures to gain equality. Washington was on a speaking tour in New York City when he fell ill. He asked to be taken home to the South to be buried. He made it back to Tuskegee where he died.

Tuskegee Institute

1. From the passage, what can you infer about the reasons that Booker T. Washington had for achieving all that he did?

    A. He was motivated by the desire to escape poverty, to help others live out their dreams, and by the love of learning for itself.

    B. Booker T. Washington was motivated by the criticism of his peers to excel and change his way of approaching the difficulties in racial equality.

    C. He found motivation in the work of George Washington Carver, his first teacher.

    D. Booker T. Washington was motivated by a love of the North and the need to raise money for the Tuskegee Institute.

2. Based on the passage, which of the following sentences BEST describes the relationship between Teddy Roosevelt and Booker T. Washington?

   A. Roosevelt and Washington did not get along.

   B. Booker T. Washington taught Roosevelt how to raise money.

   C. Washington had Roosevelt visit his home on many occasions.

   D. Washington and Roosevelt admired each other and agreed on many issues.

3. In the passage, what two challenges did Booker T. Washington have to resolve?

   A. 1) He convinced other black professionals that teaching at Tuskegee was a good job by writing a book about the institute. 2) He had to raise money to keep the institute growing by befriending Andrew Carnegie.

   B. 1) He first overcame the limits on former slaves by getting an education. 2) He had to overcome charges that he was too accommodating to the white leaders. He stood by his belief of working to provide economic equality for all citizens.

   C. 1) Overcoming poverty and 2) convincing Teddy Roosevelt that Washington was right about the importance of the peanut crop in Alabama.

   D. 1) He experienced conflict by being born in the South and so moved to New York. 2) He had to stand up to the other black leaders who said he was too harsh in his racial views.

THEME

Whereas facts and specific examples usually support the main idea of a nonfiction passage, more subtle details suggest the main idea of a fictional passage. We use the word **theme** in discussing the central idea of short stories, novels, poetry, and plays. The theme is thought of as the message that the entire passage is communicating to the reader. Sometimes this message is difficult to discover, like a message hidden in a bottle. That is when the reader needs to put together all the details in the passage. Look at the example below.

> The youth gave a shriek as he confronted the thing. He was, for moments, turned to stone before it. He remained staring into the liquid-looking eyes. The dead man and the living man exchanged a long look. Then the youth cautiously put one hand behind him and brought it against a tree. Leaning upon this he retreated, step by step, with his face still toward the thing. He feared that if he turned his back the body might spring up and stealthily pursue him.

From *The Red Badge of Courage by* Stephen Crane

1. Which of the following statements is the best theme for the passage?

   A. The living and the dead form bonds of love.

   B. Death should not be feared.

   C. Never speak badly about the dead.

   D. Confronting death can be terrifying.

While the first three choices contain general truths, they do not apply specifically to this passage. For example, "A" focuses on love between the living and the dead, while the details in the passage convey fear and dread. Likewise, "B" ignores the fear so apparent in the description. Finally, "C" is incorrect because the youth never speaks badly about the dead person. His shock is so great that all he can do is shriek in fear.

Therefore, answer "D" is the best choice. It describes the overall message of the passage and is based upon the details presented.

Tips for Finding the Theme

1. Read the passage carefully.

2. Think of one statement that summarizes the overall message of what you read.

3. Make sure the details in the passage support your answer. Something in a statement may be true but not relevant to the passage.

4. Make sure your answer summarizes the message of the entire passage, not just one part.

Practice 5:   Theme

Read the following passages. Then choose the best statement of the theme.

As the old man walked the beach at dawn, he noticed a young man ahead of him picking up starfish and flinging them into the sea. Finally, catching up with the youth, he asked why he was doing this. The young man explained that the stranded starfish would die if left until the morning sun.

"But the beach goes on for miles, and there are millions of starfish," commented the old man. "How can your effort make any difference?"

The young man looked at the starfish in his hand and then threw it safely in the waves. "It makes a difference to this one," he said.

– Anonymous

1.   What is the best statement for the theme?

   A.   The morning sun will kill stranded starfish.
   B.   Starfish must be saved from extinction.
   C.   Saving even one life can make a difference.
   D.   Saving millions of starfish is a waste of time.

In *Between Parent and Teenager,* Dr. Haim Ginott told this story: As Jean walked along the beach with her mother, she asked, "Mom, how do you hold a husband after you've found him?"

Her mother gave her a silent lesson in love. She scooped up two handfuls of sand. One she squeezed hard. The more she squeezed, the more sand escaped. The other she held lightly, and the sand remained.

Jean said, "I see."

2. What is the best statement for the theme?
    A. Learn the dangers of love.
    B. Learn the principles of sand science.
    C. Learn the many themes of love.
    D. Learn the difference between love and possessiveness.

A man was going down from Jerusalem to Jericho, when he fell into the hands of robbers. They stripped him of his clothes, beat him, and went away, leaving him half dead. A priest happened to be traveling the same road, and when he saw the man, he passed by on the other side. So too, a Levite, when he came to the place and saw him, passed by on the other side. But a Samaritan, as he traveled, came where the man was; and when he saw the man, he took pity on him. He bandaged his wounds, pouring on oil and wine. Then he put the man on his own donkey, took him to an inn and took care of him. The next day he took out two silver coins and gave them to the innkeeper. "Look after him," he said, "and when I return, I will reimburse you for any extra expense you may have."

– The Bible

3. What is the best statement of the theme?
    A. Robbers can be dangerous on the roads.
    B. Try to avoid areas where there is crime.
    C. Innkeepers take good care of their customers.
    D. A good neighbor loves those in need.

UNIVERSAL THEMES IN LITERATURE

Some situations, relationships, and emotions are common to all humans no matter when and where they live. Literature often focuses on these **universal themes** of common human experiences. These themes can be explored in all genres of literature. A universal theme must transcend time and place; it must address human experience that is not unique to a particular time period or cultural boundary. Some of the most common universal themes include good and evil, war and peace, discord, and of course, love in all of its varieties, complexities, and stages. Family relationships, life and death, and a young person reaching maturity (coming of age) are also common universal themes.

Writers explore these universal themes in all genres of literature. Within each of the genres, the themes can also be treated in various ways. For example, Shakespeare treats the theme of true love as serious and tragic in *Romeo and Juliet*, but in the comedic play by George Bernard Shaw, *Arms and the Man*, Shaw portrays love as a game of chance that in reality has little influence over the fate of the characters.

Practice 6: Identifying Universal Themes

Make a list of five fiction books you have read and five movies you have seen. Next to the title of each one, identify the universal theme. Write a sentence or two explaining why you decided on your answer. Compare lists with classmates. If you listed some of the same titles but have different answers, discuss your answers.

COMPARING AND CONTRASTING UNIVERSAL THEMES IN LITERATURE

Literature that offers insights into universal themes can give you many compelling ideas to think about. Many authors have explored the same themes in a variety of ways, including different genres. Reading more than one work that deals with a specific universal theme can greatly expand how you think about the theme.

When looking at one universal theme reflected in the works of authors writing in different genres, be sure to analyze each work in the same way you would otherwise: consider the development of characters, plot, setting, conflicts, and so on. In addition, consider how the genre itself might affect the meaning of the work.

Practice 7: Comparing and Contrasting Universal Themes

Read literary selections, which you choose or your teacher recommends, that offer insights into the same universal theme and fit into different genres. Discuss how the themes are similar. Some suggestions are listed here.

Universal Theme	Genre	Suggested Work
giving selflessly without expecting something in return	short fiction	"The Gift of the Magi" by O. Henry
	fable/children's story	*The Giving Tree* by Shel Silverstein
	poem	"How Do I Love Thee?" by Elizabeth Barrett Browning
the struggle for freedom	novel	*Fahrenheit 451* by Ray Bradbury
	nonfiction	*I Know Why the Caged Bird Sings* by Maya Angelou
	poem/song	"Bruce's Address at Bannockburn" by Robert Burns
parent / child relationships	drama (short)	"Mind the Gap" by Meredith Oakes
	drama (full length)	*King Lear* by William Shakespeare
	novel	*The Joy Luck Club* by Amy Tan

CHAPTER 6 REVIEW

Read each of the literary selections for content, and answer the questions that follow each one.

The Courage That My Mother Had

The courage that my mother had
Went with her, and is with her still:
Rock from New England quarried;
Now granite in a granite hill.

The golden brooch my mother wore
She left behind for me to wear;
I have no thing I treasure more:
Yet, it is something I could spare.

Oh, if instead she'd left to me
The thing she took into the grave!-
That courage like a rock, which she
Has no more need of, and I have.

– Edna St. Vincent Millay

1. This selection could best be described as

   A. a biography.   B. a story.   C. a poem.   D. a drama.

2. What is the most likely wish of the narrator in this passage?

   A. She wants to sell the brooch her mother left her.
   B. She wishes that she was as brave as her mother.
   C. She does not like where her mother was buried.
   D. She resents that she did not inherit more valuables.

Excerpt from "The Monkey's Paw"

The man sat up in bed and flung the bedclothes from his quaking limbs. "Good God, you are mad!" he cried, aghast.

"Get it," she panted; "get it quickly, and wish—Oh, my boy, my boy!"

Her husband struck a match and lit the candle. "Get back to bed," he said unsteadily. "You don't know what you are saying."

"We had the first wish granted," said the old woman, feverishly; "why not the second?"

"A coincidence," stammered the old man.

"Go and get it and wish," cried the old woman, and dragged him toward the door.

The old man turned and regarded her, and his voice shook. "He has been dead ten days, and besides he—I could only recognize him by his clothing. If he was too terrible for you to see then, how now?"

"Bring him back," cried the old woman, and dragged him toward the door. "Do you think I fear the child I have nursed?"

– W. W. Jacobs

3. This selection is BEST described as a(n)

    A. essay.   B. drama.   C. mystery.   D. autobiography.

The Art of Kite Flying

When first learning to fly a kite, a person should be in the right frame of mind, the right location, and have the right kind of kite for the weather.

The right frame of mind comes first since it is what controls and communicates the wishes of the flyer to the kite. Pick a day where you have no other activities planned. Understand that you are choosing to spend this time to be in the moment with the wind, sun, and fragile paper wings.

Now you are ready to choose the place or location to fly your kite. This should be a place of grass and flowers but no trees. A parking lot is not a good choice; it disgraces the spirit of the flight.

Lastly, the kite that you choose will also choose you. It will be a bond that must be felt even when you're standing in front of a display of thousands of kites in a rainbow of colors.

Know the weather existing in your area when planning to fly the kite. A soft southwestern wind, a zephyr, will require a different sort of kite from harsher northern gales. Next, you will read in detail about the kinds of kites that are high-flying and highly compatible with most personalities.

4. This selection is BEST described as a(n)

    A. short story.   B. essay.   C. poem.   D. novel.

The Real Paul Revere

"The British are coming! The British are coming!" Most of us remember these words from Paul Revere's famous midnight ride between Lexington and Concord, Massachusetts in 1775. He was warning the American patriots about British troops gathering to fight them. Even though this is the most popular memory of Paul Revere, he was actually a man of many skills. Among his attributes, the ones that stand out most are his artistic talents, his political leadership, and his role in raising a large, successful family.

Born in Boston on January 1, 1735, Paul Revere grew up in a family of 11 children. His mother, Deborah, raised the children and kept the house, and his father, Appolos, was a silversmith. At 13 years old, Paul Revere began learning how to become a silversmith from his father. He learned well. When Paul was 19, his father died, and Paul inherited his father's silversmith business.

His artistic talents grew rapidly, and he created many beautiful drinking cups, pitchers, bowls, tea pots, bells, and serving plates. Many of these pieces are in American museums today. Paul Revere also created metal plates that were used to print newspapers of the day. One of his most famous prints shows the Boston Massacre on March 15, 1770. This print was circulated throughout the 13 colonies and even in England. In the 1790s, Revere also learned to manufacture rolls of copper sheets on a large scale. These were of such high quality that they were used to cover the top of the Massachusetts state house and the bottom of the famous American war ship, the Constitution. He finally formed a business called the Revere Copper and Brass Company. Even today, when Americans want quality cookware, they buy Revere Ware.

Another of Revere's talents was his political leadership. On December 16, 1773, he and his workers staged the Boston Tea Party on a ship in Boston's harbor.

They dressed as Indians and dumped all the tea chests from England into the harbor to protest the high tax on tea. After the Boston Tea Party, Paul Revere became one of the important leaders who visited towns in New England to tell citizens about the unjust laws of Great Britain. In addition, Revere helped to hide important papers about the plans for the rebellion against the British government. He also helped John Hancock and Samuel Adams evade British soldiers.

Revere's experience as an engraver also helped the revolution. Using old copper plates, he printed money for the American soldiers so they could buy supplies. He printed mostly British money because that was the way people bought products. He was doing this illegally so he had to be guarded day and night so the British soldiers would not try to kill him. John Adams and Benjamin Franklin later asked him to print money for the new American Congress.

Finally, Paul Revere raised a large and successful family. His first wife, Sara Orne, bore him eight children before dying in childbirth in 1773. His second wife, Rachel Walker, also bore him eight children. Sadly, Revere lost six of his children as babies or young adults, but the rest survived and went on to success. One son, Joseph Revere took over his father's copper business, as did grandson John Revere later on. Maria Revere married the US Consul to Singapore. Son John Revere became a professor of medicine at Jefferson Medical College. Paul Revere's granddaughter, Grace Revere, had two marriages to successful surgeons. Grandsons Edward and Paul Joseph died in battles during the Civil War, with Paul Joseph rising to the rank of colonel (a monument to him and the 20th Massachusetts Infantry that he led stands today at the battlefield of Gettysburg). When Paul Revere died in Boston on May 10, 1818, his family had grown to 51 grandchildren.

Paul Revere was more than a messenger riding on a horse, shouting and warning Americans about a British attack. He gave back to his country many talents and is one of our greatest heroes. When he died, many mourned his passing. Today he lives on in his famous silver art pieces, and his many acts of bravery will always be remembered. Over 1000 persons now carry on the Revere name in the United States.

5. This selection is BEST described as a(n)
   A. autobiography.   B. poem.   C. biography.   D. short story.

6. Which of the following BEST describes the author's style in this passage?
   A. informative, while using words that convey pride about an American hero
   B. poetic and descriptive, including vivid imagery to describe people and events
   C. simple and unbiased, like a description that would be found in encyclopedias
   D. romantic and adventurous, giving it the feel of an action-adventure novel

7. What is the main technique used to characterize Paul Revere?
   A. dialogue   C. motivations
   B. a foil   D. description

8. Based on the passage, which of the following sentences BEST describes the main event that led to many of Revere's accomplishments?
   A. His father passed away when Paul was just a young boy.
   B. The American colonies were fighting for freedom from British rule.
   C. There was a great deal of competition among silversmiths.
   D. Everything that Revere did, he had to keep secret and hidden.

9. If you were to include this passage with a group of passages that have the same universal theme, which of the following would be the BEST choice?
   A. a legend about an early American folk hero; an article about colonialism throughout history; an essay about the American Revolution
   B. a paper about the art of copper production; a book about early American craftsmen; a biography about Betsy Ross as a patriotic American
   C. a book about the life of Florence Nightingale; an article about someone receiving recognition for a heroic deed; a story about how Jackie Robinson overcame prejudice in sports
   D. a historical document about famous American families; an essay about how ancestors influence their families; a Web site about genealogy (family tree)

10. Write a brief explanation for your choice in number 9 above.

Chapter 7
Literary Devices and Story Structure

This chapter covers the following South Carolina end-of-course exam items:	
Reading 2.2	*Demonstrate the ability to evaluate an author's use of stylistic elements such as tone, irony, and figurative language.*
Reading 2.5	*Demonstrate the ability to describe with specific examples how the narrator's point of view or the author's choice of narrator affects a work of fiction.*
Reading 2.8	*Demonstrate the ability to analyze the impact of conflict (internal and external) on plot and character in a literary work.*
Reading 1.2	*Demonstrate the ability to make connections between a text read independently and his or her prior knowledge, other texts, and the world.*

In this chapter, you will learn about **literary devices** and **story structure**, as well as additional skills for the analysis of literature. In Chapter 6, you studied the genres, characters, and themes in works of literature. You learned how an author reveals characters to the reader and how the characters must interact. They must work together the same way the organs or parts of a body work together. Literary devices also are like parts of the body. They allow characters to move and to exist within a text in a logical way. Literary devices and story structure reveal to the reader how characters understand the world in which they exist. In addition, your own experience in the world, your prior knowledge, and how you apply these to your reading, can help you further analyze the literature you read.

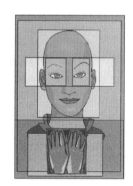

LITERARY DEVICES

Literary devices are what authors use to create their works of literature. They include elements that help to set up background information and to place characters in **time** or in a **sequence** of events. Another type of device is **figurative language**, which is a way of expressing something without using only plain, dry facts. Figurative language employs imaginative and powerful language to express ideas and to make a story come alive.

TIME AND SEQUENCE

Both time and the sequence of events in a work of literature may be arranged in several ways for the logic of the story. A logical time frame, even if it shifts with narration, is important for understanding a work.

Time	may move straight forward from the first event to the last event, such as in John Steinbeck's novel *The Pearl*. However, the author may feel that the story will be better remembered or understood by mixing up time. One example is Amy Tan's novel *The Joy Luck Club*, in which time moves from the past to the present and back to the past, following the storytelling of each character.
Sequence	is the order in which events happen in a story. The sequence may not go in a straight time order but may go back and forth in time with the use of **flashbacks**. One common use of flashback is to have a narrator describe events, as when Holden Caulfield describes what led to his breakdown in *The Catcher in the Rye* by J.D. Salinger. **Foreshadowing** is another way that time is changed; however, with foreshadowing, clues are used to bend time a little towards the future.

The diagram below shows the events of a story line that moves forward in a straight path: a baby girl is born, as a toddler is bitten by a spider, reads a book about a famous researcher, and after becoming a researcher, she is bitten by a spider and dies.

Now, look below at the diagram of the same story line events. Notice how a writer can also use flashbacks and foreshadowing to move backward and forward in time.

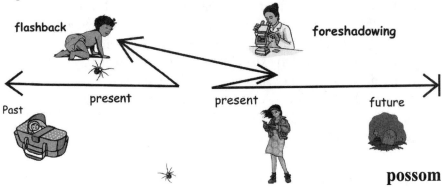

A baby girl is born. As a child, she is outside swinging and sees a spider. She remembers (**flashback**) being painfully bitten by a spider as a toddler. As she grows and attends school, she reads a book (**foreshadowing**) about a famous woman who researches poisonous spiders for cures to their poison. The girl becomes the same type of researcher. In the middle of a successful career, a deadly spider bites her, and she dies.

FIGURATIVE LANGUAGE

Figurative language can be used to build the story and ideas in it with words that are powerful and that help readers experience the emotions. For example, the phrase "time flies" does not really mean that time is a creature with wings. The factual wording of the thought may be "time always moves forward quickly," but this phrasing has much less feeling. Figurative language and vivid images allow readers to experience a story through the written words describing sights, smells, tastes, sounds, and touch.

FIGURATIVE LANGUAGE

Alliteration	the repetition of the same consonant sounds in lines of poetry or prose. Examples: 1) "Leader beloved, and long he ruled," – *Beowulf* (repetition of "l" sounds). 2) "**W**hat **w**ould the **w**orld be, once bereft/Of **w**et and **w**ildness?" – Gerard Manley Hopkins, "Inversnaid" (repetition of "w" sounds).
Allusion	a reference to a well-known place, literary or art work, famous person, or historical event. In today's world, these references are often related to pop culture. Allusions are dependent on the reader being familiar with the work or item being referred to. **Example**: You tell your friends that your nephew reminds you of Bart Simpson; they would have a definite picture of the boy's personality!
Analogy	an extended explanation or description of something unfamiliar or difficult to explain by comparison with something familiar. **Example**: "Life is like a box of chocolates; you never know what you're going to get." – Forrest Gump.
Euphemism	using mild words to describe something instead of using possibly offensive terms. **Examples**: 1) **passed away** for died, 2) **perspire** for sweat, 3) **restroom** for bathroom, 4) **sanitation engineer** for trash collector, 5) **remains** for corpse.
Hyperbole	exaggeration to create an effect. **Examples**: 1) I was so surprised, you could have knocked me over with a feather. 2) I would rather die than eat brussels sprouts. 3) If you hum that tune one more time, I'll explode.
Imagery	the use of words or phrases that evoke the sensations of sight, hearing, touch, smell, or taste. For example, Edgar Allan Poe opens "The Fall of the House of Usher" with "During the whole of a dull, dark, and soundless day in the autumn of the year, when the clouds hung oppressively low in the heavens . . ." Poe's word choices help the reader picture the day and the mood.

Irony

a contrast or incongruity between what is stated and what is meant (**verbal irony**), or between what is expected to happen and what actually happens (**irony of situation**). 1) For an example of verbal irony, imagine that you and some of your friends have been working on a project for school. It's been a long, hot, and tiring day. One friend suddenly announces to the group, smiling, "I've had about as much <u>fun</u> as I can stand for one day. I'm out'a here!" That person is using verbal irony to express a wish to go home, saying that it's been too much fun—but meaning the opposite, that it's really been too much work. 2) In the movie *Gladiator*, a lowly, imprisoned gladiator defeats the powerful but evil emperor of Rome. This is an example of irony of situation.

Metaphor

a direct comparison between two unlike things *without* using the words "like" or "as." Examples: 1) The sun was a ball of fire. An **extended metaphor** is when a metaphor is set up and other items are compared within that metaphor, or along the same lines as the first metaphor. In William Shakespeare's  play, *As You Like It*, the world is compared with a stage. Within that metaphor, people are compared with actors. An entire story, poem, or book may be a metaphor for a concept. For example, Robert Frost's poem, "After Apple Picking," on the surface describes harvesting fruit and how the apple-picker looks forward to a long rest; one common interpretation, however, is that the entire poem is a metaphor for the approaching end of life, with "sleep" symbolizing death.

Onomatopoeia

words that imitate the sound they are naming. **Examples**: 1) woof, meow, splash, boom, hiss, buzz, pitter-patter 2) "The *moan* of doves in immemorial elms; / And *murmuring* of innumerable bees," – Alfred Lord Tennyson.

Oxymoron

two or three words that combine opposite or contradictory ideas such as "wise fool," "sweet sorrow," or "jumbo shrimp."

Paradox

contradictory ideas existing together to point to a deeper truth. **For example**, a poem attributed to Francis of Assisi states, "For it is in giving that we receive,/ in pardoning that we are pardoned,/ and in dying that we are born to eternal life."

Personification

giving human qualities to something not human. **For example**, 1) "Sky lowered, and muttering thunder, some sad drops/Wept at completing of the mortal sin." – John Milton, 2) "The oak trees whispered softly in the night breeze." – John Steinbeck.

Rhyme	when words, usually those at the ends of lines, have the same sounds. **Examples**: 1) "Tyger! Tyger! burning bright / In the forests of the night" – William Blake (**bright** and **night** rhyme.) 2) "Happy the man who, safe on shore, / Now trims, at home, his evening fire; / Unmov'd, he hears the tempests roar, / That on the tufted groves expire:" – Philip Freneau (**shore/roar** and **fire/expire**).
Rhythm	the arrangement of stressed and unstressed syllables into a pattern. While rhythm is almost always found in poetry, quality prose writing also involves regular patterns that appeal to the reader. Read the following example out loud: "Vanishing, swerving, evermore curving again into sight,/ Softly the sand beach wavers away to a dim gray looping of light." – Sidney Lanier
Simile	comparison between two things using "**like**" or "**as**." **Examples**: 1) "Sometimes I feel **like** a motherless child" – African-American spiritual, 2) "My love is **like** a red, red rose" – Robert Burns, 3) Free **as** a bird.
Symbol	any object, person, place, or action that has a meaning in itself and that also represents a meaning beyond itself, such as a quality, an attitude, a belief, or a value. For example, a skull and cross bones are often a symbol that warns of poison, and a dove with an olive branch is a symbol of peace. In Nathaniel Hawthorne's short story "The Minister's Black Veil," the black veil symbolizes secret sin.

Study the types of figurative language, and apply what you learn to the practice passages on the next several pages. Refer to the list above as you need to.

Practice 1:   Time and Figurative Language

Read each of the following passages. Then on your own paper answer the questions about literary devices.

Excerpt from "Common Sense" by Thomas Payne

1   The heart that feels not now is dead; the blood of his children will curse his cowardice
2   who shrinks back at a time when a little might have saved the whole, and made them
3   happy. I love the man that can smile in trouble, that can gather strength from distress, and
4   grow brave by reflection. 'Tis the business of little minds to shrink; but he whose heart is
5   firm, and whose conscience approves his conduct, will pursue his principles unto death.
6   My own line of reasoning is to myself as straight and clear as a ray of light. Not all the
7   treasures of the world, so far as I believe, could have induced me to support an offensive
8   war, for I think it murder; but if a thief breaks into my house, burns and destroys my
9   property, and kills or threatens to kill me, or those that are in it, and to "bind me in all
10 cases whatsoever" to his absolute will, am I to suffer it?

1.   Where do you find *paradox* in this passage?

2. Which lines in the passage contain an *analogy*?
   A. 1 – 2   B. 3 – 4   C. 5 – 7   D. 8 – 10

3. In your own words, describe the *analogy*.

4. Which lines in the passage are an example of *hyperbole*?
   A. 2 – 3   B. 3 – 4   C. 6 – 7   D. 8 – 9

5. Which line in the passage is an example of a *simile*?
   A. 5   B. 6   C. 7   D. 8

A Traditional Folk Song

1	You ought to see my Cindy
2	She lives way down south;
3	She's so sweet the honey bees
4	Swarm around her mouth.
5	Oh, Cindy is a pretty girl.
6	Cindy is a peach;
7	She threw her arms around my neck.
8	And hung on like a leech.
9	And if I were a sugar tree
10	Standing in the town
11	Every time my Cindy passed
12	I'd shake some sugar down.

6. Which of the following group of lines from the song contains a *hyperbole*?
   A.   lines 1 – 2   C.   lines 5 – 6
   B.   lines 3 – 4   D.   lines 9 – 10

7. Which of the following lines contains an example of a *metaphor*?
   A.   line 5   B.   line 6   C.   line 7   D.   line 8

8. Write the sets of words that *rhyme* in this song.

9. Cite some examples of *alliteration* in the song.

10. Where do you find *irony* in this song?

11. Describe an example of *imagery* in this song.

Excerpt from the Notebooks of Leonardo da Vinci

I am fully conscious that, not being a literary man, certain presumptuous persons will think that they may reasonably blame me, alleging that I am not a man of letters. Foolish folks! Do they not know that I might retort as Marius did to the Roman Patricians by saying that they, who deck themselves out in the labors of others will not allow me my own. They will say that I, having no literary skill, cannot properly express that which I desire to treat of, but they do not know that my subjects are to be dealt with by experience rather than by words, and experience has been the mistress of those who wrote well. And so, as mistress, I will cite her in all cases. Though I may not, like them, be able to quote other authors, I shall rely on that which is much greater and more worthy—on experience, the mistress of their Masters. They go about puffed up and pompous, dressed and decorated with the fruits, not of their own labours, but of those of others. And they will not allow me my own. They will scorn me as an inventor, but how much more might they—who are not inventors but vaunters and declaimers of the works of others—be blamed.

12. Identify an example of *allusion* in this selection.

13. Identify examples of *imagery* in this passage.

14. Give an example of *personification*.

15. Give an example of *foreshadowing* in this passage.

A Fishing Trip

The traffic began moving again. Josh was certainly glad to be finished building houses in the Spartanburg area. Now, he was ready to relax with his son, David, for a couple of weeks at Sumter National Forest. Josh knew that David would be a little tired since today was the last day of David's tenth grade year; it had been a tough one for him. So, Josh drove slowly in the right-hand lane down Highway 9 on the way home to Jonesville, giving David time to unwind before he had to get in the truck. Glancing in his rear view mirror, Josh saw a school bus and thought about his last day of school in the tenth grade. Josh's dad had been in jail again, for the third time. Josh could still see and hear the cell door bars with their mocking clanging: so much like the bells at school and so not like them.

Shaking off his sad memory, Josh looked forward to the vacation ahead. When he got home, he'd pack the tent, sleeping bags, food, and cooking gear in the truck. Then he'd pick up David. They would be together for the whole vacation, secluded in the woods. They'd fish the Tyger River with the new rods they had given each other for Christmas, hike the Chatooga Trail, and relax and talk in their camp. The cool air and water would refresh their minds and spirits. Josh could already smell the freshly caught catfish sizzling over an open fire and could already hear the stories that he and David would share.

16. Who is the *protagonist* in the story?
    A. David   B. Josh   C. narrator   D. the forest

17. The story most likely takes place
    A. in the early morning.
    B. in the late evening.
    C. in the late afternoon.
    D. around midnight.

18. The example of a *flashback* is when
    A. the traffic gets heavy.
    B. Josh thinks about catfish
    C. Josh mentions hiking the trail.
    D. a school bus brings a memory to Josh.

We Wear the Mask by Paul Laurence Dunbar

1   We wear the mask that grins and lies,
2   It hides our cheeks and shades our eyes,–
3   This debt we pay to human guile;
4   With torn and bleeding hearts we smile,
5   And mouth with myriad subtleties.

6   Why should the world be over-wise,
7   In counting all our tears and sighs?
8   Nay, let them only see us, while
9   We wear the mask.

10 We smile, but O great Christ, our cries
11 To thee from tortured souls arise.
12 We sing, but oh the clay is vile
13 Beneath our feet, and long the mile;
14 But let the world dream otherwise,
15 We wear the mask!

19. What does the mask *symbolize* in this poem?

20. Cite two other examples of *symbols*.

21. How does the author's use of *rhythm* in lines 5, 9, and 15 affect the poem?

22. Cite two examples of *alliteration* in the first stanza.

23. Dunbar wrote poetry about the oppression African-Americans experienced in the early 1900s. Based on this information, what else might the poem's mask symbolize? Explain.

Practice 2:   Literary Devices

A. Passage Practice. Locate the literary devices used in poems or stories from your literature book. Then, compare your answers with your classmates.

B. Team Activity. Review 2 or 3 stories, plays or poems you have read in class, and then get into teams. Using index cards, write a literary device on the front of the card and an example from the literature you reviewed on the back. Teams quiz each other by showing the example, and the other team has to name the literary device the example illustrates.

C. Time. With a partner or with a group, tell a 2 – 3 minute story about something you or a friend experienced recently. First, tell the story from the first event to the last event. Then, tell the story a second time, but start in the middle or at the end and then go back to the beginning. What are the advantages of telling the first version of the story? The second version? Are there disadvantages to either version? Write your stories, and share them with your class or teacher.

STORY STRUCTURE

The human body needs not only the organs working together but also must also have a structure to hold everything in place. The skeleton is the frame or structure for the human body. If the skeleton is not strong, it will not stand for long. In a similar way, authors use **story structure** to organize and build stories. For a story, if the structure is not strong, the story will fail to keep the reader's interest.

A story can be told in many different ways. A good writer will use structural tools, or devices, such as **point of view**, **setting**, **plot**, **mood**, and **tone** to build the story in the most effective way. Study the following list of structural devices and their features to help you better understand stories.

POINT OF VIEW

The first step in building the story structure is its **point of view**: the perspective, or outlook, from which a writer tells a story. There may be a character narrating the story, or there may be an unknown speaker describing the action and thoughts of all main characters. For example, Mary Shelley writes *Frankenstein* from the first person point of view, but she uses three different narrators to tell their own stories: Dr. Frankenstein, the creator of the monster; the monster itself; and Walton, the last man to speak to both.

FEATURES OF POINT OF VIEW

First Person	The narrator tells the story from the "I" point of view. In *The House On Mango Street*, Esperanza tells her story as the main character.
Second Person	The speaker is talking to you and so uses the pronoun "you." This is not often used in most literature, but the second person reference is fairly common in poetry, short essays, and songs. For example, the songs "You Are My Sunshine" and "You've Got a Friend," and Jamaica Kincaid's story "Girl" use the second person point-of view.
Third Person	The speaker tells a story describing characters as "he," "she," or "they" as in *The Pearl* by John Steinbeck.
• **omniscient**	The narrator is capable of knowing, telling, and seeing all that happens to the main characters. In Leo Tolstoy's *Anna Karenina*, the narrator describes all the actions and the inner thoughts of the main characters.
• **limited**	The narrator tells the story knowing only what is seen, heard, and felt by the thoughts and viewpoint of one character, usually the main character. Ralph Ellison wrote the short story "King of the Bingo Game" using this point of view.

Deciding what point of view the author is using to tell a story is a first big step in understanding how that story will work. When you determine what the point of view is, you are ahead in understanding the characters and actions.

SETTING

Setting is the backbone or background for the action of a story, including time, place, and general surroundings of the characters. A setting can be realistic, as it would be in a historical novel, or it can be completely imaginary, as in science fiction or fantasy. For example, the setting of Puritan colonial New England is an important part of Nathaniel Hawthorne's *The Scarlet Letter*.

FEATURES OF SETTING

- **Time** when the story occurs, for example, the historical period or season of the year. *The Scarlet Letter* takes place in the 17th century.

- **Place** where the story happens, including such things as geographic place, scenery, or arrangement of a house or room. *The Scarlet Letter* is set in Boston, Massachusetts. In the marketplace where sinners were exhibited and shamed, some of the story's most important events happen.

- **General Surroundings** daily habits of characters including job and cultural, religious, or emotional spirit of the area. In *The Scarlet Letter*, the main characters are high members of the Puritan religious community.

PLOT

The events in a story (what happens in it) is the **plot**. If you are reading a book and a friend asks what the book is about, you would probably begin telling him about the plot. Every story has to have more than setting and characters. Something has to happen to the characters!

When we discuss plot, it is generally broken down into several parts. The **introduction**, or exposition, brings the reader into the story. Generally, the author gives the setting, introduces the characters (or at least some of them) and begins to tell the reader about the conflict. Events leading up to the **climax** or turning point are called the **rising action,** and events afterwards are the **falling action**.

The **resolution** is the final section of the plot. Usually, the conflict is ended in some way—a mystery may be solved, problems are worked out, or some other suitable solution to the conflict occurs.

PLOT AND ITS FEATURES

Plot events in a story, or how the story works out. The plot of Herman Melville's *Moby-Dick* follows Captain Ahab chasing a great white whale.

Introduction	opening of a story where the author describes a *setting*, introduces the *characters*, and reveals the *conflict*. Exposition is another term for introduction. Not all of this information is present in every introduction. For a specific reason, the author may wait until later to include some of this material. The narrator's point of view is usually revealed in the introduction. The personality of the narrator and the point of view will affect how the plot is seen to be developing. In *Moby-Dick*, the very first sentence tells us the narrator and point of view: "Call me Ishmael." In the first chapters, the reader learns about the major characters and the dangerous whaling voyage they are about to undertake.
Conflict	the struggle between different forces in a story which is also the main interest. This struggle can be with nature, with one's self, with others, or with society. The main conflict in *Moby-Dick* is between Ahab and the whale.
• **Foreshadowing**	clues or hints of events to come. When Captain Ahab has his own coffin built, it foreshadows his death in *Moby-Dick*.
• **Suspense**	looking forward to a story's next event. When the ship sets sail, Ishmael knows Captain Ahab is on board but doesn't actually see him for several days. This keeps the reader in suspense.
Climax	the turning point in a story. Events leading up to this are called the *rising action* and events after are the *falling action*. In *Moby-Dick*, the climax is when Ahab realizes he is obsessed with the desire to kill the whale, but he can't stop himself.
Resolution	final events of a plot; the solution of a mystery, an explanation of something, or outcome of events. By the end of *Moby-Dick*, the ship has sunk, and the entire crew has perished except for Ishmael, who lives to tell the story.

CONFLICT

In respect to literary plots, the term **conflict** has the same meaning that we use in everyday conversations—a struggle between opposing forces. Some authors and readers consider conflict to be the most important part of the plot. The main conflict affects all parts of a story; it drives the events and the characters. Conflicts in literature are classified as either internal or external. **Internal conflicts** are those that take place within a single character. These types of conflicts are sometimes called man vs. himself. (Of course, by "man" we mean any human being.) A character who has to make an important life decision would be an example of someone experiencing an internal conflict. Some examples include Gollum in *The Lord of the Rings,* who must decide whether to help Frodo or thwart his effort to return the ring, and John Nash, who struggles to regain his mental health in *A Beautiful Mind.*

External conflicts are those caused by forces outside of a character. These conflicts can be man vs. nature, such as in the books *Robinson Crusoe* and *Lord of the Flies* or the movie *Castaway*, or man vs. man, which is present in countless books, movies, and other literary works. Another type of external conflict is man vs. society, in which someone, or a group of people, struggles against some aspect of culture or society. The Disney movie *Mulan* is a good example: Mulan wants her family to be proud of her, so she disguises herself as a young man and goes to war in her father's place. Certainly, she would not have been allowed to do such a thing; Chinese society would not allow a girl to become a warrior.

In various genres of literature, plot will usually contain more than one type of conflict. The reality TV show *Survivor* would be an example containing all the types of conflict. Some participants have internal conflicts (man vs. himself) about their actions and behaviors. All of the participants are competing against one another (man vs. man) and against conditions (man vs. nature). There are often elements of man vs. society when the participants struggle to break free of the rules of society that they are used to living under.

IMPACT OF CONFLICT ON PLOT

In some stories, the major conflict may create the entire plot. For example, in a James Bond movie, the conflict of man vs. man—Bond vs. the villain—is the basis of the entire plot. All events related to the main plot are centered around the struggle between those two opposing forces. In other stories, there may be several conflicts playing out at once.

Conflict is the element that drives the plot along a particular path. A story's plot might be running along smoothly when some particular conflict arises and the entire plot takes a different twist. Many books and movies have been written about characters enjoying a successful life and rewarding career, when a major illness or accident strikes, and they have to come to terms with the event and learn a whole new way of life.

Internal conflict will have its primary effect on the character experiencing it, but the character's actions may affect the entire plot. When examining the impact of various conflicts, look at the source and the effects of the conflict, and how both are related to the plot. If you are trying to determine the impact of a conflict on plot, identify some of the following points: Has it been present all along, or is it new in the story? Does the conflict affect all of the characters or primarily one character? What or who has been affected directly by this conflict? What or who has been affected indirectly? The information you collect from these questions will form the basis to answer any questions about the impact of conflict on plot.

MOOD AND TONE

Mood	the atmosphere (or soul) of a literary work. The author carefully chooses and develops the voice, persona, or narrator to give the story the feelings the author wants to show to the readers. The writer creates a mood through the point of view and the details of the setting and plot. All of these elements of a story must support the writer's feeling or mood. In "The Cask of Amontillado," Poe creates a mood, a feeling, of mystery and gloom. 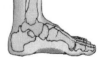
Tone	a feeling or impression given to the reader through word choice and language in the work of literature. The reader experiences a tone of humor and mischief in the novel *Tom Sawyer* by Mark Twain.

Some Types of Mood and Tone (learn what these words mean)

angry	dramatic	mocking	sad
anxious	fearful	optimistic	satirical
boring	happy	pessimistic	suspenseful
calm	humourous	poetic	sympathetic
cynical	lighthearted	relaxed	tragic
depressed	lofty	threatening	remorseful
lackadaisical	gloomy	tense	nervous
hysterical	lethargic	pensive	tearful
expectant	disgusting	macabre	beguiling

Just as the parts of a body may be identified and studied, you can identify the parts of a work of literature and study them. This is the key to understanding how the parts work together. You will see by this study how literary devices and story structure can guide you to a greater understanding and appreciation of literature.

Practice 3: Story Structure

Read each of the following passages. Then answer the questions that follow.

Excerpt from *Les Miserables* by Victor Hugo

Three days after his arrival, the Bishop visited the hospital. The visit ended, he had the director requested to be so good as to come to his house.

"Monsieur the director of the hospital," said he to him, "how many sick people have you at the present moment?"

"Twenty-six, Monseigneur."

"That was the number which I counted," said the Bishop.

"The beds," pursued the director, "are very much crowded against each other."

"That is what I observed."

"The halls are nothing but rooms, and it is with difficulty that the air can be changed in them."

"So it seems to me."

"And then, when there is a ray of sun, the garden is very small for the convalescents."

"That was what I said to myself."

"In case of epidemics,—we have had the typhus fever this year; we had the sweating sickness two years ago, and a hundred patients at times,—we know not what to do."

"That is the thought which occurred to me."

"What would you have, Monseigneur?" said the director. "One must resign one's self."

This conversation took place in the gallery dining-room on the ground-floor. The Bishop remained silent for a moment; then he turned abruptly to the director of the hospital.

"Monsieur," said he, "how many beds do you think this hall alone would hold?"

"Monseigneur's dining-room?" exclaimed the stupefied director. The Bishop cast a glance round the apartment, and seemed to be taking measures and calculations with his eyes.

1. The story is told from the point of view of
    A. the Bishop.   C. a first person narrator.
    B. the director.   D. a third person narrator.

2. At the end of the selection, the mood is
    A. calm.   B. tragic.   C. hopeful.   D. boring.

3. The main conflict in this passage is a struggle with
    A. society.   B. one's self.   C. the supernatural.   D. nature.

4. The setting of this passage is
    A. a dining-room   B. the Bishop's   C. a meeting   D. a hallway.
        at the hospital.   home.   room.

5. Which of the following is the BEST statement of the plot in this passage?
    A. The Bishop wants to assist with the crowded conditions at the hospital.
    B. The hospital director wants to purchase the home of the Bishop.
    C. The two men fear that an epidemic will soon break out among patients.
    D. They are considering how to enlarge the hospital's little garden.

The Civil War, or a Party?

When the phone rang, I was struggling with the introductory paragraph of my essay about the Civil War. I jumped about ten feet because I'd been so absorbed with trying to figure out a good topic for this horrendous paper that had been frying my brain.

"Hello," I said into the receiver, as I waited for my heart to slow down.

"Hey! Guess who's having a party! Jesse's back in town just for one day, and I'm having a quick get-together so we can all hang out."

It was Rianne, with the best news I'd heard all day. I felt a great weight lift off me just thinking about doing something fun for a change.

"Sounds great," I said. Then my heart sank. "Oh, but I have this paper I have to finish. I'm stuck on what point to make about the Civil War that will sound good and get me a decent grade."

There was a giggle at the other end of the line.

"I had Mrs. Thompson for American History last semester," Rianne volunteered. "That's an easy one. How about 'The Economic Consequences of the Civil War on the South.' Sounds impressive, but it's actually easy. You know how the South was fighting to keep slavery, because it was a major part of how they ran farms and plantations? Well, think about what abolishing slavery did."

"Oh, yeah, I get it!" I felt relieved and ready to explore this concept in my essay.

"Alright, hurry up and finish that thing," Rianne said, "and get over here by six."

6. What is the best statement of the plot in this passage?
   A. A friend coming in from out of town keeps the narrator from finishing an essay.
   B. A friend helps the narrator with an idea for an essay so they can have a party.
   C. The narrator doesn't want to finish an essay until motivated by a reward—a party!
   D. The narrator's actions show what it's like to crumble under peer pressure.

7. Who is the narrator of this story?
   A. Rianne
   B. a first person narrator
   C. a third person narrator
   D. Jesse

8. The main conflict in the story is between
   A. Rianne and the narrator.
   B. Jesse and Rianne.
   C. how to finish the paper *and* join the party.
   D. the narrator and completion of the essay.

Practice 4: Structural Devices

A. Passage Practice. Read this passage. Identify the point of view, setting, plot, character(s), irony, and mood in the passage. Compare answers with your classmates.

Excerpt from *The Red Badge of Courage* by Stephen Crane

Upon his fellows he beamed tenderness and good will. "Gee! ain't it hot, hey?" he said affably to a man who was polishing his streaming face with his coat sleeves.

"You bet!" said the other, grinning sociably. "I never seen such dumb hotness." He sprawled out luxuriously on the ground. "Gee, yes! An' I hope we don't have more fightin' till a week from Monday."

There were some handshakings and deep speeches with men whose features were familiar, but with whom the youth now felt the bonds of tired hearts. He helped a cursing comrade to bind up a wound of the shin.

But, of a sudden, cries of amazement broke out along the ranks of the new regiment. "Here they come ag'in! Here they come ag'in!" The man who had sprawled upon the ground started up and said, "Gosh!"

The youth turned quick eyes upon the field. He discerned forms begin to swell in masses out of a distant wood. He again saw the tilted flag speeding forward.

The shells, which had ceased to trouble the regiment for a time, came swirling again, and exploded in the grass or among the leaves of the trees. They looked to be strange war flowers bursting into fierce bloom.

B. Mood and Tone. Review the types of moods and tones listed in this chapter. Which ones would accurately describe the mood in short stories and poems in your literature book?

...IOR KNOWLEDGE TO ANALYZE LITERATURE

...arned in the last chapter, analysis means to break something into parts and examine or study those ... .hat is exactly what you need to do in order to analyze literature. Questions based on literary analysis will focus on the basic components of literature such as themes, characters, plots, settings, and literary devices. There are an almost endless number of possibilities to the questions that you could be asked. Take some time to review all the components and elements of literature if you are unsure about them.

In order to answer any questions related to analysis of literature, you have to read the question very carefully. Then, of course, you have to read the literature very carefully and closely examine the elements or components the question is asking about. Look at all of the answer choices, eliminate ones that do not correctly address what was asked, and then choose the best answer.

In addition to carefully reading the passage and interpreting what you read, it is also important to apply knowledge about other texts, your experiences, and the world in general. You do this every day. Think, for instance, about movies you have seen. When you see a new film, do you notice that some scenes may remind you of other films? Perhaps the new movie ends in a similar way to one you have seen before, or it may have the same "feel" as another movie (which usually comes from the expectations set up by its genre; that's why action films are similar to one another, romantic comedies all have some things in common, and so on).

An example of applying past experience in this way is a brief analysis of some scenes in the film *The Matrix*. When Neo is instructed to follow the white rabbit, and again later when Morpheus asks him how far down the rabbit hole he will go, the film makes **allusions** to the book *Alice in Wonderland* by Lewis Carroll. When Cypher tells Neo, "Buckle up, Dorothy, because Kansas is going bye-bye," the character is making an **allusion** to *The Wizard of Oz* (both examples of analysis come from knowing other works and literary elements). The way Neo falls into the water upon being released from his pod can be seen as a **metaphor** for baptism (analysis that comes from knowing literary elements and general world knowledge). As you can see, there are a number of ways to use your prior knowledge of other works, literary elements, and general experience in the world to help you analyze something new.

The skill of applying prior knowledge to analyze a text is also similar to (and aided by) being able to "read between the lines," also known as making inferences. You can review Chapter 5 for details about making inferences and drawing conclusions.

Practice 5: Using Prior Knowledge to Analyze Literature

You will use your unique experiences and knowledge of other works and the world when you analyze texts, which you will practice here. To help simulate some prior knowledge, some facts are given, along with an excerpt from the novel *The House of a Thousand Candles* by Meredith Nicholson. Read the facts and passage carefully, and answer the questions that follow. Note any prior knowledge you use.

Facts
1. The dust jacket on the novel contains the following "teaser" copy: *When his rich, eccentric grandfather dies, John Glenarm (an unemployed engineer who likes to gallivant around the world) inherits an unfinished estate, with the stipulation that he must remain alone in the house for a year. The grandfather's missing fortune is supposedly hidden in the crypts and tunnels of the mansion, nicknamed The House of a Thousand Candles because the old man preferred candles over electricity. As young Glenarm mulls it over, he has no idea what mystery and thrills await him.*
2. The novelist Meredith "Nick" Nicholson (1866 – 1947) lived and wrote in a residence called The House of a Thousand Candles, and he names this—his first novel—after it.
3. Quite a few films have been made about different adventures people go through to inherit something, and perhaps you have seen some of these. A few examples are: *Snow Dogs, Brewster's Millions, The Bachelor,* and *Billy Madison.*

Excerpt from *The House of a Thousand Candles* by Meredith Nicholson

I reached across the table for the paper, and he gave the sealed and beribboned copy of John Marshall Glenarm's will into my hands. I read it through for myself, feeling conscious meanwhile that Pickering's cool gaze was bent inquiringly upon me. These are the paragraphs that interested me most:

I give and bequeath unto my said grandson, John Glenarm, sometime a resident of the City and State of New York, and later a vagabond of parts unknown, a certain property known as Glenarm House, with the land thereunto pertaining and hereinafter more particularly described, and all personal property of whatsoever kind thereunto belonging and attached thereto,—the said realty lying in the County of Wabana in the State of Indiana,—upon this condition, faithfully and honestly performed:

That said John Glenarm shall remain for the period of one year an occupant of said Glenarm House and my lands attached thereto, demeaning himself meanwhile in an orderly and temperate manner. Should he fail at any time during said year to comply with this provision, said property shall revert to my general estate and become, without reservation, and without necessity for any process of law, the property, absolutely, of Marian Devereux, of the County and State of New York.

"Well," he demanded, striking his hands upon the arms of his chair, "what do you think of it?"

For the life of me I could not help laughing again.

There was, in the first place, a delicious irony in the fact that I should learn through him of my grandfather's wishes with respect to myself. Pickering and I had grown up in the same town in Vermont; we had attended the same preparatory school, but there had been from boyhood a certain antagonism between us.

He had always succeeded where I had failed, which is to say, I must admit, that he had succeeded pretty frequently.

When I refused to settle down to my profession, but chose to see something of the world first, Pickering gave himself seriously to the law, and there was, I knew from the beginning, no manner of chance that he would fail.

1. The novel begins with the narrator, John Glenarm, reading a will; from the way it begins, which answer BEST describes how the story will move in time?

    A. The will signifies the end of the grandfather's life, so the story will now move backward in time to provide details about the mansion and its owner.

    B. The will is actually being read at the end of the events in the story, and now a flashback will reveal how it all started during John's travels.

    C. Although John's decision about whether to pursue the inheritance is in the future, many flashbacks will be needed to fill in details about the old man.

    D. The reading of the will is the beginning of the story, which will now move forward to tell whether John accepts the challenge and what happens.

2. The author's style can set up certain expectations (foreshadowing) of how the story will unfold. Which choice BEST describes what is likely to happen in this story?

    A. The narrator laughs at the challenge, so he won't pursue it and will go back to traveling. The story will follow his travels.

    B. The will mentions Marian Devereux prominently; this will probably be a love story or a romantic comedy.

    C. The narrator will accept the challenge, though he doesn't want to be stuck in the house for a year. It will be an adventure.

    D. The challenge sounds eerie, and the narrator is being lured to the house for sinister reasons; it will be a tale of horror.

3. As the passage shows, the story is told in first person, with John serving as narrator. What is the BEST reason for the author making this choice of narrator?

    A. Telling the story from John's point of view will best show how he is affected by events.

    B. Readers need to know everything that's happening, and only John can explain it all.

    C. John is narrator at the beginning, but that may change as the novel progresses.

    D. John is the main character and the protagonist, so he needs to be the narrator.

4. Which pair of adjectives is the BEST description of the tone of this passage?

    A. mysterious / expectant   C. nervous / agitated

    B. calm / pensive   D. funny / satirical

5. For each answer you chose above, go back and explain how you made your choice and what prior knowledge, in any, you used.

CHAPTER 7 REVIEW

Read the following selections carefully, and then answer the questions.

Requiescat*

by Oscar Wilde

(means "may she rest" in Latin; Wilde wrote this poem for his sister, Isola, who died very young)

Tread lightly, she is near
Under the snow,
Speak gently, she can hear
The daisies grow.

All her bright golden hair
Tarnished with rust,
She that was young and fair
Fallen to dust.

Lily-like, white as snow,
She hardly knew
She was a woman, so
Sweetly she grew.

Coffin-board, heavy stone,
Lie on her breast,
I vex my heart alone,
She is at rest.

Peace, Peace, she cannot hear
Lyre or sonnet,
All my life's buried here,
Heap earth upon it.

1. This selection is BEST described as

   A. an essay.   B. non-fiction.   C. biography.   D. poetry.

2. Which sentence BEST describes the theme of the selection?
   A. When there is snow on the ground, be careful where you walk, especially in graveyards.
   B. Loved ones who have died are at peace though we may continue to mourn them.
   C. The departed return as ghosts to watch the seasons change and see who visits their graves.
   D. When someone close to us dies, we should bury something very special with them.

3. The point of view in the selection is BEST described as
   A. second person.   B. omniscient third person.   C. first person.   D. limited third person.

4. Which phrase from the selection contains a simile?
   A. Tread lightly, she is near
   B. Lily-like, white as snow
   C. All her bright golden hair
   D. Heap earth upon it

5. Which phrase from the passage BEST creates a tone of sadness?
   A. Speak gently, she can hear
   B. Coffin-board, heavy stone
   C. She that was young and fair
   D. All my life's buried here

6. Which pair of nouns BEST describes the mood of the selection?

A. fear/panic   C. wonder/surprise

B. bitterness/longing   D. admiration/jealousy

The Cave

It was one of the coldest days of winter when the four high school seniors began their journey into the mountains. Chad, a football player; Doug, an apprentice auto mechanic; Steve, a deer hunter; and Mike, a computer whiz all had one thing in common: they ate together at lunch. For weeks, they had planned this trip. Steve's father owned about 600 acres of land near the North Carolina border. The previous month, Steve had seen an old limestone cave he'd heard stories about and had been waiting for the best time to explore it. Winter break had just begun, so the boys were ready for high adventure.

After an hour's drive, they reached the edge of the forest that surrounded the cave. They parked Chad's SUV and unloaded the exit markers, rope, and helmets with cave lights attached. They carried their gear two miles through thick underbrush before reaching the cave's entrance. Mike screamed, "There's smoke coming out of that hole!"

"Will you hush, ya little book worm, don't ya know that caves are always warmer than the outside in the wintertime? That's just mist!" Steve said.

The cave entrance was slippery and muddy. Spiders crawled through the opening, and there were signs of bats regularly flying in and out at night. Once the boys passed the entrance, however, there were no more bugs.

"It sure is a lot warmer in here than outside," Doug muttered.

They crawled, jumped, and sloshed their way through the cave. Crystal stalactites and stalagmites decorated the cave floor and ceiling with stunning beauty. Chad reached out to grab one of the alluring crystal formations. "Don't you touch that!" Steve yelled. "I've heard talk from long ago that there's some sorta cave guardian here. The story's that the Guardian is supposed to be really mean and nasty, and it strikes whenever someone tries to steal part of the cave's formations." Chad dropped his hand, and the group continued crawling forward.

Slightly farther along, the passage opened up into a huge cavern. The ceiling soared 100 feet above. Beautiful crystal formations resembling amethyst and topaz sparkled under the light of their helmet lamps. Mike shrieked when he tripped over a bone on the cave floor.

"Don't worry, Mike. It's probably some animal that crawled down here and died a long time ago," Steve said.

While the rest were occupied comforting Mike, Chad carefully examined a two foot long crystal formation. Unable to resist any longer, he reached up and broke off a shard. Suddenly, a low growl filled the cavern. "What was that?" everyone asked. Two yellow eyes shown through the darkness from a ledge near the ceiling.

A gravelly voice bellowed, "Get! Out!"

The group broke into a run. As Steve led everyone out of the cave, he yelled, "Don't look back! Whatever ya do, don't look back!" They could feel a presence behind them all the way to the cave's entrance. Once free from the darkness of the cave, the boys jumped, tripped, and ran through the forest as fast as they could. They were near exhaustion by the time they reached the SUV. Steve gasped, "Chad, get us outa here!" Chad fumbled for his keys and jumped in. Then, Steve heard something behind him. Turning around, he saw the Guardian coming at them. Steve told everyone, "Mike and I are gettin' in front of the car. When y'all see the Guardian, run it over."

Shaking with fear, Mike and Steve waited for the Guardian to catch up with them before they started racing to the SUV. As soon as the spider-like creature was in front of him, Chad floored the gas pedal running over the Guardian. A flash of blue light flared from beneath the car, and the Guardian was nothing but a pile of wiggling crab legs.

"Let's get outa here for good," Steve shouted.

7. The selection is BEST described as
   A.   romance.   B.   autobiography.   C.   poem.   D.   science fiction.

8. Which of the following sentences BEST suggests a conflict in the passage?
   A.   Once the boys passed the entrance, however, there were no bugs.
   B.   "Don't worry Mike; it was probably some animal that crawled down here and died a long time ago," Steve said.
   C.   They were near exhaustion by the time they reached the SUV.
   D.   "Don't you touch that!" Steve yelled. "I've heard talk from long ago that there's some sorta cave guardian here,..."

9. Which of the following sentences BEST describes the theme of the passage?
   A.   An SUV is more reliable than friends in a difficult situation.
   B.   Caves can be beautiful and educational places to visit.
   C.   Strong bonds of friendship can overcome difficult obstacles.
   D.   Caves and caving trips are very common in the mountains near North Carolina.

10. Which pair of nouns BEST describes the mood of this passage?
   A.   joy and happiness   C.   pride and prejudice
   B.   suspense and resolution   D.   trust and faith

11. The point of view in this selection is BEST described as
   A.   omniscient third person.   C.   first person.
   B.   second person.   D.   limited third person.

12. Which of the following sentences BEST describes the climax of the passage?
   A.   "A flash of blue light flared from beneath the car, and the Guardian was nothing but a pile of wiggling crab legs."
   B.   "Unable to resist any longer, he reached up and broke off a shard."
   C.   "A gravelly voice bellowed, 'Get! Out!'"
   D.   "As Steve led everyone out of the cave he yelled, 'Don't look back! Whatever ya do, don't look back!'"

13. What is the BEST description of the setting of the passage?

    A. a cave in the hot Arizona desert

    B. deep in the rolling hills of South Carolina

    C. a cave in rainy, forested mountains

    D. a cave in the muddy backwoods of the Rockies

14. Which of the following responses BEST describes the relationship between Steve and Mike?

    A. As a confident outdoors person, Steve acts as a sort of big brother to Mike: fussing at or comforting the fears of Mike.

    B. Steve and Mike are always competing against each other for the leadership position of the group.

    C. Mike willfully disobeys all of Steve's instructions and so brings the anger of the cave Guardian down on the group.

    D. Mike is the brother of Steve's father, so Mike is Steve's uncle.

Excerpt from *The Lost City* by Joseph E. Badger, Jr.

Far away towards the northeast, rising above the distant hill, now showed an ugly-looking cloud-bank which almost certainly portended a storm of no ordinary dimensions.

Had it first appeared in the opposite quarter of the horizon, Bruno would have felt a stronger interest in the clouds, knowing as he did that the miscalled "cyclone" almost invariably finds birth in the southwest. Then, too, nearly all the other symptoms were noticeable,—the close, "muggy" atmosphere; the deathlike stillness; the lack of oxygen in the air, causing one to breathe more rapidly, yet with far less satisfying results than usual.

Even as Bruno gazed, those heavy cloud-banks changed, both in shape and in colour, taking on a peculiar greenish lustre which only too accurately forebodes hail of no ordinary force.

His cry to this effect brought the professor forth from the shed-like shanty, while Waldo roused up sufficiently to speak:

"To say nothing of yonder formation way out over the salty drink, my worthy friends, who intimated that a cyclone was born at sea?"

15. Which of the following BEST describes how the storm is personified in this selection?

    A. The storm is personified as a killer.

    B. It is described as a quickly-approaching monster.

    C. The storm is referred to as being born.

    D. The personification is that of a wheezing old man.

16. Which of the following phrases is the BEST example of the mood of this selection?

    A. "a storm of no ordinary dimensions"

    B. "the deathlike stillness"

    C. "the lack of oxygen in the air"

    D. "hail of no ordinary force"

17. Which of the following BEST describes the setting of this passage?
    A. The characters are outdoors somewhere near the sea.
    B. The setting is in a large city at night.
    C. The story is placed in some countryside in the heat of day.
    D. The characters are on a dock as night is falling.

18. In this passage, which type of figurative language is BEST developed?
    A. hyperbole   B. paradox   C. onomatopoeia   D. imagery

19. Which phrase is the BEST example of foreshadowing?
    A. an ugly-looking cloud-bank which almost certainly portended a storm of no ordinary dimensions
    B. Bruno would have felt a stronger interest in the clouds
    C. the miscalled "cyclone" almost invariably finds birth in the southwest
    D. those heavy cloud-banks changed, both in shape and in colour, taking on a peculiar greenish lustre

20. Which of the following is the BEST example of irony in the selection?
    A. The characters expected a sunny day, but a storm is coming.
    B. The professor was hiding but was called out to watch the storm.
    C. Waldo thinks the approaching storm could be called a cyclone, even though it appears over land.
    D. Bruno watched for a cyclone, but a storm formed over the water.

21. Which of the following phrases is the BEST example of a metaphor in the selection?
    A. ugly-looking cloud-bank   C. the close, "muggy" atmosphere
    B. shed-like shanty   D. the salty drink

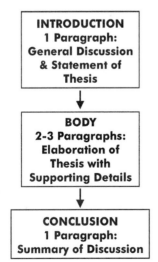

Chapter 8
Planning the Extended Response

This chapter covers the following South Carolina end-of-course exam items:	
Writing 1.1	*Demonstrate the ability to choose a topic, generate ideas, and use oral and written prewriting strategies.*

Whenever you write, you go through a process that helps you decide what words to put down, how to organize them, and what to include to best express your ideas to a given audience. Most of the time, this is done subconsciously, meaning you don't even realize you're doing it. However, learning to understand and use this process better can help improve your writing skills.

In this chapter, you will learn about the **basic structure of an extended response** (such as a paragraph or an essay), and you will review the **writing process**, including **choosing a topic**, **creating a thesis**, **generating ideas** using **prewriting strategies**, and **organizing ideas into an effective response.**

BASIC STRUCTURE OF AN EXTENDED RESPONSE

> **INTRODUCTION**
> **1 Paragraph:**
> **General Discussion & Statement of Thesis**
>
> ↓
>
> **BODY**
> **2-3 Paragraphs:**
> **Elaboration of Thesis with Supporting Details**
>
> ↓
>
> **CONCLUSION**
> **1 Paragraph:**
> **Summary of Discussion**

A five-paragraph extended response should include three main parts: **introduction**, **body**, and **conclusion**.

The **introduction** is the first paragraph of your extended response. It gets the reader's attention, prepares the reader for what will follow, and states the **thesis** of the extended response. The thesis of an extended response is much like the main idea of a paragraph.

The **body** consists of three paragraphs which support the thesis. Each paragraph is focused around a topic sentence which can be drawn from the key points of the thesis. In turn, the topic sentence of each paragraph is supported by the details explained in the rest of that paragraph.

The **conclusion** is the last paragraph of your extended response. It reinforces the thesis of your essay with a vigorous summary of your argument. It ties everything together and convinces the reader of the rightness of your position.

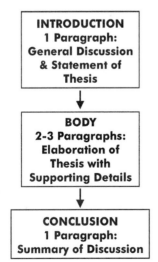

THE WRITING PROCESS

Whether you are composing a letter, an in-class extended response, or an essay assigned as homework, your writing does not appear magically. You must follow a process. You have to think, write, review, and then repeat these steps. Study the writing process described below.

AN OUTLINE OF THE WRITING PROCESS

THINK

1. If you are given a **writing prompt**, read it carefully. Make sure that you understand what question the writing prompt is asking and who your audience is.

OR

2. Choose the **topic** well for your essay. Make sure it is not too broad to cover in the length of writing you have been assigned, or too narrow that you will not have enough to say about it.

3. Generate **ideas**. Make a list of every idea that comes into your head regarding the topic. Don't judge the ideas as good or bad yet.

4. **Focus** your ideas. From your list, choose some ideas that you can use for your essay, forming a **thesis** and making a plan for how you will present your ideas.

WRITE

5. Write a **draft** based on your plan. Use complete sentences to develop your ideas into paragraphs.

REVIEW

6. **Revise**. Check over your draft for coherence, transitions, and sentence variety and structure. Delete any unnecessary words, phrases, or sentences.

THINK

7. Think about any other ways you can **improve** what you have written.

WRITE

8. Write the **final copy** of your extended response or essay.

REVIEW

9. **Proofread**. Neatly correct punctuation, spelling, capitalization, word choice, grammar, and sentence formation. Also check formatting (like line spacing and margins) if you are composing on a computer.

It may seem like there are many steps to follow when you only have a limited amount of time to write an extended response. For now, go through the steps slowly, learning each one thoroughly. As you practice, these steps will become like second nature to you. Then, you will be well prepared for any writing assignment you face, including timed extended responses on exams.

CHOOSING A TOPIC

Sometimes you will be given specific instructions for what to write. For example, when you are responding to literature you might be asked to write about how the setting of a story serves as a symbol for its meaning (as in Eudora Welty's "A Worn Path"). In this case, your teacher is looking for a specific response, so the topic has been chosen for you. Other times, you will only be given general guidelines or a broad prompt. You will have to choose a topic and develop it.

Whether you are writing to answer a particular question or you must decide on the specific subject, you will follow the steps of the writing process. You will also want to be sure that you are addressing the correct audience. Also, as you write, be careful that you do not steer away from the topic.

Here is an example of a possible writing prompt for an extended response assignment for which you must choose the specific topic to write about. Read it carefully, then answer the questions below. Once you have answered, look at the analysis of the possible answers.

Are All the Gadgets Good for Us?

In many ways, modern technology makes life easier. Computers, cell phones, PDAs, and other communication devices allow people to work faster, access more information, and stay in touch no matter where they are. For example, the World Wide Web is an immense resource for education and business alike. Many people argue, however, that getting dependent on "gadgets" can actually be counter-productive. For example, if the computers aren't functioning, people can't work. Instead of getting fresh air, people watch TV or play video games. They use cell phones even when they could be talking to the person right in front of them. They spend their time programming, fixing, and using machines rather than living "real life."

Do you think that tools like computers, PDAs, pagers, and cell phones have more positive or negative effects? You will write an essay about your opinion of modern technology, providing support for your position. Your essay may appear in the school newspaper.

1. Based on the assignment described above, which of the following titles represents an essay that BEST addresses the question?

   A. "Latest Technology is Too Complicated for Many People"
   B. "Are Your Computer and Cell Phone Your Best Friends?"
   C. "Our Love-Hate Relationship with Computers"
   D. "Is It Rude to Use Cell Phones in Public Places?"

2. What audience should you speak to in your assignment?

    A. your teacher

    B. the PTSA

    C. the general public

    D. students at your school

To choose the correct answer for the first question, you first need to **read the prompt carefully**. In this case, the assignment said to decide whether technology had more positive or negative effects. Thus, the topic chosen needs to address either the positive or negative effects of technology on people's lives.

Next, you can look at the possible answers to **see if any can be eliminated** because they are too broad or too narrow. If you do this, you can eliminate answers C and D because they are too narrow: C addresses how people feel about computers, and D explores the etiquette of using cell phones.

This leaves us with A and B. Answer A is a title for an essay that discusses how complicated technology is to use. While this is a problem that may *lead* to negative effects (like not being able to use the new DVD player because you can't figure out how to program it), it really **does not address the prompt**. Answer B is correct because the title implies that someone who constantly uses technology may end up with "gadgets" being the most important things in life.

The second question asks what audience should be addressed in the essay. If you don't recall, **read the prompt again for clues**. The prompt says that essay may be printed in the school newspaper. Therefore, answer D is correct. Your essay should be written with your fellow students in mind as the audience.

So, to choose a topic for an assignment, begin by understanding the prompt and what audience should be addressed. Use the following exercises to practice coming up with appropriate topics for assignments.

Practice 1: Choosing a Topic

A.

In addition to the many animals we can see easily, including both pets and wild creatures, there are many that we don't often see. Entire worlds full of life exist under the waters of the earth. Have you ever read about or seen a program about the strange fish that live near the bottom of the ocean, or the fish and amphibians in lakes, or the beavers that live in the dams they make on rivers?

In some cases, animals that exist today have not yet been discovered. Scientists exploring the Amazon jungles have found new species of birds and insects. Even some species that have been identified have not been described and studied in detail.

1. Which title below belongs to a paper that shows the BEST understanding of the passage?

    A. "The Fascinating Life of the Sea Urchin"

    B. "Pollution Is Threatening Ocean Life"

    C. "Where to Look for Fish and Amphibians"

    D. "Fish Can Make Wonderful Pets"

2. For what audience should this paper be written?

    A.   your fellow students   C.   the contest judges

    B.   your biology teacher   D.   the general public

3. Which of the following would be most helpful in choosing a topic based on this passage?

    A.   a newspaper reporter   C.   a zoologist

    B.   a pet rescue representative   D.   a park ranger

4. If you chose the green sea turtle as your topic, which of the following would be LEAST appropriate for your research?

    A.   a visit to a planetarium

    B.   a visit to an aquarium

    C.   observing turtles laying eggs on the beach

    D.   an interview with a reptile specialist

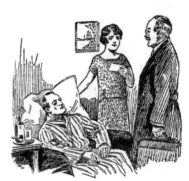

Decades ago, it was common for doctors to make house calls (to come to a home to check on someone who was sick or injured). Today, people who are ill or hurt have to travel to the doctor's office or to the emergency room. Most people say that this is the only solution because doctors could not possibly visit as many people as can come to see them. Others would like to see a return to the days when doctors made house calls, so that sick or injured people can stay in bed and rest. That way, they also will not make other people sick or be exposed to further harm themselves. Some doctors are starting to make house calls again because they can focus on each patient, even though they can see fewer patients each day.

5. Which of the following topics would be most appropriate for further research on house calls?

    A.   one that talks about how much paperwork there is to fill out every time someone has to see a doctor

    B.   one that describes the history of doctors making house calls and explains why the practice changed

    C.   one that argues that more people should get medical degrees because there are not enough doctors

    D.   one that points out how doctors can treat patients anywhere today thanks to portable modern equipment

6. Who is the BEST audience for this essay?

    A.   other students   C.   the public

    B.   your friends   D.   your teacher

7. If you wanted more information on this topic, who would you LEAST want to interview?

    A.   someone over 80 who grew up with doctor house calls

    B.   your primary care physician

    C.   your dentist

    D.   a physician's assistant

B. For English class, you have been assigned an essay for which you need to narrow down your topic. The guidelines are that the essay should be about something that is very important in your life: it could be a sport or an instrument you play, a special friend or pet, or some event that you will never forget.

Choose your topic. On your own paper, write down your topic and how you decided on it, as well as a possible title for your essay.

CREATING A THESIS

Once you have a topic for your response to the writing prompt, what you say about it will be focused around the **thesis** or controlling idea. The thesis is the main point—the idea you are trying to prove. It is what you want to say. The thesis must be broad enough to invite discussion but narrow enough to be manageable in the length of writing you have been assigned. It summarizes the topic and purpose of your essay in one sentence and includes the **general topic**, **your focus**, and **supporting points**.

Look at the following example:

General Topic	Focus	Supporting points
Television affects young children	in a negative way	• showing them adult programs • commercials make kids want things • takes time from play activities

A sentence which states the thesis would look like this:

> Television has a negative effect on young children because they can watch programs that are not meant for their age, see commercials for products they don't need, and miss out on playtime they do need.

The statement of the thesis for your essay is similar to the topic sentence of a paragraph. It provides the reader with valuable information about what is to come, and it gives you a kind of compass to keep your essay on track. You can then use each of the supporting points from your thesis to form topic sentences for the body paragraphs.

Practice 2: Creating a Thesis

A. Below are several topics, some of which have been focused in a specific way. For others, you will choose a way to focus the topic. Fill in the focus blanks where needed, and provide three supporting points. The first is completed for you, and the second is partially filled in

1.

General Topic	Focus	Supporting points
school uniforms	not a good idea	• look bad • limit individual choice of what to wear • expensive to buy two sets of clothes

2.

General Topic	Focus	Supporting points
school uniforms	a good idea	• less distracting • promotes professional dress • _____

3. If the general topic is **part-time jobs for students**, which of the following could be a focus?

   A. teaches you to budget your time   C. choosing a career
   B. rewarding but time-consuming   D. learning the value of money.

4. If the general topic is **why my parents should buy me a car**, which of the following would **NOT** be used as a supporting point?

   A. I can go anywhere with my friends anytime I want to.
   B. I took driver's education and got my license on the first try.
   C. My parents won't have to take me anywhere.
   D. I can help out the family by running errands.

5. If the general topic is **why we should get a dog**, and the focus is companionship and security, which of the following would **NOT** be a good supporting point?

   A. We are home alone after school until 7:00 p.m.
   B. If someone strange comes to the door, the dog will bark and warn us.
   C. When we go on vacation, the dog can go to a kennel.
   D. The dog can sleep with the little kids so they won't be scared on stormy nights.

6. If the general topic is **commercials on television are good and bad**, which of the following would **NOT** be a good choice for a focus?

   A. commercials teach us about new products, but is it the truth?
   B. commercials entice us to buy things we don't need.
   C. commercials for adult-only products should be on after 10:00 p.m.
   D. commercial ads for the Super Bowl cost ten million dollars.

B. For each of numbers 2 through 6 above, write a statement of the thesis for an essay in which you will defend your position. Use your own paper to write your thesis statements. Share them with your teacher.

GENERATING IDEAS

Once you have decided on a topic, you can begin generating ideas to use in your response. You may have many good ideas, but they aren't useful until you get them out of your head and onto the paper. There are many ways to get your ideas organized and ready to incorporate into your writing. Two prewriting strategies, **brainstorming** and **freewriting**, are discussed here.

BRAINSTORMING

One way to explore possibilities for your essay is through brainstorming. Begin writing down whatever comes to mind regarding the topic and questions provided by the writing prompt. Do not worry about grammar or spelling, and don't make any decisions about the ideas as you write them. Just let them flow freely from your thoughts. Your purpose is to create a **list of ideas and details** that you can use to develop your essay. For example, look at the brainstorming list below which is based on the following prompt:

Does television affect young children positively or negatively? Explain your answer.

What's wrong with television?	learn new information
kids are quiet	kids need exercise
they should be out playing	safe places to play?
educational programs	Barney, Sesame Street, Sponge Bob
see lots of commercials!	kids like TV
too many hours in front of the tube	tv is violent
sitting around playing video games	what if parents aren't home
kids watch too much TV	

As you can see, brainstorming helps you generate ideas for your essay, and it also can help you clarify your thoughts. As the ideas flowed freely onto the page, the student who wrote this list developed an opinion about the effects of television on young children.

Practice 3: Brainstorming

1. Which of the following could be added to the brainstorming list above about children and television?

   A. plasma TV screens   C. DVD players vs. videos

   B. eating while watching TV leads to obesity   D. High Definition TV

The following is a brainstorming list for "Why I Need an Allowance."

   1. It would teach me responsibility.   3. The other kids get an allowance.

   2. I should be paid for my chores.   4. I would learn to budget money.

2. Which of the following would be the BEST to add to the list above to convince your parents?

    A.   There are child labor laws.

    B.   I would take on more responsibilities at home.

    C.   I would quit asking for money all the time.

    D.   I would learn a lot from having more money to spend.

FREEWRITING

Freewriting is another way to write down ideas that you can use for an essay. When some people are asked a question, they just start talking to help them think out loud. Sometimes, this is how people find out what their thoughts are. When you freewrite, you simply start writing and see what happens. Don't worry about grammar and spelling. If you get stuck and don't know what to put next, write "I don't know what to write." Just let the ideas flow. Look at the following freewriting sample about the topic of school uniforms.

school uniforms are stupid. I want to wear what I want to wear. Can you see me in one of those silly skirts? Those colors are always so bad. Who woudl want unifiorms anyway? How much do they cost. I couldl never get a date if I were wearing a uniform. I don't know what to write Schoool uniforms stifle student individuality. Everyones an individual we don't need to look the same. What are the benefits. As long as clothing is clean and respectable, why do we all have to wear the same thing? Think of the added expense of buying two sets of clothes. Clothes that can conly be worn at school and closthes t home, I wouldn't be caught dead in one of those schoool uiformns otuside fo school

Obviously, the student who wrote this has some strong opinions that could lead to a good essay.

Practice 4: Freewriting

A. Try freewriting about each the following topics:

1. The need for improved public transportation in your area.

2. Life contains many joyful moments. What was the happiest day of your life?

3. School activities such as field trips, plays, and concerts can be fun and educational. What was your favorite school activity last semester?

4. Cheating in school is the wrong way to get an education. How should students who are caught cheating be punished?

B. Read the following freewriting sample about an old sick dog. Then choose the best answer for the questions that follow.

What To Do About My Old, Sick Dog

My dog is old. Poor vision. Has to try four times to jump up on my bed. I love him. He sleeps with me. Cries more now. I think he has aches and pains. Vet says he's getting old. He was adopted - like me - not sure how old he is. A good guess is 11 or 12. What will I do? Put him down? Listen to him cry? What should I do? Are there pain pills for dogs?

Give him aspirin. Parents don't want more vet bills. He's expensive, but I love him. How much longer will he live?

5. Which of the following statements is the LEAST relevant to the topic?

A. Vet says he is getting old.

C. What will I do?

B. He was adopted like me.

D. I think he has aches and pains.

6. Matt is willing to take his sick dog to the veterinarian. Which of the following topics would the veterinarian most likely be able to explain?

A. costs for the dog's treatments and medicines

B. whether or not to put the dog down

C. how long the dog will live

D. the dog's life before adoption

7. Next week, Matt's teacher wants a 500-word essay on this freewriting topic. What should be Matt's next step?

A. add more freewriting statements to Matt's existing freewriting

B. cross out several topics in Matt's existing freewriting

C. destroy the current freewriting and start over

D. identify the dog's illness on the internet and include a description in the essay

FOCUSING IDEAS

Obviously, you cannot create an essay directly from a brainstorming list or a freewriting sample. The ideas don't follow any logical order. Also, there are too many ideas. You can't use them all. You need to choose a group of related ideas that you can develop into a coherent, well-organized essay. **Clustering** is another prewriting strategy that can help you organize your thoughts and develop the thesis for your essay.

CLUSTERING

Clustering is one helpful way to start organizing your ideas by grouping related thoughts together. In the clustering process, you put the main question of the writing prompt in the center of the page, and draw a circle around it. Then you draw branches off from this circle to add topics and supporting details.

Sample Clustering for Effects of Television on Young Children

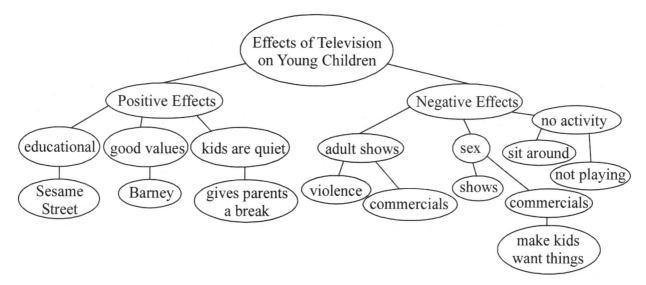

The clustering process can help you narrow your ideas, but these ideas still need to be limited further. You can choose only one portion of your cluster to develop your essay. For example, in the cluster diagram above, there are more ideas grouped around the negative effects of television. This indicates interest, enthusiasm, and support for this idea, and would, therefore, make a good focus for an essay.

Practice 5: Clustering

Choose four of the topics from the previous practices, and create a clustering diagram for each one. (You will use these diagrams later, so keep them in a safe place, like your portfolio or writing folder.)

ORGANIZING IDEAS

Your thesis is like the destination you have chosen for a journey. The ideas you have gathered in your clustering diagram are the stops you want to make along the way. You still need to decide how you will get to your destination, putting your stops in the proper order. An **outline** helps you plan your journey.

OUTLINE

An outline lays out the plan for your essay in a very structured way. It is the road map you will follow in writing your draft. You will get to your destination more easily if your road map looks like the following:

I. **Introduction**: General discussion including statement of controlling idea

II. **Body**

    A. **Paragraph 1**: Topic 1 (from statement of controlling idea) and supporting details

    B. **Paragraph 2**: Topic 2 (from statement of controlling idea) and supporting details

    C. **Paragraph 3**: Topic 3 (from statement of controlling idea) and supporting details

III. **Conclusion**: Summary of discussion

An outline for the essay about the effects of television on young children might look like this:

I. **Introduction**: Television affects young children negatively because they can watch programs that are not meant for their age, see commercials for products they don't need, and miss out on playtime they do need.

II. **Body**

    A. Television exposes children to adult programs.

        1. Theft

        2. Murder

        3. Sex

    B. Commercials increase children's wishes for needless products.

        1. Children find it difficult to tell reality from pretend

        2. Products bring happiness

    C. Television takes away from children's playtime.

        1. Lack of play with others

        2. No fresh air and movement

III. **Conclusion**: Young children should watch less television

OUTLINE SHORTCUT

An outline can be very helpful for organizing an extended response when you have more than 90 minutes to complete the assignment. However, sometimes you must complete writing assignments within a class period or other limited testing time.

One way to save time is to use your clustering diagram to create an outline shortcut in place of a complete outline. You can look at the clustering diagram you have already produced, and write "CI" next to the circle that will be your **controlling idea**. Then, choose two or three circles from which you can form your body paragraphs, and put them in order by writing 1, 2, or 3 next to them. You may even want to group a few ideas for one paragraph by circling them. With this shorthand notation, you have made a kind of outline that will help you write your introduction around the thesis and support it with the body paragraphs according to the order you have chosen. Then you can summarize your key ideas in your conclusion.

See below how the clustering diagram from Page 146 can be used in this way.

Sample Outline Shortcut for Effects of Television on Young Children

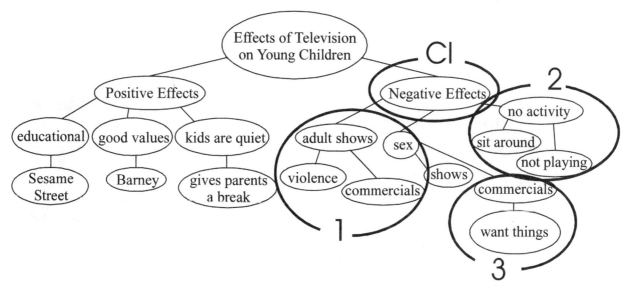

Practice 6:   Organizing Ideas

A. Choose the BEST outline for the following writing prompt.

1.   You have noticed that the cafeteria at school seems to serving the same dishes over and over. You have also heard friends complain that choices often don't include what they need to be eating. Write a letter to the principal requesting a wider choice of foods in the school cafeteria.

    A. I.   Introduction: The cafeteria needs a greater variety of foods, with energy foods for athletes, low fat foods for kids watching their weight, and better choices for vegetarians.

        II. Body

           A. Athletes need energy.

               1. protein, lean meats

               2. carbohydrates

           B. Overweight people need fewer calories

               1. grilled items

               2. less fried food

               3. fruits, vegetables

           C. meat substitutes & more salads for vegetarians

III. Conclusion: A wider variety of choices and items for specific diets is needed in the cafeteria.

B. I. Introduction: The cafeteria does not offer a variety of food, there is never enough of the best dishes, and the side items are dull.

   II. Body

     A. The cafeteria needs different foods.

       1. something other than chicken

     B. make more of the favorites

       1. always running out

       2. only things no one wants left by late lunch period

     C. better side items

       1. variety of vegetables, prepared in different ways (not just boiled)

       2. use more herbs and spices to make them less dull

   III. Conclusion: A greater variety, more of the favorites, and more interesting side dishes will have everyone enjoy having lunch in the cafeteria.

C. I. Introduction: Students would benefit greatly if the cafeteria served dishes like those at surrounding restaurants, which have more variety, better taste, and greater appeal.

   II. Body

     A. model food in cafeteria on variety of restaurant offerings

       1. pizza, sushi, burgers, wraps, tacos, hot wings, submarine sandwiches, etc.

       2. easy to get examples by looking at nearby restaurant menus

     B. restaurants are busy because their food tastes good

       1. use ingredients more like restaurants

     C. restaurant food more appealing—why?

       1. better sauces and sides

       2. better presentation

   III. Conclusion: Students would prefer eating in the cafeteria if it served a variety of foods like those in nearby restaurants, with the better taste and appeal of restaurant foods.

B. Choose two of the topics for which you have generated ideas in any of the previous practices, and develop outlines for each one.

C. Choose two of the clustering diagrams you have made, and organize each one into an outline shortcut.

CHAPTER 8 REVIEW

Save the work you do in this chapter review. Your work with the topics you choose here will continue in the next chapter.

A. Read the sample brainstorming list for the writing prompt below. Then, on a separate sheet of paper, write down your brainstorming ideas surrounding the topics in prompts 1 through 4.

Sample writing prompt: The school's marching band needs to decide how it will raise money for this year's travel to band events. It has invited ideas from all students for new ways to do so (and the winning idea gets a prize). What do you think would be a good way for the band to raise funds?

Sample brainstorming list:

fall & winter items, since that's when the funds are raised		something everyone needs	
calendars	candy	light bulbs	T-shirts
hats, scarves	candles	pens	note pads
greeting cards	fruit	coffee	books
wrapping paper	holiday music CDs	computer software	
Christmas wreathes		coupons for local restaurants	
Christmas trees		have an auction for donated prizes	

Prompt 1: Some people think that the arts (visual arts, music, drama) are secondary to the basics of education such as math, science, and English. They propose that the arts be available as after-school activities and supplemental courses but not take time and resources away from the core curriculum. Others argue that the arts are fundamental to a well-rounded education. How do you think that teaching of the arts should be handled in schools?

Prompt 2: Stopping at or driving through a fast food restaurant can save time when people are in a hurry or don't want to cook. A recent film called ***Supersize Me*** helped point out something many people feel, that eating burgers, pizza, and other fast food too often is not healthy. It can also be expensive as opposed to eating at home or taking a fresh food snack, like fruit, with you. Do you think it is alright to eat fast food, and how often? Or, are there alternatives that are possible even when you're on the run?

Prompt 3: Your local newspaper is sponsoring a contest with a $10,000 prize. The contestants must write a two-page essay which answers the question, "If you were granted one wish to change the world, what would you change?" Write a convincing essay for the judges.

Prompt 4: Your school district is considering changing to a year-round school schedule with month-long breaks in December and July. Many students are in an uproar because they enjoy having a long summer vacation to take extended trips. However, many teachers and parents support the proposal because students would remember more information. Which do you think is a better school calendar? Why?

B. Read the freewriting example below that creates ideas about the sample prompt for Part A. Then, on your own paper, freewrite your ideas surrounding the brainstorming you did for prompts 1 through 4.

Sample freewriting:

> *The band cuold sell something seasonal since fundraising starts in fall. Christmas stuff wuld be popular, but then not everyone celebrates Xmas - maybe have other things for other holidays? calendars for the next year are good. something non-religious would be good for everyone, like candles or fruit. Fruit sounds great because its healthy and everyone misses it in winter. It should be something everybody can use, everyday kinds of things. Not everyone drinsk coffee - maybe teas? and people probably have too many t-shirts. Special pens with the band and school name might be nice. Combine ideas: maybe a calendar with the school name - have one made that has pictures of the band and the teams? maybe too expensive to produce. Too many people/places are already selling entertainment books, but maybe getting prizes donated and having an auction would work - but that's a lot of work to organize - not like everyone just selling what they can of one item.*

C. On a separate sheet of paper, take each of the ideas from prompts you have been working on, and organize them by clustering. From these clusters, notice common details, and write a controlling idea. See the sample below.

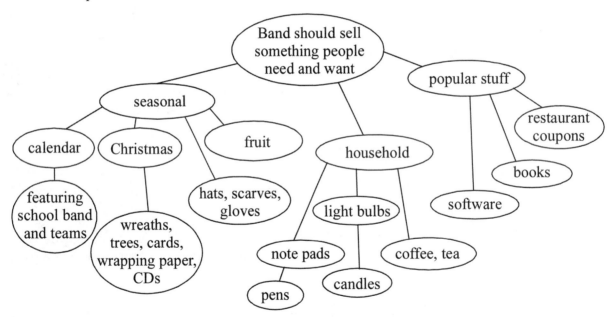

If you combine the clustering diagram with the freewriting ideas, some directions begin to emerge. These can be expressed in a preliminary thesis statement. Remember that you can revise your thesis later, as you refine your topic.

thesis: To raise funds this year, the band should sell something that most people need and want so that it will sell well, something people can use around the house, and something that is seasonal but non-religious.

D. Use your clustering diagrams from Part C to create outline shortcuts for your four ideas. The shortcut below is an example.

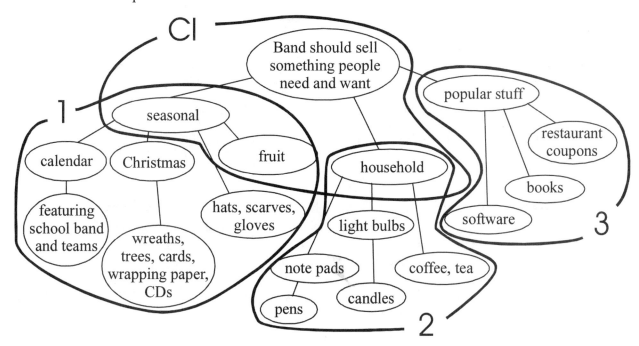

E. On a separate sheet of paper, create an outline for each prompt based on the clustering diagrams you designed in Part C. See example below.

Example:

I. Introduction: To raise funds this year, the band should sell fruit because it's something that most people need and want and will buy, something people can use around the house, and something that is seasonal but non-religious.

II. Body

    A. something seasonal because of selling period

        1. calendar would be great but expensive to make

        2. Christmas items sell well, but some people don't celebrate Christmas

        3. hats, scarves: would need variety of colors and styles

        4. fruit is the best choice because it's for everyone; citrus is ripe in winter

    B. something people can use around the house

        1. light bulbs, candle, note pads, pens are staple items but not very exciting

        2. not everyone drinks coffee or tea

        3. fruit is best choice because it's healthy and people buy it anyway

    C. other popular items

        1. Computer software and some books are popular, but they are expensive.

        2. entertainment books/coupons already sold by many other organizations

III. Conclusion: Fruit would be the best thing to sell because it's something healthy that people want and need, there is good fruit available in the winter, and it's great to have fresh fruit around the holidays.

Additional Activities:

1. As a class, choose one of the following topics to discuss.

   - raising the driving age to 18
   - voting on the internet
   - using cell phones while driving
   - no homework policy for high school students
   - benefits of studying a foreign language

   - offensive bumper stickers
   - surveillance cameras at school
   - praying in school
   - race prejudice in school
   - your favorite cars

Once your class has chosen a topic, each student, individually, should create a brainstorming list of ideas regarding that topic. Then, students should gather in small groups to share, compare, and further develop their lists. The class should then create a large brainstorming list by writing ideas on the chalk board. Finally, the class should choose which ideas would make the strongest extended response

2. Choose another topic from #1. On your own, freewrite on this topic for about 10 minutes. Then gather in small groups to share, compare, and further develop your freewriting. Finally, as a class, create one extensive freewriting sample on the board or overhead projector. Then choose the ideas that would make the best extended response.

3. In #1, you developed a brainstorming list, and in #2, you created a freewriting sample. Now, choose either one, and develop a clustering diagram. Then discuss your clustering in a small group. Finally, contribute your best ideas to a clustering diagram for the entire class.

4. Review your clustering diagram from #3. Then circle and label the part of your cluster that would be an outline shortcut. Use the sample outline shortcut on page 152 as a guide.

5. Based on your outline shortcut from #3, create a thesis for your extended response. Write it down, and then compare it with the thesis from other students in the class. Make sure it includes your topic, your focus, and your supporting ideas.

Chapter 9
Drafting the Extended Response

This chapter covers the following South Carolina end-of-course exam items:	
Writing 1.2	*Demonstrate the ability to generate drafts that use a logical progression of ideas to develop a topic for a specific audience and/or purpose.*
Writing 1.3	*Demonstrate the ability to develop an extended response around a central idea, using relevant supporting ideas.*
Writing 1.4	*Demonstrate the ability to revise writing for clarity, sentence variety, precise vocabulary, and effective phrasing through collaboration, conferences, and self-evaluation.*

Some people like to write several drafts, changing and improving each one significantly. Other writers try to be more precise the first time and may write only two or three drafts. For in-class writing, you usually have only enough time to write one draft, revise it, and proofread it. That is why it is important for you to practice writing extended responses now, so it will be easier for you to do when you have only a limited amount of time.

This chapter will help you improve your writing skills by providing practice in the following areas:

- **Developing Clarity and Precise Vocabulary**
- **Using Transitional Words**
- **Developing Coherence**
- **Writing the Draft**

DEVELOPING CLARITY AND PRECISE VOCABULARY

Your draft is an attempt to convey your ideas accurately and in an interesting way to the reader, so you need to be aware of the **audience** for which you are writing. Once you have identified your audience and decided which **tone** and **language** would be appropriate, you will select certain words and phrases to reflect these decisions. Your **vocabulary** is an important way to interest the reader, accurately convey your ideas, and provide convincing reasons for your position on a topic. Improving word choice involves selecting **specific words**, using a **dictionary** and **thesaurus**, being aware of **connotations and denotations**, and **avoiding clichés and sweeping generalizations**.

SELECT SPECIFIC WORDS, NOT GENERAL WORDS

One aspect of good word choice is selecting **specific and concrete words** rather than general or abstract words. Avoid vague, overused words like *thing*, *nice*, *great*, *bad*, *good*, and *a lot*. These words have many meanings, but none are very clear or specific. Specific words provide the reader with a clear image of what you are describing. Take, for example, this sentence:

Example 1: When he hit the home run, the crowd cheered.

The sentence tells the basic facts, but it could be improved significantly with a more detailed description. Consider the following questions: Who hit the ball? How did he hit it? Where did it go? How did it get there? In what way did the crowd cheer? To answer these questions, one might write the following:

Example 2: When John's mighty swing sent the ball hurtling over the right-field fence, the crowd leapt to its feet and burst into wild cheers.

In the revised sentence, the writer gives detailed answers to the above questions and provides a vivid picture of what happened. Good descriptions are more interesting and more persuasive.

Practice 1: Using Specific Words

A. Choose the BEST answer to rewrite each of the following sentences using specific words for more vivid description. Look for specific, concrete words and description that suits the meaning of the original sentence.

1. The dog barked all night long.
    A. The dog was barking all night, so I had to get up and put in some ear plugs.
    B. The mutt next door yipped from the time I went to bed until the sun came up.
    C. The poor dog could not sleep, and he wandered around making lots of noise.

2. He wanted a new video game, but he didn't have any money.
    A. He liked playing video games, and he was tired of all the old ones he already had.
    B. What he really wanted was a new game and a new system on which to play it.
    C. He longed to try his hand at the new adventure game, but his wallet was empty.

3. It was very cold and windy on the shore.
    A. As the chilling wind came in from the sea, we shivered and our teeth chattered.
    B. We all felt cold standing on the shore because we had not worn the right clothes.
    C. It seemed to get colder as we stood there, on the shore, in the cold and the wind.

4. I was so happy to get a new scooter for my birthday.
   A. It was so nice of my cousins to get me the scooter I wanted so much for my birthday.
   B. When I pulled the yellow wrapping off the bright metallic scooter, I shrieked with surprise.
   C. I absolutely loved the scooter I got for my birthday, and it made me very happy.

BE AWARE OF CONNOTATIONS AND DENOTATIONS

One important part of word choice is knowing the difference between the **denotations** (dictionary meanings) and the **connotations** (emotional associations) of words. For example, the words *slender* and *skinny* both mean "thin." However, if you called a person slender, that compliment might get you a date. On the other hand, calling the same person skinny might be offensive. In a similar way, the words *determined* and *stubborn* both refer to persistence and an unwillingness to be moved from a particular position. However, determined carries a positive connotation, while stubborn is usually considered a negative word. You might want to review connotations and denotations in Chapter 1.

AVOID CLICHÉS AND SWEEPING GENERALIZATIONS

Avoid using **clichés** in your writing. These familiar expressions include popular phrases such as "busy as a bee" and "to make a long story short." These dull, overused expressions interfere with your message. Simple, straightforward language is often more effective. Take a look at the examples in the next table.

Clichés	Simple Language
busy as a bee	very active
to make a long story short	to summarize
cute as a button	endearing
stop beating around the bush	get to the point
save it for a rainy day	save it for when you need it

Also, avoid sweeping generalizations like the following: "No one ever calls me." Unless used for dramatic effect in a story, words like *always, never, ever, no one, everybody,* and *everywhere* are most often not true and show an overly simple understanding of the topic being discussed. Unless they really are true (as in the case of the statement "I have never flown in an airplane" for someone who truly never has), replace these unrealistic claims with more accurate descriptions. Look at the following examples:

Sweeping Generalization	Accurate Description
No one ever calls me.	I rarely get phone calls.
It always rains on my birthday.	It seems like every year it rains on my birthday.
Everybody knows that Cincinnati has the best team.	Many people believe Cincinnati will win the championship again.

Practice 2: Connotations and Denotations, Clichés and Sweeping Generalizations

A. Use a dictionary to help you describe the connotations and denotations of the following words:

1. watch, glance, stare
2. walk, stroll, meander
3. run, sprint, scurry
4. shivering, trembling, quaking
5. strong, sturdy, tough

B. For each of the following sweeping generalizations, choose the BEST revised accurate description.

1. I'll never learn how to type fast on the computer.

    A. I am having trouble learning to use the computer.
    B. It is a real challenge for me to type very quickly.
    C. Typing is overrated, and I'll keep writing by hand.

2. Nobody rides trains anymore.

    A. Trains are noisy and slow, so no one travels by railroad now.
    B. People don't take trains anymore because they don't run often.
    C. Today, most people travel by car and airplane rather than by train.

3. Student names are always misspelled in the school newspaper.

    A. There seem to be quite a few mistakes in spelling student names in the school paper.
    B. The newspaper editors are careful with faculty names, but not about student names.
    C. The school newspaper has excellent stories, but the reporters are not very good spellers.

4. She wants go to the dance more than anything in the world.

    A. She will be happy for the rest of her life if only she is able to go to this dance.
    B. The dance promises to be a spectacular event, so she really wants to attend.
    C. If she can't go to the dance, she won't be able to show her face at school again.

USING TRANSITIONAL WORDS

By now you see that, when you write, you need to clearly state your main idea, and then you need to justify it with supporting ideas and detail. Using **transitional words** and an appropriate organizational pattern are two ways to make supporting ideas flow well from your central concept.

Transitional words are used in different ways depending on the organizational pattern of your essay. These patterns, such as time order, comparison-contrast, and so on, are described below. After each description, you will find some common transition words used in conjunction with this pattern.

TIME ORDER

You can use transitional words to show **time order**, that is, when events happen in relation to each other: one event before another, one after another, or both at the same time. Read the following example to see what happens when transitional words are missing.

> **Example 1:** Our family has a daily routine to get us to work and school. My father leaves the house. He wakes up my brother and me. I get up and take a shower. My brother takes a shower. I get dressed. My mother gets our lunches ready. We eat breakfast. We jump in the car and drive to school. Mom drops us off on her way to work.

Example 1 is choppy because it is missing transitional words to clarify the order of events. Without these words, the reader wonders how the father can leave the house, and then wake up his children. Below is a corrected example with transitional words underlined.

> **Example 2:** Our family has a daily routine to get us to work and school. Before my father leaves the house, he wakes up my brother and me. I get up first and take a shower. Then, my brother takes a shower while I'm getting dressed. Meanwhile, my mother gets our lunches ready. After breakfast, we jump in the car for the drive to school. Lastly, Mom drops us off on her way to work.

Using transitional words is a simple and effective way to present your ideas and descriptions clearly. The chart below provides you with examples of transitional words that show time order.

Transitional Words for Time Order			
after	again	and then	as
as long as	as soon as	at the same time	before
currently	during	eventually	finally
first	gradually	immediately	in the future
later	meanwhile	now	second
soon	suddenly	then	third
until	when	whenever	while

ORDER OF IMPORTANCE

Transitional words can help emphasize the **importance of some ideas over others.**

> **Example 3:** You should always be aware of your surroundings in parking lots at night. Look over the lot carefully for potential danger spots, for example, areas of low visibility and areas which do not have parking attendants. Be sure you have a defensive weapon, such as pepper spray or a loud noisemaker, in your hand as you walk to your vehicle. Before entering your vehicle, look through the windows to make sure no one is hiding inside.

Notice how the writer did not use transitional words to indicate whether any steps are more important than others. Below is a corrected example with underlined transitional words showing the order of importance.

Example 4: You should always be aware of your surroundings in parking lots at night. First, look over the lot carefully for potential danger spots, for example, areas of low visibility and areas which do not have parking attendants. More importantly, be sure you have a defensive weapon, such as pepper spray or a loud noisemaker, in your hand as you walk to your vehicle. Above all, before entering your vehicle, look through the windows to make sure no one is hiding inside.

As you can see, using these transitional words helps to rank the steps required to reduce the potential danger of parking lots at night.

Transitional Words for Order of Importance		
above all	especially	first
in fact	in particular	of highest importance
more importantly	most importantly	

CAUSE AND EFFECT

Linking **causes and effects** is an important aspect of writing a convincing persuasive extended response. You can use transitional words to make these connections clear. Read the example below.

Example 5: Students cause problems for themselves and others coming in late to class. They can miss important information. The teacher may have already started talking about the lesson. They disrupt other students. They come in and walk through the rows of seats. Other people can't see or focus on the lecture. Students should get to class on time.

The cause and effect relationship in Example 5 is not clear because the paragraph is missing transition words. Read Example 6, and notice how the transition words and phrases (underlined) can bring clarity to this paragraph by signaling the effect of students who come to class late.

Example 6: Students cause problems for themselves and others as a result of coming in late to class. They can miss important information, because the teacher may have already started talking about the lesson. They disrupt other students. If they come in and walk through the rows of seats, then other people can't see or focus on the lecture. Therefore, students should get to class on time.

Transitional Words for Cause and Effect				
as a result	because	for this reason	if...then	since
so	so that	therefore	thus	whenever

COMPARISON

Transitional words help a writer show **comparisons**, that is, how certain ideas or subjects are similar. Example 7 lacks these transitions.

> **Example 7:** The United States and the USSR did not want to enter World War II. They had been forced to enter the fighting because of sneak attacks. The Soviets were caught off guard when Hitler broke his non-aggression treaty and invaded the Soviet Union on June 22, 1941. The United States suffered a surprise attack when the Japanese struck the US naval base at Pearl Harbor on December 7, 1941. From that time on, the two countries were allies in fighting the Axis powers of Germany, Italy, and Japan.

Due to the lack of transitional words in Example 7, the similarities between the United States' and the Soviet Union's entry into World War II are as clear as they could be. In fact, the first sentence is awkward. The few well-placed transitions shown in Example 8 make the passage more effective and easily understood.

> **Example 8:** <u>Neither</u> the United States <u>nor</u> the USSR had wanted to enter World War II. <u>Both</u> countries had been forced to enter the fighting because of sneak attacks. The Soviets were caught off guard when Hitler broke his non-aggression treaty and invaded the Soviet Union on June 22, 1941. <u>Similarly</u>, the United States suffered a surprise attack when the Japanese struck the US naval base at Pearl Harbor on December 7, 1941. From that time on, the two countries were allies in fighting the Axis powers of Germany, Italy, and Japan.

"Neither" and "nor" may not sound like comparison words, but they point to negative similarity. The other underlined transitional words make the comparisons between the US and the USSR clearer. Also, note the importance of "from that time on" in the last sentence to show the order of events.

Transitional Words for Comparison		
also	as well as	at the same time
both	equally important	in the same way
likewise	neither…nor	similarly

CONTRAST

Transitional words also help a writer make **contrasts**, or differences, clearer. Read the example below to see how a contrasting paragraph needs transitions.

> **Example 9:** You may consider caves and mines the same kind of holes in the ground. They are really quite different. Underground streams and rivers form caves over millions of years through erosion. Humans use machines to dig mines over the course of only a few months. The rapid removal of rock during the mining process requires the use of supports to prevent a mine's ceiling from collapsing. The slow, natural formation of caves makes these supports unnecessary. The slow process of cave formation allows natural gases to escape slowly and safely.

Miners must be cautious of the explosive and poisonous gases that are rapidly released as the earth is blasted open. As you can see, human excavation of the earth is often rapid and dangerous. Nature's development can be gradual and peaceful.

Example 9 makes sense without transitional words, but it does not flow well. The writer lists ideas but does not connect them. Read Example 10 to see how transitional words can help the flow of the ideas in the paragraph.

Example 10: You may consider caves and mines the same kind of holes in the ground, <u>but in reality</u>, they are quite different. Underground streams and rivers form caves over millions of years through erosion. <u>In contrast</u>, humans use machines to dig mines over the course of only a few months. The rapid removal of rock during the mining process requires the use of supports to prevent a mine's ceiling from collapsing. <u>However</u>, the slow, natural formation of caves makes these supports unnecessary. The slow process of cave formation <u>also</u> allows natural gases to escape slowly and safely, <u>whereas</u> miners must be cautious of the explosive and poisonous gases that are rapidly released as the earth is blasted open. As you can see, human excavation of the earth is often rapid and dangerous, <u>while</u> nature's development can be gradual and peaceful.

Transitional Words for Contrast			
although	and yet	but	despite
even so	even	though	however
in contrast	instead of	in spite of	nevertheless
on the one hand	on the other hand	rather than	still
whereas	while		

Use transitional words to help the reader see the relationship between your ideas. These relationships include time order, order of importance, cause and effect, comparison, and contrast.

Practice 3: Transitional Words

A. Read the paragraphs below, and decide how each paragraph would be best organized.

There are many things to remember as you get ready to go back to school. Develop a positive attitude about the upcoming school year. Make sure you understand your class schedule. You know your classes. You should buy plenty of school supplies such as pens, paper, notebooks, and a calculator. Take time to inventory your clothes, and make sure you have the clothes you need. These tasks are completed. You will be ready for the new school year.

1. How could this paragraph BEST be organized?

    A. time order

    B. order of importance

    C. cause and effect

    D. comparison/contrast

Both your beliefs and your actions are important in leading an exemplary life. Your beliefs should guide you to knowing how to act in all situations. If your actions do not match what you believe, people will not listen to what you say. If you act in a way that seems good to others, but you have no beliefs to explain your actions, people may label you as shallow. Be certain and careful with both your beliefs and your actions in order to be an example to others.

2. What is the BEST organization pattern for this paragraph?

    A. time order

    B. order of importance

    C. cause and effect

    D. comparison/contrast

When we went to visit my aunt and uncle in Orangeburg this summer, we couldn't take Rascal, our beagle. My uncle is very allergic to dogs. We had to decide whether to board him at the vet's. We could also hire a dog sitter to come take care of him at our house. At the vet's, he would have people around most of the time. There would be other animals. He might get fleas. He might be disoriented and sad not to be home. At home, he would be more comfortable. He would get lonely. The sitter might not come exactly when he needs to go out or should eat. It was tough, but we finally decided to hire the sitter so Rascal could be at home. It turned out she did a great job.

3. What is the BEST way to organize this paragraph?

    A. time order

    B. order of importance

    C. cause and effect

    D. comparison/contrast

I like to prioritize the duties I feel towards those around me. I feel duty-bound to care for and protect my parents, brothers, and sisters. I try to take care of my extended family and close friends. I consider it necessary to serve my country in the case of foreign attack. These three circles of obligation complete the priorities I feel in my social and civic life.

4. What is the BEST organization pattern for this paragraph?

    A. time order

    B. order of importance

    C. cause and effect

    D. comparison/contrast

Ordering something as simple as a pizza requires several steps. You should look through the tower of coupons that has grown from daily advertisement mailings. You must endure the arduous process of finding out what everyone wants on their pizza. Call the pizza place and wait on hold. You are ready to hang up and make your own pizza. Distract your mind from the growing hunger in your stomach by getting your money ready. The delivery person arrives, run out to the car, grab the pizza, and shove the money in the person's hand. You can enjoy the lukewarm pizza that you earned with all your hard work.

5. Which organizational pattern is the BEST choice to use for this paragraph?
    A. time order
    B. order of importance
    C. cause and effect
    D. comparison/contrast

The preparation required for a test is quite similar to the preparation needed for a sports event. Training for any sports event requires daily practice to keep the athlete's body in good condition. Test preparation requires daily practice and review to keep the scholar's memory up to date. The night before a sporting event, the athlete must get plenty of rest. A scholar must rest his or her mind, so it will be fresh for the big event of the test. A good athlete will take pride in a nutritious diet that provides the building blocks for a strong body. A scholar must feed the mind with nutritious food to increase mental skill. Test-taking may not have the same glamour as athletic competition, but both activities require preparation in order to achieve success.

6. What is the BEST way to organize this paragraph?
    A. time order
    B. order of importance
    C. cause and effect
    D. comparison/contrast

B. Rewrite each paragraph on a separate sheet of paper, inserting the correct transitional words or phrases.

DEVELOPING COHERENCE

Coherence means sticking together. You want the ideas of your essay to "stick together," that is, to be connected and to lead from one to the other in a logical way. Tying your ideas together is an important part of helping the reader understand your writing. Three ways you can link the ideas and paragraphs in your extended response are **planning an order**, **using transitions**, and **repeating key words and phrases**.

PLANNING AN ORDER

Organizing your ideas in a certain order is the first step to developing a coherent extended response. If something is out of order or doesn't belong, it can throw off the reader and interfere with understanding of what you wrote. Look at the following example.

I was walking toward home, and suddenly I noticed two big guys tormenting a kid that lives down the block from me. I didn't know what I would do when I got there, but I broke into a run toward them. One of the bullies threw the kid's book bag aside. They were pushing and slapping the little guy.

Notice how the events seem out of sequence. How might you change this paragraph? Take a look at the revised example below in which the sentences have been rearranged. Another option would be to rewrite.

I was walking toward home, and suddenly I noticed two big guys tormenting a kid that lives down the block from me. They were pushing and slapping the little guy. One of the bullies threw the kid's book bag aside. I didn't know what I would do when I got there, but I broke into a run toward them.

USING TRANSITIONS

In the last section, you saw how transitional words link ideas from one sentence to another. They also link ideas between paragraphs to make the whole extended response "stick together." Without these transitional words and phrases, the writing becomes less interesting or even less understandable.

REPEATING KEY WORDS AND PHRASES

While you don't want to say the same thing over and over, repeating certain key words and phrases can improve the reader's understanding of the topic. By including key words or ideas from your controlling idea in the topic sentences of your paragraphs, you will make it easier for the reader to follow your train of thought. These repeated words are like landmarks along the road of your extended response, reminding the reader where you have been and where you are going. For example, look at the following plan for an extended response in which the topic sentences repeat key words from the controlling idea:

Controlling Idea: Citizens of the United States could greatly improve the country by obeying the law, protecting the environment, and being kind to other people.

Topic Sentence: The first and most basic step to improving the country is to obey the law.

Topic Sentence: In addition to obeying the law, citizens can make this country even more beautiful by protecting the environment.

Topic Sentence: A third way to make the United States a better place to live is for citizens to reach beyond their own self-interest and be kind to one another.

You can also repeat key words or phrases throughout the essay, not only in topic sentences.

Practice 4: Developing Coherence

Read the following passage, the answer the questions that come after it.

(1) Many people are familiar with the Civil War monument and museum of Fort Sumter. (2) How many know that Fort Sumter is named after a true patriot and hero who served his country long before the Civil War? (3) Fort Sumter has a very interesting

museum that is open year-round. (4) General Thomas Sumter (1734 – 1832) started his famous military career in the French and Indian War. (5) He fought heroically against the British to win freedom in the American Revolution. (6) He became a U.S. Representative and Senator from South Carolina, and he served a year as minister to Brazil. (7) He founded the town of Stateburg. (8) Sumter never gave in to British occupation, fought for many years to ensure America's independence, and continued to serve his country after the Revolution. (9) He was called "the gamecock of the Revolution" because of his tenacious fighting style.

1. What is the most logical place to put sentence number 9?
   A. immediately after sentence 4
   B. immediately after sentence 5
   C. immediately after sentence 6
   D. correct as is

2. Which sentence interrupts the logical progression of ideas?
   A. sentence 2
   B. sentence 3
   C. sentence 6
   D. sentence 7

3. Which sentence provides the most support for the central idea that Thomas Sumter was a true patriot and hero?
   A. sentence 4
   B. sentence 5
   C. sentence 7
   D. sentence 8

4. What type of transition words would help make this passage more coherent?
   A. time order transitions
   B. order of importance transitions
   C. cause and effect transitions
   D. comparison and contrast transitions

CHAPTER 9 REVIEW

1. Rewrite the following paragraph, using vivid images and concrete words to enhance the description.

   There is a park not far from the center of town. At its edges, a variety of trees provide shade. In the center is an open field and a baseball diamond. Many people use this area for different sports and recreation. They can also just relax there and take in nature. In nice weather, many people gather in the park. All summer long, there are festivals and other fun activities that keep the area lively. The park is a favorite place for young and old alike.

2. The paragraph below contains clichés and sweeping generalizations. Rewrite the paragraph in Standard American English.

   I have a bone to pick with Lindsey Savage. Two shakes of a lamb's tail after his election, he is raising a ruckus. "The county roads need fixing," he says, "so let's add 1%

to the sales tax." Lindsey Savage is so crooked he has to screw on his socks. The extra money for road improvements will just go to line the pockets of his sidekicks in the road construction business. Then they'll just piddle around and waste our money. If you hate more taxes, make a beeline for the county commission meeting next Tuesday night. Voice your opinions, or we're up the creek without a paddle.

3. In Chapter 8, you practiced planning an extended response. Choose two of the four topics for which you did freewriting, clustering, and outlines. Review the work you have done so far, and complete an extended response draft for both topics you chose. (Complete the others if you want further practice.) Save your draft, so you can work with it further in the next chapter.

ADDITIONAL ACTIVITIES

On your own or in a group, skim through 3 – 4 articles in magazines such as *Time*, *Newsweek*, *People*, *Sports Illustrated*, etc. Describe examples of clarity and specific vocabulary. Point out examples of transitional words and key words and phrases. How do those words and phrases improve the coherence of the articles?

Chapter 10
Revising the Extended Response

This chapter covers the following South Carolina end-of-course exam items:	
Writing 1.4	*Demonstrate the ability to revise writing for clarity, sentence variety, precise vocabulary, and effective phrasing through collaboration, conferencing, and self-evaluation.*

Even if you plan your extended response very carefully and try to write your draft precisely, you will still have room for improvement. Remember, writing is a process of thinking, writing, and reviewing. Once the draft is finished, it is time for reviewing, which includes revising and proofreading. This chapter will help you with revising, and the next chapter will show you how to proofread.

Revising is looking again at the draft of your extended response with the intention of making changes to improve it. Revising involves the steps shown below.

- **Adding Clarifying Information**
- **Deleting Unrelated Sentences**
- **Eliminating Unnecessary Words**
- **Correcting Shifts in Tense or Person**
- **Checking for Parallel Sentence Structure**
- **Developing Sentence Variety**

There are still some errors in the extended response which the next chapter will address. For the rest of this chapter, you will practice some revising skills.

ADDING CLARIFYING INFORMATION

When you write your draft, you know what you mean, but you want to be sure it will be clear to your audience. As you revise your extended response, imagine that you are the intended audience reading the extended response for the first time. You want to make sure the reader has enough information, so that he or she has no unanswered questions. Ask yourself if added information, more details, or another example would make your writing clearer. The following sentence provides a good example.

Example 1: At its next meeting, the school board will consider the proposal.

The writer may have provided enough information for someone who is familiar with the situation described. However, another reader might ask, "Which school board?" "What proposal?" or "When's the next meeting?" The writer must add information to make the description clearer, as in the following sentence.

Example 2: Next Thursday night, the city school board will consider the proposal to expand the recycling program in all schools.

With this sentence, the reader doesn't have to be a member of that particular school district in order to understand what the writer is describing. All the necessary information is provided. You want to write the same kind of sentences for the reader of your extended response.

Practice 1:   Adding Clarifying Information

Revise the following sentences by adding clarifying information.

1.   We went to my aunt's house, and I forgot my watch there.

_____

_____

2.   We didn't have any time to shower after the game.

_____

_____

3.   Those kinds of shoes are too expensive.

_____

_____

4.   My new glasses will help me get better grades.

_____

_____

DELETING UNRELATED SENTENCES

In some cases, you may want to add information, ideas, or examples to your sentences. In other cases, you will want to eliminate information, ideas, or examples if they do not relate directly to the topic of your extended response. Look at the paragraph following.

I got a lot of great deals at the Clothing Mart. All the shoes were 50% off, so I bought two new pairs. I bought 4 new shirts because they were on sale—buy one, get one free. I'm so glad my friend Chris was there to help me pick out clothes. The pants were reduced by only 10%, but I really liked a green pair, so I bought it. I've never seen such a great sale.

Each sentence in the paragraph relates to the writer's purchasing new clothes at a big sale. The author's appreciation of Chris' help, however, does not fit well in the paragraph. This sentence is not related closely enough to the other sentences, so it weakens the coherence of the paragraph. Deleting the fourth sentence will make the paragraph more concise and coherent.

Practice 2: Deleting Unrelated Sentences

Read each of the following paragraphs, and choose the unrelated sentence from the choices below it.

1. My sister collects so many different things, it's a wonder she still fits everything into her room. She started when she was little, gathering Barbie doll clothes and accessories. I think her collection is museum-worthy by now. Next, she started collecting those little spoons that you can buy when traveling around. Most have cities or states on them. What's the use of having a bunch of spoons you can't even use for eating? Now, she's into eggs made out of all kinds of materials. Some are stone, some are ceramic, some are jeweled, and other are too myste- rious to even guess about. I'll never figure out what she sees in any of that junk!

    A.   Next, she started collecting those little spoons that you can buy when traveling around.
    B.   Most have cities or states on them.
    C.   What's the use of having a bunch of spoons you can't even use for eating?
    D.   Now, she's into eggs made out of all kinds of materials.

2. My first day in high school was pretty challenging. For the first time, I changed to a different class every fifty minutes. The school was huge, and I got lost during every move. I showed up to every class late. To top it all off, the combination to my locker didn't work, so I had to carry all of my books the entire day. I was not looking forward to going home, either, because I had to mow the lawn. My only consolation was that the other students in my classes were really friendly, and the teachers were understanding of what happens that first day.

    A.   The school was huge, and I got lost during every move.
    B.   I showed up to every class late.
    C.   To top it all off, the combination to my locker didn't work, so I had to carry all of my books the entire day.
    D.   I was not looking forward to going home, either, because I had to mow the lawn.

3. When Leah turned the corner and entered the perfume shop at the mall, she got more than she bar- gained for. The most horrid smell in the world assaulted her nose. Customers and sales associates in this store were coughing and gagging! Leah pinched her nose immediately and ran for her life. After running for about fifty feet with her nose pinched, she released her nose and breathed some fresh air. There's nothing like fresh air to increase your mental functioning. After that incident,

Leah thought it would be best to go home. The next morning she read about someone placing a stink bomb in the store as a prank.

    A.   After running for about fifty feet with her nose pinched, she released her nose and breathed some fresh air.

    B.   There's nothing like fresh air to increase your mental functioning.

    C.   After that incident, Leah thought it would be best to go home.

    D.   The next morning she read about someone placing a stink bomb in the store as a prank.

4.   Spicy food is absolutely my favorite. In fact, I can't eat anything bland anymore. When we have humdrum chicken breasts and mashed potatoes for dinner, I reach for the Tobasco. Even breakfast has to be spicy, so on weekends, I like to make myself a Mexican omelette with jalapeno slices and pepper-jack cheese. As a snack, I really like a mix that I found at the grocery store which has pretzels, peanuts, and cajun corn sticks, all covered in fiery spice. I'm not happy until my taste buds are blazing! I wonder if my tastes will change as I get older.

    A.   In fact, I can't eat anything bland anymore.

    B.   When we have humdrum chicken breasts and mashed potatoes for dinner, I reach for the Tobasco.

    C.   Even breakfast has to be spicy, so on weekends, I like to make myself a Mexican omelette with jalapeno slices and pepper-jack cheese.

    D.   I wonder if my tastes will change as I get older.

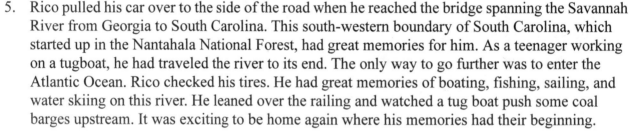

5.   Rico pulled his car over to the side of the road when he reached the bridge spanning the Savannah River from Georgia to South Carolina. This south-western boundary of South Carolina, which started up in the Nantahala National Forest, had great memories for him. As a teenager working on a tugboat, he had traveled the river to its end. The only way to go further was to enter the Atlantic Ocean. Rico checked his tires. He had great memories of boating, fishing, sailing, and water skiing on this river. He leaned over the railing and watched a tug boat push some coal barges upstream. It was exciting to be home again where his memories had their beginning.

    A.   The only way to go further was to enter the Atlantic Ocean.

    B.   Ricco checked his tires.

    C.   He had great memories of boating, fishing, sailing, and water skiing on this river.

    D.   He leaned over the railing and watched a tug boat push some coal barges upstream.

Eliminating Unnecessary Words

Along with unrelated sentences, you want to eliminate unnecessary words. Good writing does not necessarily involve lengthy sentences full of big words. Good writing expresses ideas clearly through effective words—the fewer the better. As an example, read the following sentence.

    Example 1: As I was reflecting the other day, I thought about the very great number of people who, as of yet, have had very little experience of their own with using the Internet by going on-line.

This sentence includes various words that do not help the reader understand the writer's intended idea. In fact, these extra words cloud the meaning. Read the following sentence without the extra words.

Example 2: Two days ago, I thought about the many people who have never used the internet.

This shorter sentence provides the same information, but it does so more directly and clearly.

As you write your draft, don't worry too much about extra words. Let the ideas flow. However, when you are revising, eliminate unnecessary words, and replace them with a simpler way of expressing the same ideas. Use the chart below to help you.

Unnecessary Words	Simple Language
due to the fact that	because
with respect to	about
hurried quickly	hurried
at that point in time	then
conduct an investigation	investigate
circular in shape	circular
there are many students who join	many students join
has a preference for	prefers
it is my belief that	I believe that
she is the kind of person who doesn't tolerate rudeness	she doesn't tolerate rudeness
In Nathaniel Hawthorne's novel *The Scarlet Letter*, he writes about	In *The Scarlet Letter*, Nathaniel Hawthorne writes about

CORRECTING SHIFTS IN TENSE OR PERSON

While you are writing, you don't want to shift gears abruptly. You want to keep the ride smooth, not giving the reader any unexpected surprises. One way to do this is to avoid shifts in tense or person.

SHIFTS IN TENSE

It is important to keep one verb tense throughout your extended response. Once you choose present or past tense, stay with it. Read the following passage, and notice how the underlined verbs shift from present tense to past tense.

Example 1: It <u>is</u> the last game of the championship. Tamara, the girl who <u>is</u> always picked last when forming teams, <u>sits</u> on the bench and <u>cheers</u> her team, the Rockets, against the visiting team, the Panthers. Earlier in the game, Louise, the star pitcher of the Rockets, <u>sprained</u> her arm in the opening pitch.

The shifts in tense make the reader unsure about how the narrator is related to the action. See how much more smoothly the passage below reads because it keeps the same tense.

Example 2: It <u>was</u> the last game of the championship. Tamara, the girl who <u>was</u> always picked last when forming teams, <u>sat</u> on the bench and <u>cheered</u> her team, the Rockets, against the visiting team, the Panthers. Earlier in the game, Louise, the star pitcher of the Rockets, <u>sprained</u> her arm in the opening pitch.

SHIFTS IN PERSON

"Person" refers to the point of view of the writer, as outlined in the chart below.

Point of View		
Person	Use	Pronouns
first person	the writer speaks	I or we
second person	the writer speaks to the reader	you
third person	the writer speaks about someone or something	he, she, it, or they

Shifts in person have a similar effect to shifts in tense. They can cause confusion by making the reader unsure of the writer's perspective. Consider the following passage.

Example 3: When I saw the water bubbling up from the ground, I knew there was a pipe leaking under there. I started digging slowly because you never know if you might hit the pipe or an electrical cord. You just have to be careful. As I dug deeper, I found the leak. You can just imagine how happy I was to find it.

 In everyday speech, shifting from I to you is quite common. However, this practice does not follow the rules of Standard English. In Example 3, the writer tells a personal story about an underground water leak. The writer begins speaking from the perspective of the first person, then shifts to the second person, then back to first and finally, back to second. These shifts interfere with the clarity and flow of the passage. Compare the revised passage below.

Example 4: When I saw the water coming up from the ground, I knew there was a pipe leaking under there. I started digging slowly because I knew I might hit the pipe or an electrical cord. So, I dug carefully. As I dug deeper, I found the leak. I was very happy to find it.

Example 4 gives the reader a clear sense of where the narrator stands in relation to the story. The narrator maintains the first person point of view, rather than shifting points of view.

Practice 3: Correcting Shifts in Tense or Person

1. Choose the sentence in which tense and person are consistent.

    A. A person who wants to learn how to play piano must be dedicated because you have to practice every day.

    B. A person who wants to learn how to play piano must be dedicated because he or she has to practice every day.

    C. To learn how to play piano, they have to practice every day and you must be dedicated.

    D. People who want to learn how to play piano must be dedicated because every day you must practice.

2. A. I was walking to the laundromat when I saw Philip, and I talk with him.

    B. Seeing Philip as I walk to the laundromat, I talked with him.

    C. As I walked to the laundromat I saw Philip, and I talked with him.

    D. Walking to the laundromat, I see Philip and I talked with him.

3. A. A typical first-year student has trouble adjusting to a new schedule, but after a while, they learn their schedule.

    B. After a while, you learn your schedule but a typical first-year student has trouble adjusting to their new schedule.

    C. Having trouble adjusting to a new schedule, a typical first-year student learned it after a while.

    D. Typical first-year students have trouble adjusting to new schedules, but after a while, they learn their schedules.

4. A. I went to the bank to make a deposit, but I couldn't because you know how long the line gets.

    B. Going to the bank to make a deposit, I couldn't because I knew how long the line got.

    C. I went to the bank to make a deposit, but I couldn't because the line was too long.

    D. So I go the bank making a deposit, but I can't because the line get too long.

5. A. One needs to take out huge loans before they can go to college.

    B. Before they can go to college, you need to take out huge loans.

    C. You might need to take out a huge loan before you can go to college.

    D. The student takes out huge loans before they can go to college.

6. A. It is the first of October, and I plan on driving into the mountains to see the leaves change color.

    B. It was the first of October, and I am planning on driving into the mountains to see the leaves change color.

    C. As it was the first of October, I planned on driving into the mountains and saw the leaves changing color.

    D. You should plan on driving into the mountains around the first of October to see the leaves, and it will have changed color.

7. A. An athlete never knows when they might suffer an injury.
   B. An athlete never knows when he might suffer an injury.
   C. You never knew when athletes suffer an injury.
   D. When an athlete will suffer an injury, they never knew.

8. A. So many children go hungry every day, while other people threw food in the trash.
   B. You have children going hungry every day, while they throw food in the trash.
   C. So many children go hungry every day, while other people throw food in the trash.
   D. Many children goes hungry every day, yet other people they wastes food in the trash.

9. A. People don't think it will happen to them, but a bad illness made them lose their job and home.
   B. People don't think it will happen to them, but a bad illness can make you lose your job and home.
   C. A person don't think it will happen to him, but a bad illness could make them lose their job and home.
   D. People don't think it will happen to them, but a bad illness could make them lose their jobs and homes.

10. A. Because a growing baby is so small, any drugs a pregnant mother took affected the baby greatly.
    B. Because a growing baby is so small, any drugs taken by a pregnant mother affect her baby greatly.
    C. Because growing babies is so small, any drugs a pregnant mother took affects their baby greatly.
    D. Because a growing baby was so small, any drugs pregnant mothers take affects her baby greatly.

CHECKING FOR PARALLEL SENTENCE STRUCTURE

Parallel sentence structure means that the parts of the sentence which are equally important are also similarly expressed. In other words, verbs match with verbs, adjectives with adjectives, prepositional phrases with prepositional phrases, and so on. Note the parallel structure in the following famous sentences.

I came; I saw; I conquered.
– Julius Caesar

Ask not what your country can do for you; ask what you can do for your country.
– John F. Kennedy

For I was hungry and you gave me food; I was thirsty and you gave me something to drink; I was a stranger and you welcomed me.
– Jesus Christ

These sentences have a rhythm and power because they are written in parallel structure. Writing that is not parallel can be difficult to read, and it is not Standard American English. Read the following examples.

Not Parallel: Billy knows how to play basketball, sing opera, and can even cook gourmet meals.

Parallel: Billy knows how to play basketball, sing opera, and cook gourmet meals.

Not Parallel: The three best things about summer are eating ice cream, swimming at the pool, and no school.

Parallel: The three best things about summer are eating ice cream, swimming at the pool, and not going to school.

Practice 4: Checking for Parallel Sentence Structure

Choose the BEST example of parallel sentence structure from each of the following sets of sentences.

1. A. The coach told us to go to bed early, to eat a good breakfast, and don't arrive late for the game.

    B. The coach said we should go to be early, eat a good breakfast, and don't be late for the game.

    C. The coach told us to go to bed early, eat a good breakfast, and arrive on time for the game.

2. A. The school lunches need more fresh fruit, less fried food, and there should be more choices.

    B. The school lunches need more fresh fruit, less fried food, and more choices.

    C. The school lunches lack fruit, feature fried food, and lack variety.

3. A. We searched for Tiger upstairs, downstairs, and under the house.

    B. We searched for Tiger upstairs, downstairs, and crawled under the house.

    C. We searched for Tiger upstairs, then we checked downstairs and looked under the house.

4. A. My hobbies include reading books, watching movies, and I have a stamp collection.

    B. My hobbies include reading books, watching movies, and collecting stamps.

    C. My hobbies are reading books, movie watching, and a stamp collection.

5. A. In this class, we will learn to blend various colors, to use different types of paper, and how to draw realistic portraits.

    B. In this class, we will learn blending various colors, using different types of paper, and how to draw realistic portraits.

    C. In this class, we will learn to blend various colors, to use different types of paper, and to draw realistic portraits.

6. A. Did you make your bed, wash your clothes, and clean your room today?

    B. Did you make your bed, wash your clothes, and cleaned your room today?

    C. Did you make your bed, washed your clothes, and cleaned your room today?

DEVELOPING SENTENCE VARIETY

Sentence variety involves writing sentences of different structures and lengths. It includes using different types of words and phrases. These variations make your writing more interesting to the reader. Three ways to develop sentence variety are by combining simple sentences into longer ones, starting a sentence with something other than the subject, and using a question or exclamation occasionally.

COMBINING SIMPLE SENTENCES

Simple, direct sentences are often the best way to convey ideas. However, if these simple sentences become repetitive, they make the writing uninteresting. Compare the two examples below.

Example 1: We went to the basketball game. We were late. There was a huge crowd of cheering fans. The team won. Everybody celebrated in the parking lot. Then, some jubilant fans had parties at their houses. It was a great night.

Example 2: After arriving late to the basketball game, we joined the huge crowd in cheering our team to victory. Hundreds of people continued the celebration into the parking lot and then on to the homes of jubilant fans. What a night!

Example 1 is a list of simple sentences, and the repetition is boring. In Example 2, the writer has combined several of these simple sentences into a few longer ones. Both passages tell the same story, but the second one is more interesting to read because of sentence variety.

STARTING A SENTENCE WITH DIFFERENT BEGINNINGS

Most sentences begin with a subject, continue with a verb, and end with an object. Adjectives and adverbs may appear along the way. This pattern works well as long as your writing doesn't get repetitive and boring. Therefore, from time to time, start a sentence with something other than the subject. Look at the following examples:

Begin with an adverb:

Replace "I found myself suddenly in a bad situation." with
"Suddenly, I found myself in a bad situation."

Begin with a prepositional phrase:

Replace "We stopped at the ice cream stand on the way home." with
"On the way home, we stopped at the ice cream stand."

Begin with a participial phrase:

Replace "The children ran into the candy store, screaming with joy." with
"Screaming with joy, the children ran into the candy store."

The examples above show different ways of forming sentences. They also show how a modifier is best understood when it is placed near the noun or verb it is modifying.

USING A QUESTION OR EXCLAMATION

Finally, using a question or exclamation occasionally can provide a welcome change of pace for the reader. Compare the following two examples:

Example 3: I didn't like it when my best friend told me he was going out with my ex-girlfriend. It was the worst feeling I've ever experienced.

Example 4: How would you like it if your best friend told you he was going out with your ex-girlfriend? Well, I know. It's the worst feeling I've ever experienced!

Examples 3 and 4 show how to use a question or exclamation to add variety to your writing. Example 4 also shows how a shift in person can be used effectively.

Practice 5: Developing Sentence Variety

Rewrite the following paragraphs by varying the sentences.

1. My best friend is a guy. We've known each other forever. Other girls ask me about him. They ask me why we are good friends. I tell them he is funny. He thinks of weird stuff. He tells me this stuff to hear me laugh. Sometimes I just tell him that he is too strange. He will listen to my opinion. He says that he is glad that he knows someone who will both laugh and tell him different.

2. You never know what effect you can have on other people. Sometimes it can be a big effect. Our school held a talent show. My friends and I did a lip sync to a song by 'N Sync. The crowd cheered. Everyone thought it was great. After the show, everyone wanted to tell us how great we were. I shook everybody's hand.   I had a little fever that day. I found out later that I had step throat. A lot of students were out sick the next week.

3. There's a new student in our school. His name is Omar. Most of his friends are in the chess club. He wasn't very popular. He wanted to run for student council. There was another student who was coming up for re-election. Her name is Theresa. Omar's friends were excited about his campaign. They put up a lot of posters all around the school. Omar gave a good speech. He had some good ideas. This was the first time he did something like this. He won by a small margin.

4. Almost every day, our neighbor across the street practices his golf game in the driveway. When he swings, he hits the ball between houses and into the back yard. Most of the time, the ball goes so far that it flies over his yard and into the yard behind his. One of these days, he's going to break a window in somebody's house.

CHAPTER 10 REVIEW

A. Read the sample extended response, which was written based on the writing prompt below. Using the skills you practiced in this chapter, choose the best answers for revising this extended response.

Writing prompt: Write a letter to your school counselor explaining what career field you wish to enter and why you have chosen that field. Include details and convincing information to show your counselor that you are serious about your career choice.

Example:

Dear Counselor Branson,

(1) The career field I would most like to pursue is to work with animals. (2) I have always loved animals and have had many pets in my life. (3) I know how to take of them. (4) They sense that I understand them. (5) My mother always says it's almost as if I can talk to them. (6) I would like to become a pet groomer because I think it makes the pets happy to be clean and groomed, because it's a booming business because people love their pets, and because there are parts of other jobs with animals—like being a veterinarian—that I would not like.

(7) The first reason I want to be a pet groomer is to make the animals themselves happy. (8) I believe that dogs, cats, and other animals are happier when they look nice and feel clean, just like people. (9) In the wild, or with other pets, animals groom each other. (10) They thrive on the attention and togetherness, as well as getting clean. (11) Animals even like a little massaging of the muscles they use all day, just as people do. (12) It would also mean that I could spend some time with many different animals and get to know them.

(13) Secondly, people spend a lot of money on their pets. (14) Pets are like part of the family, and people spend practically as much on them as they do on their children. (15) Or, if they don't have kids, pets receive all the attention. (16) As a pet groomer, you can have a very profitable business, especially if you are good with the animals and put them at ease.

(17) Finally, I chose grooming as a way to spend time with animals as well as to have a profitable career after looking at other options. (18) One working career I gave a great deal of consideration was that of becoming a veterinary animal doctor. (19) But I think that it would make me unhappy to see animals sick or injured. (20) Also, it would be terrible to have to put a pet to sleep, even if that was the best thing for it because of some problem it had. (21) I also considered the job of a trainer, but again I would not want to be mean or discipline an animal, even if it was for its own good.

(22) All in all, my dream is to work with animals in some way, and it seems that being a groomer will fulfill this dream. (23) Groomers provide a service by helping animals, grooming can provide a solid income, and they have fewer negative aspects to their jobs than other people who deal with animals. (24) I plan to study and work hard to make this dream come true!

Sincerely,

Sarah Williams

Sarah T. Williams

1. What is the BEST way to add clarifying information to sentence number 3?

   A.   "I know how to take tender loving care of many animals."

   B.   "I know how to take of them because I've had many pets over the years."

   C.   "I know how to take care of dogs, cats, ferrets, gerbils, rabbits, and other animals."

   D.   Leave the sentence as it is.

2. Which sentence in paragraph 2 should be taken out because it gives unrelated information?

   A.   sentence number 8

   B.   sentence number 10

   C.   sentence number 12

   D.   None of the sentences should be taken out.

3. What is the BEST way to eliminate unnecessary words in the sentence "One working career I gave a great deal of consideration was that of becoming a veterinary animal doctor."

   A.   "One type of work I gave consideration was a veterinary animal doctor."

   B.   "One career I considered was becoming a veterinarian."

   C.   "Maybe I should become a vet."

   D.   Leave it as is.

4. What is the most effective way to combine the information in sentences 19 and 20?

   A.   "But it would be terrible to see sick and injured pets, and I sure wouldn't want to have to put any animals to sleep."

   B.   "Sometimes, though, sick or injured animals even have to be put to sleep, and that would be a terrible part of having that job."

   C.   "However, I would not like to see animals sick or injured, or have to put a pet to sleep, even if that was the best thing to do."

   D.   "But veterinarians have some disadvantages like having to treat sick and injured animals or having to put pets to sleep."

5. How would you correct shifts in person in paragraph 3?

   A.   Change the entire paragraph to first person.

   B.   Change sentences 13, 14, and 15 to second person.

   C.   Change the sentence number 16 to third person.

   D.   Eliminate sentence 16 completely.

6. Which of the following is the BEST way to revise for parallel sentences structure in sentence 23?

    A. "Groomers provide a service by helping animals, they can make a solid income, and they have fewer negative aspects to their jobs than other people who deal with animals."

    B. "Groomers provide a service by helping animals, they can make a solid income, and grooming has fewer negative aspects to than other professionals that deal with animals."

    C. "Groomers not only help animals, but they make a solid income, and they also have fewer negative aspects to their jobs than other people who deal with animals."

    D. Leave the sentence as is.

Chapter 11
Proofreading the Extended Response

This chapter covers the following South Carolina end-of-course exam items:	
Writing 1.5	*Demonstrate the ability to edit for language conventions such as spelling, capitalization, punctuation, agreement, sentence structure (syntax), and word usage.*

You've written and revised your extended responses, and now you are ready to hand them in to your teacher, right? Well, they are almost ready, but not even the best writers turn in a piece of writing before they do a careful proofreading. **Proofreading** is the process of checking your extended response for errors in capitalization, punctuation, spelling, and grammar as well as for repeated words or omitted words. Before turning in your final copy, take time to look for these small, but costly, errors.

In this chapter, you will review proofreading notation, and then practice proofreading for errors in the following areas of writing:

- **Capitalization**
- **Punctuation**
- **Grammar and Usage**
- **Spelling**
- **Sentence Formation**

If you or your teacher feels more practice or review of grammar would be beneficial, read the text and complete the exercises in American Book Company's companion resources, *Basics Made Easy: Grammar & Usage Review* book and software.

PROOFREADING NOTATION

When you write an extended response in class, be careful to use legible handwriting for your final draft. When your turn in an essay done as homework, you will most likely have typed it (your teacher will tell you what format is required). However, you may still find a last-minute correction to make. In either case, remember that if your paper cannot be read, it cannot be graded. So, write neatly and clearly even for your proofreading corrections.

Proofreading notation refers to certain ways of making corrections that are standard among writers. Below is an example of how you might make corrections to the fourth paragraph from the extended response called "Children Watch Too Much TV."

Commercials are another problem with television. As well as advertising shows with adult situations, commercials persuade children to buy products th~~e~~at they do not need. ~~Thats'~~ That is how television pays for itself: C̸ompanies pay to put commercials on television,^ and they hope children will buy ~~there~~ their stuff. The voice on commercials tell ^s children that they will be happy if they buy a certain toy or cereal. They will be like other children.' ~~A~~nd a other children will like them if they have those products. It is difficult enough for adults to tell the difference between reality ^and pretending in commercials. How ~~are~~ is a three-year-old supposed to do that?

Notice how the proofreading marks are written neatly and clearly so that they do not interfere with reading the passage. Develop standard abbreviations and notations for editing your writing. Though you do not necessarily need to use these standard markings, your teacher may use them for evaluating practice extended responses.

EDITING AND PROOFREADING CHART

Symbol	Meaning	Example
sp	spelling error	They're ~~Their~~ back from vacation. (sp)
cap	capitalization error	I live in the E̸ast, but my sister lives in the W̸est. (cap)
. ? !	end marks	Where are you going/(?)
,	comma	Hello' Mr. Ripley (,)
^	add	Ray went to the store.
/	change	Television teaches ~~kids~~ children manners.
frag	fragment	Near Kokomo. (frag)
RO	run-on	He tripped he fell. (RO)
t	tense error	Yesterday I walk ^ed to school. (t)
s-v	subject-verb agreement	Keisha and I loves to shop. (s-v)
mod	misplaced modifier	Quickly, Sam ate the sandwich. (mod)

CAPITALIZATION

Capitalization involves the practice of using a mixture of capital letters ("A") and lower case letters ("a"). In the early development of English, writers used only capital letters. Now, in modern English, there are rules for capitalizing certain words in order to emphasize their importance. One example is the first word of a sentence, like the word *One* which began this sentence. Another example of words that are capitalized is proper nouns, like "Myrtle Beach, South Carolina." There are many other examples of times when a word should be capitalized. Think for a moment about the examples that you know.

Looking for errors in capitalization is an important proofreading skill. You will practice this skill in the following exercise.

Practice 1: Capitalization

Carefully read the letter below, proofreading for errors in capitalization. Circle all of the words with capitalization errors, including words that should have been capitalized and were not, as well as words which should not have been capitalized but were. **Hint:** There are forty-eight (48) words with capitalization errors to find.

july 24, 2004

dear mr. Golden,

My Family and i finally went on our vacation to the grand canyon in arizona. we got there on a Wednesday Morning. My brother, will, and I both wanted to go on the Helicopter tour first, but mom and dad said-"Later!"

When we first walked to the Edge of the South Rim, our jaws dropped, and we exclaimed "oh, wow!" at one time. Mom took a step back. "Oh," She said, "I don't think I can hike this!"

Some german Tourists, hearing our english voices, stopped by us at that moment to ask about the horseback tours. We helped them find the Camp office, and we spoke with kelly o'hara, the Park Ranger on duty. after giving us information about the Canyon and reassuring Mom about the bright angel Trail, Ranger o'hara asked if we were from the south. I guess our accents are more noticeable than i had thought...

Since I know that you, as my english Professor, will be asking for this later, Maybe you could look over my Outline for the Annual "what I did this summer" paper.

I. Memorial day pool Visit

A. sunburn

1. Second degree burns

sincerely yours,

Leigh Harpar

INTERNAL PUNCTUATION

Internal punctuation refers to the writing marks that are used within the structure of a sentence. They include commas, colons, semi-colons, apostrophes, and quotation marks. The appropriate use of these marks add clarity and logic to your writing.

COMMAS

The action of writing an extended response has a certain flow and thought process in drafting and even in revising. This flow can create an engaging paper, but it can also lead to omissions of certain punctuation. **Commas** are often forgotten in the flow of writing. Proofreading for any missing commas is important for the clarity of your paper.

Commas can signal a contrast, set off extra information, or separate items in lists. There are other uses for commas as well. Consider what you know about using commas, and then begin the next exercise.

Practice 2: Commas

Read the story below carefully, looking for all missing commas. Insert commas where they are needed, and circle them or mark them with a highlighter. **Hint:** There are thirty-five (35) commas that are missing.

What's in a Car's Name?

In our college library I fingered the book's jacket in disbelief. The title had to be a joke or was it? The letters stood out lemon yellow on a cobalt blue background spelling out the words *How To Name Your Car*. I told my best friend Renatta "Hey look at this!"

"Well yeah" she remarked in a bored tone "I saw a book kinda like that in my lit class by T. S. Eliot about how to name your cat. Crazy huh?" Still curious I headed to the nearest table to find out why this book would have been written and what it said.

When I began reading the book I realized that it detailed not only car names but also who would choose to name a car. Apparently Westerners who have not gone past the high school level in their education are more likely than other people to name their vehicles especially their mud-caked trucks and open-air jeeps. Sitting at that table I felt my past revealed exposed. My parents with their two semesters of college between them had named our huge maroon station wagon—had named her "Battle Axe." It was a righteous and well-deserved title. My family also according to the book fell into the common masses category by referring to this hulking machine with the pronoun "she." In her glory days she plowed into several smaller cars—usually in the shopping center parking lot where my mother vainly tried to overcome the "blind spot" that came with the car. Battle Axe always came away unscarred from the crashes but the other cars weren't so lucky.

After fourteen years we got our next car on May 17 1996. This new "she" had been pre-owned by my grandparents who lived in Fort Collins Colorado. She was a pale yellow black-topped Chevelle with a sweet 350 engine—she could move out! What did we name her? We named her "Cream Puff." She and her name lasted until the puff from her engine became a bluish-black oily cloud of smoke.

For myself I have named cars; however with my college experience it seems as if I don't have enough sense to remember to use the names and the cars don't last as long. I've used the names "Blue Meanie" "Behemoth" and "W. G."or "Wise Guy"—HE was quite a car. This soon-to-graduate South Carolina female has at least broken through the sexist mold when naming her cars.

COLONS, SEMI-COLONS AND APOSTROPHES

The **colon** signals that there is a bit of information that the sentence needs. It most often sets off a list, a quotation, an appositive (renaming), an explanation or an example. Colons are also used in number phrases like time notations or Biblical references. Two major rules about colons are

1. <u>never</u> place a colon right after a verb (between the verb and its object), and

2. <u>never</u> use a colon to separate two independent clauses with a coordinating conjunction between them.

You may use a **semi-colon** to separate two independent clauses which are closely related to one idea. (For more emphasis, you may also use a colon in this case, especially to emphasize the second clause.) Another common use of the semi-colon is to separate items in a list when the item names contain commas.

Apostrophes do not separate anything; they signal either possession or missing letters in contractions.

To improve your proofreading skill, consider the guidelines above and consider how you normally use these punctuation marks. Then complete the following exercise.

Practice 3: Colons, Semi-colons, and Apostrophes

First, carefully read the story below and continuing on the next page for content. Next, insert the missing punctuation marks and circle or highlight them. **Hint:** There are eleven (11) colons, semi-colons, and apostrophes missing in the passage.

Now Were Cooking!

You wouldnt play football without shoulder pads or a helmet, and no one would even think of trying to paint a picture without paints, brushes, and a canvas. Well, its just as important to be prepared when youre in the kitchen! When youre planning to cook or bake, one of the most important "ingredients" is to prepare everything you will need in fact, its best to have it all close at hand.

First, take a look at the list of ingredients you will need. Measure out the correct amounts of everything you need. If you dont have enough measuring cups or spoons, transfer the measured amounts to small bowls or other containers. Also, be sure to check early, even a day or two in advance, if you have everything you will want. That way, you can still run out and get something thats missing.

Next, read the rest of the recipe you plan to prepare it should tell you what equipment is required. Usually you will need the following mixing bowls, utensils, measuring cups and spoons, and pots and pans (or bakeware, if the food is going in the oven). Place all of this equipment within reach, but not where itll be in your way.

Finally, dont forget about timing. If the recipe calls for anything to be prepared ahead, chilled, melted, or anything like that, make sure you have that done before you start on the rest. Once youre ready to actually add heat to your dish, either on the stove top or in the oven, carefully follow directions about how long to keep the food at what temperature. You can use the timer on the range however, if it there isnt one or its not working, use a regular alarm clock. Simply set the alarm for the number of minutes needed. For example, if it's 4 15 p.m., and the dish should simmer for 40 minutes, set the alarm for 4 55 p.m.

Having everything you need at your fingertips will make cooking or baking a pleasure whereas, if you fail to prepare, it can be a frustrating and disappointing experience. "Always be prepared" is a good motto not just the Boy Scouts need to keep it in mind!

QUOTATION MARKS

Quotation marks are signals, framing words that belong to someone other than the author. When used in fiction, quotation marks help to keep the voices of different characters from becoming confused. There are two types of quotation marks:

- **double quotation marks (" ")** are used to signal direct quotes or some titles
- **single quotation marks (' ')** are used to signal quotes within quotes

Practice 4:   Quotation Marks

Carefully read the story below, first for content. Then, look for missing quotation marks, and add the quotation marks where needed. Next, circle or highlight the ones you added. **Hint:** There are eight (8) pairs of double " " marks and one (1) pair of single ' ' marks missing.

Summer Blight

Race you to that mimosa! challenged Sophie, pointing to a slender pink-dotted tree.

You're on, dork, snorted Terrell, and the loser has to bring everybody sodas.

We took off, with me—dead last as usual. We fell under the scant shade of the tree, panting and sweating from the summer's heat. I rolled onto my back to look up through the mimosa's fern-like leaves.

Did you know that these trees were all killed by a blight years back? I asked. My aunt Beryl always talks about climbing these trees as a kid, but they were huge then. Now the blight's over and the mimosas are growing again, but they're all scrawny, like this one here. Wonder when they'll be big enough to be good climbin' trees again...

Sophie sat up, frowning and fussing, Don't try to change the subject. You know it's you that has to get the sodas, and while you're at it, you might as well bring food, too.

Terrell agreed with her (as usual) that as the fartherest-back-of-all-time loser I should bring anything they wanted. My speech had backfired—making them hungrier and thirstier than ever. I tried again.

With this drought going on, the worst in history even, I think we should forget the sodas. Just remember, I said raising a hand into the air, that old saying, Don't spit; you just might need it. And I think...

Sophie and Terrell threw dust, thistles, and rude names at me until I got up and trudged off, feeling as much a loser as Charlie Brown in the comic strip Peanuts. Then, as I got closer to our screened door, I started daydreaming about what would happen if I fell in a hole or was taken by aliens. Sophie and Terrell—well, I expect that they would just wither up and blow away like blighted mimosa shoots.

GRAMMAR AND USAGE

Grammar and usage refers to the ways that writers put together words, phrases, sentences, and paragraphs. When you are proofreading, you want to make sure that you have followed the rules for Standardized American English. Look for mistakes in the usage of **nouns**, **articles**, **pronouns**, **adjectives**, **adverbs**, **negative words**, **verbs**, and **subject-verb agreement**. Usage can also refer to formal and informal language. When you are writing for a school report you will want to use formal language and sentence construction.

NOUNS AND ARTICLES

Nouns are words which name people, places, things, ideas, and concepts. **Common nouns** name general examples of these. **Proper nouns** name specific people, places, things, ideas, and concepts and are capitalized. Proper nouns are capitalized and common nouns are not. There is a special group of nouns called collective nouns. **Collective nouns** name single units made up of many members. Two examples are a **school** of fish and a **committee** of delegates.

Nouns may be **possessive**, showing ownership or a relationship. There are several different ways to form the possessive of a noun. Two of the guidelines are as follows: for a singular noun, add an *'s*; if the noun is plural and ends in *s*, then add only an apostrophe after the letter *s*.

In English, **articles** like *the* or *a* are closely associated with nouns. These small words often give the reader essential information about the noun they accompany. There are three forms of articles:

definite–"the"   indefinite–"a / an"   zero–no article

1. The first form, the **definite article**, is *the*. It can be used with any type of noun. *The* marks a thing that is known to readers either by general knowledge, the context of the rest of the writing, or by the information in the noun phrase.

> **Example 1:** **The** first star I see tonight...

> **Example 2:** A mudslide in Southern California claimed ten lives. It is **the** worst mudslide in 10 years.

> **Example 3:** **the** Atlantic Coast, or

the hurricane that struck South Carolina in 1989

There are three instances where *the* is always needed:

- Before the word *same* (**the same** time zone)
- Generally before a written (ordinal) number (**the first** star I see)
- Before a superlative statement (**the best** music)

2. The second form, the **indefinite article**, *a / an*, does not identify a certain thing. The writer may know of the noun item but does not expect the reader to know it. The indefinite article *a / an* can only be used with singular nouns. The article *a* is used before words that begin with a consonant letter or sound. The article *an* is used before words that begin with a vowel letter or sound.

> **Example 1:** I went to **a** concert.   He worked on **a** railroad.

> **Example 2:** She had **an** egg for breakfast.   They drove for **an** hour to get to the fair.

3. The third form, the **zero article**, means no article at all. No articles are used with plural or uncounted nouns. Often, vague generalizations are made with no article.

> **Example 1:** We will serve <u>hot tea</u> with lunch.

> **Example 2:** <u>Trees</u> give off oxygen, benefitting our atmosphere.

> **Example 3:** Religious texts are founded on <u>faith</u>.

Practice 5:   Nouns and Articles

Choose the correctly written sentence from each set below, based on whether a **definite article**, **indefinite article**, or **no article** should be used.

1. A. The school collected canned goods to donate for **the** World Hunger Day.

   B. The school collected canned goods to donate for **a** World Hunger Day.

   C. The school collected canned goods to donate for World Hunger Day.

2. A. **The** bus we arrived on had a flat tire and had to be replaced by another bus.

   B. **A** bus we arrived on had a flat tire and had to be replaced by another bus.

   C. Bus we arrived on had a flat tire and had to be replaced by another bus.

3. A. People say Alaska is too cold for a vacation, but **the** cruise in or around Prince William Sound is really beautiful.

   B. People say Alaska is too cold for a vacation, but **a** cruise in or around Prince William Sound is really beautiful.

   C. People say Alaska is too cold for a vacation, but cruise in or around Prince William Sound is really beautiful.

4. A. News about church matters often come straight from **the** Vatican City.

   B. News about church matters often come straight from **a** Vatican City.

   C. News about church matters often come straight from Vatican City.

5. A. Scientists believe that **the** most similar known planet to Earth's atmosphere and gravity is Saturn's moon, Titan.

   B. Scientists believe that **a** most similar known planet to Earth's atmosphere and gravity is Saturn's moon, Titan.

   C. Scientists believe that most similar known planet to Earth's atmosphere and gravity is Saturn's moon, Titan.

6. A. Right up there with Tiger Woods and Ernie Els, Vijay Singh is **the** very good professional golfer.

   B. Right up there with Tiger Woods and Ernie Els, Vijay Singh is **a** very good professional golfer.

   C. Right up there with Tiger Woods and Ernie Els, Vijay Singh is very good professional golfer.

PRONOUNS

Pronouns take the place of nouns in a sentence. A pronoun must agree in number and gender with the noun it replaces. Some examples of pronouns are *I, you, she, he, it, we, they, us, their, who, that, someone, whose, none,* and *nobody.* Some of these pronouns may act as adjectives when they are followed by a noun: for example, *that, those,* or *these.* Also, there are pronouns which may begin a question: for example, *what, who,* or *whose.*

Before beginning the next practice, you may want to consider how you use pronouns or review the use of pronouns in the companion text, American Book Company's *Basics Made Easy: Grammar and Usage Review* (2001).

Practice 6: Pronouns

Choose the correctly written sentence from each set (the one which uses a pronoun correctly).

1. A. People should be aware of their surroundings, especially if **he and she** are out at night.

   B. People should be aware of their surroundings, especially if **they** are out at night.

   C. People should be aware of their surroundings, especially if **somebody** are out at night.

2. A. **We** skateboarders aren't afraid to try new things.

   B. **Us** skateboarders aren't afraid to try new things.

   C. **Them** skateboarders aren't afraid to try new things.

3. A. Mom asked **we** to take out the trash.

   B. Mom asked **I** to take out the trash.

   C. Mom asked **me** to take out the trash.

4. A. Keira wished **her** could watch the beautiful sunset all night.

   B. Keira wished **she** could watch the beautiful sunset all night.

   C. Keira wished **them** could watch the beautiful sunset all night.

5. A. **What** we didn't know is that the leftovers had already been eaten.

   B. **Which** we didn't know is that the leftovers had already been eaten.

   C. **That** we didn't know is that the leftovers had already been eaten.

6. A. You shouldn't use things that belong to **no one** else.

   B. You shouldn't use things that belong to **someone** else.

   C. You shouldn't use things that belong to **who** else.

ADJECTIVES, ADVERBS, AND NEGATIVE WORDS

Adjectives are words which modify, or describe, nouns and pronouns. Adjectives answer the questions **Which? How many?** or **What kind?** In contrast to many other languages, English almost always places adjectives before the word(s) that they modify. **Pronouns** and **articles** can also function as adjectives.

Adverbs are used to modify many different kinds of words. Adverbs can modify verbs, adjectives, or other adverbs. Frequently, adverbs end in **-ly**, but not always. All adverbs answer one of these questions: **Where? When? In what manner?** or **To what extent?**

Adjectives and adverbs are also used to compare or "weigh" differences. The **comparative** form of adjectives and adverbs (**-er**) is used to compare two things. The **superlative** form of adjectives and adverbs (**-est**) is used to compare three or more things.

Note: For words with one syllable, use the **-er** and **-est** ending. For words with two or more syllables, place *more*, *most*, *less*, or *least* in front of the comparing adjective or adverb. If the comparison is negative, use the words *worse* (two things) or *worst* (three or more things).

Two **negative words** cannot be used to express one negative idea. When they are, it is called a **double negative**. Unfortunately, it is one of the most common errors in English: for example, "I can't hardly wait for summer vacation." There are many negative words including *nothing, not, nearly, never, hardly, neither,* and *no one.*

Practice 7: Adjectives, Adverbs, and Negative Words

Read the following story for content. Then, proofread the text for correct use of **adjectives**, **adverbs**, and **negative words**. When you find an error, neatly strike through the word, and clearly write the correct form above it. **Hint:** There are thirty (30) errors.

Cake Walk

Kelly had waited eager for months before her sixteenth birthday party. Her mother promised to hold a dance party for her at the newer city community center which was only one block from theirs apartment. Kelly's wholest family was going to be there and her tenth grade class. Aunt Marilyn, the more creative person in the large family, worked as the top cake decorator in Olgetree's Grocery, the better shop in the tri-city area. She came over weeks early to ask Kelly what cake she would like for this specialer party.

"I want two cakes," Kelly declared bold. "The firstest one is for all the girls. We want a Black Forest cake. You know the one with, like, red stuff inside and the deliciousest white icing."

"I know which one you mean," her aunt replied, smiling. "Do you know how the Black Forest cake got those name?"

"Uh, no," Kelly answered vague, thinking about the next cake she wanted.

Her aunt went on happy. "Well, it came from Germany which has the deeper and dark forests in all of Europe. The 'red stuff' is really chocolate cake. The most old legends of wood sprites say that woodland spirits brought the cake to a powerful king as a peace offering. The king, however, refused the cake, and the sprites cursed him. They say that there is still magic in the most old recipes of the Black Forest Cake."

Kelly shook her head, saying, "I don't never believe in that kind of stuff, Aunt Marilyn, but that was a great story. Now about the next cake. It will be for all the guys. Make it a Devil's Food cake."

"Girl!" her aunt exclaimed. "Are you trying to make trouble?"

"Just kidding!" Kelly laughed. "I really want the kind of cake that my bestest friend likes a lot. He likes a double-fudge chocolate cake with chocolate chunks and the more bigger the better."

The cakes were baked, and the night of the party arrived with the worstest blizzard that anyone had seen. There was even lightning and thunder with the huge snowfall. In the dance room, however, there was a ton of food, a greater band, and beautiful decorations. The time for cake came, and the lights were turned out.   Kelly stood by Aunt Marilyn who held the cake, and everyone sang. Sudden, there was a tremendous crash of thunder and a blinding flash of light. The vibration was enough to start the cake sliding, with all sixteen candles burning, off the plate. It landed with a mournful squish-upside down. There was the more horriblest silence for three seconds, and then Aunt Marilyn tipped the cake more or less back on the plate, exclaiming, "Whatever you wished for will come true! Kelly, all the candles are out..."

But there was no Kelly. Someone whispered that she must have wished to disappear in the worstest way. Aunt Marilyn thought wild about the curse of the wood sprites. Then, the lights came back on, and Kelly was standing at the threshold with the second cake firm in her hands and a smile on her face. That was brightest than any amount of candles.

"Aunt Marilyn!" Kelly teased. "Remember I have never believed in none of that magic or wishes. I just do what needs doing. And tonight I am going to do my party quick before the lights go out again."

VERBS

A **verb** is a word or group of words which is a part of every complete sentence. A verb can describe action which the subject takes or receives. A verb can also link the subject to another word which describes it. Verbs must agree with the subject in a sentence in number and person, and verbs change tense to indicate the time of action.

Consider how you use verbs in sentences and in essays. Generally speaking, a verb tense should not change within an essay without a good, logical reason, but verbs do shift in number with the subject of the sentence. Think for a moment of how you use verbs, and then complete the following exercise.

Practice 8: Verbs

Read the following passage, first for content. Next, proofread for errors in verb form. Neatly strike through the errors, and clearly write the correct verb above each error. **Hint:** There are sixteen (16) errors in the text.

Big Top Follies

Were you going to the movies soon? There is a great film in town. It's been playing at the Dollar Theater, and I saw it last night. The movie are all about a circus clown and his wild ambitions. The clown goes around trying to win weird bets. For example, he betted the elephant trainer this: he could feed an elephant a wrist watch and then find the watch in the elephants' straw, still working. He lose that bet since the animal steps on the watch before the clown can save it. The clown is tried other schemes: he sang for the flamingos, he swim in the crocodile pool, he left flowers for the bearded lady, and he tried to teach the donkey to bow. These bets do not works out. The poor clown then go to the ring-leader of the circus. The clown asking him to think of a bet that he, the clown, can win. The ringleader cannot help but laugh. He do come up with a bet, though. He dares the clown to run for president. He sound serious, but it's a joke. The clown, however, agrees to it. Would you believed this silliness unless you saw it? The clown actually wins the election by a few votes, and he prevented a hand recount. I won't give the end away, but the movie is fueled by mix-ups and Jim Carrey-type humor. I was laughing about it right now. I thought about seeing it again, but the real election has been coming soon. I can just watch that.

LIE AND LAY / SIT AND SET

There are two sets of commonly confused irregular verbs. First, there is *lie* and *lay*. Lie is defined as "to recline," while lay is defined as "to place something." They are close in meaning, and in the past tense, lie is spelled lay. The other irregular verbs are *sit* and *set*, which have a similar problem: they are very close in meanings and spellings. See how these irregular verbs are used in the following sentences.

Julio <u>sat</u> in the café chair and <u>set</u> his cup on the table.

Marian said, "I am going to <u>lay</u> my book on the bed before I <u>lie</u> down."

In proofreading for errors involving the verbs *lie/lay* and *sit/set*, the first step is to remember that they exist. Also, study the chart below which shows how these verbs are used in different tenses. If you are not clear about the appropriate use of these and other irregular verbs, refer to the companion text, American Book Company's *Basics Made Easy: Grammar and Usage Review* (2001) for lists of these verbs and for practice exercises in using them.

Infinitive	Present Participle	Past	Past Participle
lie (to recline)	(is) lying	lay	(have) lain
lay (to put)	(is) laying	laid	(have) laid
sit (to rest)	(is) sitting	sat	(have) sat
set (to put)	(is) setting	set	(have) set

Practice 9: Lie and Lay / Sit and Set

Read the following historical account, first for content. Then, circle the correct verb form in the parentheses that completes the meaning of the sentence. There are eighteen (18) pairs.

Casualty of War

During World War I, the United States army kept many of its new recruits in training by (sitting / setting) up temporary camps in rural areas. One such area used by troops was the land (lying / laying) near Black Jack Mountain in Marietta, Georgia. Here, in the early 1900s, one could have seen soldiers (sitting / setting) on pine logs in between training sessions. Part of their training sessions involved learning how to fire weapons, including small cannons, which (set / sat) mini-bombs down upon faraway targets off the side of the mountain. These soldiers never guessed that in the future these pieces of ammunition would be found (lying / laying) on the ground, some still undetonated, and all kinds of people would collect them.

One of the more famous instances of this sort, at least in local lore, was that of a small boy whose father (set / sat) him up into a tree. Using a burlap sack, this father was harvesting pecans, which (lay / lie) under trees in the shadow of Black Jack Mountain. The child (sitting / setting) in the tree saw a hand-sized cannon shell which had (lain / laid) in that tree for decades. The child broke off a limb and tried to pry the shell away from the tree. The father heard his small son's voice calling, "Look what I found!" The next sound he heard was an explosion which echoed off the rocks (set / sit) into the side of Black Jack Mountain.

Struggling back to his feet after having been (laid / lain) flat by the shock wave and the shock, the child's father saw pieces of shattered pecan limbs (lying / laying) over blasted clods of red clay. They say that the man first emptied the sack of pecans, placing them back where they had (lain / laid) before he came, and then he gathered up his child, wrapping him in the rough burlap material to carry him home.

The family and the community (laid / lain) the child to rest in a cemetery near Scufflegrit Road, the turn-off to visit Black Jack Mountain. No memorial was (sit / set) near the place where this young war casualty fell; no Teddy bears nor flowers ever marked the spot. The legend lives on, though, (sat / set) forever into the hearts and minds of a generation of Georgians who grew up (setting / sitting) on front porches listening to the call of whippoorwills and to the cautionary tale of the boy who (set / sat) in the wrong tree and reached beyond himself.

SUBJECT-VERB AGREEMENT

Subject-verb agreement means that both the subject and the verb of a sentence or clause must be of the same number and person. For example, a singular subject must be paired with a singular verb, and a noun in the first person must be paired with a verb in the first person. Consider first how you use verbs to agree with subjects, and then complete the following exercise.

Practice 10: Subject-Verb Agreement

Read the following passage, first for content. Then, proofread for subject-verb agreement. If the subject and verb do not agree, neatly strike through the error, and clearly write the correct form above each part. **Hint:** There are fifteen (15) errors to be found.

Bin There?

Have you ever felt that life was stacked against you? Has you sensed that there is a burden present that presses down unrelentingly? I am experiencing that right now. It are a massive, quivering stack, consisting of squished wood fibers in rectangular shapes, menacingly growing before my face.

Yes! The "To-Be-Recyled" paper collect on my desk, daring me to dislodge it with an ill-advised move. It silently dare me to reach for paper clips or a white flag of surrender. I, now, refers to the stack as the "Re-sigh-call" for help-heap. The really bad news are that no one listens to my pathetic wails drifting through the wall of paper. Neither the management nor the office staff comes to my aid at all.

Instead, the people in my office has impeccable timing. They senses just when the stack has eroded to a manageable level. Then, they marches by with all the righteous solemnity and shallow grief of failed game show contestants, piling their orphaned projects and rejected manuscripts onto my convenient desk. There go another group now. As I fix a withering glare upon the back of the offenders (who can't be bothered to take the stuff out to the bin), the slow march continue until fading into a conference room for the finger-pointing postmortem.

After wishing, vainly, that they suffer some sort of disabling paper-cut on those pointing fingers, I calls for pizza. Moments later, I watches, with a smirk that would leave the Grinch green-er with envy, as the previously preoccupied staff scurry about. Working feverishly, they all carts away enough paper, outside to the recycling bin, so to allow pizza boxes to be centrally deposited. After the meal, who will recycle the boxes?

Yeah, I've "bin" there—head-first in the recycling bin...

SUBJECT-VERB AGREEMENT WITH COLLECTIVE NOUNS

Collective nouns name single units made up of multiple members. Collective nouns have special rules regarding agreement with verbs. If the unit is truly acting as one as in "A swarm of bees *lives* here," then the verb reflects the singular subject. However, if the unit's members act individually as in "A swarm of bees *perform* their various jobs," then the verb reflects the plural nature of the subject.

Proofreading for collective noun errors concerns the verb form used with them. Think about the logic of using the singular and plural form with the action that is occurring: is it a group or individual action? Then, complete the following exercise.

Practice 11: Subject-Verb Agreement with Collective Nouns

Read the passage that follows, noting the use of different collective nouns. Then go back, and decide if each collective noun is acting as a group or as individuals. Circle one verb in each pair to agree with the subject.

In Pursuit of Trivia

My senior class (know / knows) one thing for sure: we all love trivia. We are putting on plays showcasing our knowledge of it as well as the talents of other students.

The audience (clap / claps) when we act out animal behaviors using obscure collective nouns for groups of animals. For example, when in danger, a knot of toads (leap / leaps) into mud together; when there is a regrettable road kill incident, a murder of crows (take / takes) their favorite positions in the pecking order; and lastly, in a jungle river scene, a crash of rhinos (attack / attacks) a fishing canoe.

It is after this that the other student groups take their turns. First, the band (begin / begins) to play a thunderous medley of hits. Then, the skate club (demonstrate / demonstrates) their different special techniques, with trivial variations in moves. That is a very popular part of the show. Next, the debate team (argue / argues) about the relevancy of trivia. Lastly, the school choir (sing / sings) their favorite, though unheard of, show tunes.

I believe all this trivia mania began when the student body (was / were) challenged to discover the origin of the school's name: Eagle Lake-Eight High School. Well, it was difficult, but our class found the secret. Apparently, the school board (has / have) some members who are avid fans of Andy Griffith: the Mayberry sheriff, you know. So they chose the name to honor him; in the '70s, he starred in a television show, "Adams of Eagle Lake." It ran for only eight days before being canceled. Now that's trivia!

SPELLING

Spelling is the process of arranging letters to form words. This may seem simple, but spelling English words can be difficult. The English language has a history of taking words from other languages and trying to make the spelling of them fit into the rules of Standard American English. These rules are rather inconsistent in the first place, so it makes spelling twice as difficult. This chapter will provide you with hints and practice in finding **homonyms** and **incorrect spellings** while you proofread.

HOMONYMS

Homonyms are words that sound the same, even though they have different spellings and meanings. The best way to proofread for errors in the use of homonyms is to recognize the homonyms that you tend to misuse and look for those first. You may also want to find a list of the most commonly misused homonyms. Study the list so you can recognize common errors.

ant   **aunt**

Practice 12: Homonyms

Read the following passage for content and word meaning. Then, circle which homonym in each pair is correct for the meaning of the sentence.

Hurdles

Having a birthday can be just (plane / plain) dangerous. You don't believe me? Well, then I'd like to (advise / advice) you with a story about my recent birthday. My friends and I were hyped up for (too / two) weeks while planning my party at an extreme bike course. We could hardly (bear / bare) the wait. My parents called the course to check out (it's / its) rules and party arrangements. Finally, the day came, and my dad took us to (were / where) the course was located. (Writing / Righting) the check was the first hurdle that slowed us down, but Dad cleared that (won / one) just fine, filling in the dollars and (sense / cents) in the right places. He signed the release papers with his eyes shut. What a kidder! After all (hour / our) waiting, you can imagine we wanted to start. This was taking (two / too) long. We finally took off for the course, looking cool in our backwards caps, bike shorts, and shirts with the arms cut out so we could show off our (bare / bear) biceps. As the four of us mounted our bikes, we saw girls in the stands watching for guys; they were trying to act smooth, but we could tell we were having an (affect / effect) on them, and they were interested. In fact, they told us later at the hospital, (were / where) they had followed us, that they had never seen the human body contorted in quite those positions while hurtling through the air like (plains / planes). I won't detail every crash, but Renaldo ripped his racing shirt and his wrist, Tito twisted and tore all the tendons in his knees, Cal careened into a corner and was concussed, and I got injured just where I deserved it, (write / right) in the mouth. I needed stitches inside my cheeks and in my gums. That night, using a straw, I celebrated with mashed-up birthday cake. If I make it to my next birthday, he suggested that we rent an Extreme sports video. I was deeply (affected / effected) by his concern, but because of my swollen mouth I could not speak. So, I had to (right / write) my answer: "Yeah, I'm on that."

INCORRECT SPELLINGS

Incorrect spellings of words can make your writing sloppy, confusing, or even incomprehensible. Proper spelling is an essential part of effective writing. Because so many words in English have irregular spellings, it is important to memorize commonly misspelled words. It is also helpful to follow a plan when proofreading for spelling errors.

First, consider the spelling errors that are typical for you, and look for those types of errors. **Second**, think about the basic structure of forming words and correct any words that do not follow the structure. **Last**, use your sight memory—the memory which tells you when something just does not look right—and correct the word so it looks right. Using this plan, your proofreading for spelling should be successful.

Before you begin the practice on the following page, think about your own spelling patterns, and think about the rules for spelling that you know. In a notebook, make a list of words that you frequently misspell. Write them ten times each for practice. Be ready to use the proofreading plan (in the second paragraph above) for your spelling errors.

Practice 13:   Spelling

Read the following short extended response carefully for meaning first. Then, proofread it for spelling errors. When you find a misspelled word, strike through it neatly, and then above the word, write the correct spelling clearly. **Hint:** There are 42 spelling errors in the essay.

NPR Today

Are you tring to find an intelligent, meaningful communications source? The easyest way to find what you are seaking is to swicth your radio dial to an NPR station. The National Public Radio station is a frist class educational resource, hepling schools in your city. The public radio stations rely on listeners, ordinery peple, for funding their bugdets. Becuase of that, Thy can refuse to run commercials or to counsider big buisness interests befor their audiances' interests.

In this way, public stations can offer viry differant types of programming and can schedule the programming to meet their listeners' needs. Adults and children can unnite to support this resourse. There are shows which they can enjoiy together or individualy. The public stations, you may kow them as NPR stations, broadcast an interesting vareity of shows about sience, history, cultural movements (includeing sports results), business trends, and film. This is just a bare sampeling of the varied  broadcasts ofered to the public by the public (radio). The many station managers and jornalists, your freinds in radio, also foremat their news programs to reelly explain issues and to take time over importent events, instead of feeding their listeners sound bites from sleesy politicions' speaches.

Have you found a radio station that could offer all of this? ETV Radio, the public station in Columbea, for example, is one of the best. In Febuarary, this station will be having a fund drive for new fans to jion public radio memebership, allowing them to take control of their destinys. Tune your radio in tommorow to your local public radio station and dicsover, all over again, how good radio can be.

SENTENCE FORMATION

Sentence formation is a key writing element. To demonstrate skill in this area, you must **use end punctuation appropriately**, **correct any sentence fragments or run-ons**, **correctly identify and punctuate phrases and clauses**, and **avoid misplaced and dangling modifiers**.

END PUNCTUATION

End punctuation is one constant in the English language. There are three ways to end a complete sentence.

A **period** ends a complete statement.

    A **question mark** ends any question.

        An **exclamation point** ends a forceful or emotional statement.

These marks signal a definite end to one sentence and the beginning of the next sentence. End punctuation adds to the organization, variety, and tone of your writing.

Practice 14: End Punctuation

Read the following story carefully, and then add end punctuation as needed. Circle each added punctuation. **Hint:** There are twenty-six (26) end punctuation marks to add.

GREEN!

Has anyone out there noticed a government plot being carried out in dim grocery store aisles Yes, it's a top secret federal government plot that only certain foreign governments have paid to learn How do I know I read Stephen King novels, don't I But you, you need to look around you Look for GREEN; it's leaping out, screaming, grabbing at you everywhere you go

At one time, in years past, parents urged their children to eat green vegetables We are talking about naturally green things And just as naturally, the children turned away loudly exclaiming, "Yuck " These children are now the grown-ups driving SUVs Further study reveals an even deeper shame; these are the people who are voluntarily drinking - hold on - be prepared to be sickened They are drinking GREEN TEA Not only is this tea green, but it is flavored with other healthy things: peach, kumquat, lemon, and ginseng What's next, spinach-flavored green tea

Just to make sure that today's kids, those vital elements of target audiences, are not left out, the food industry has now funded research producing a truly grotesque, unnatural form of vegetable-GREEN KETCHUP The marketers using this research are based in Roswell, New Mexico They claim that kid experts chose this color over blue, yellow, and rainbow

But why toy with the artificially-enhanced natural red dye color at all Because as I said before, it is a government plot They are breaking down taboos-the natural order of the universe It is a law of nature, which Mrs. Einstein recorded: kids hate green food But if the government can break this taboo, breaching the limits of food color, think of all the other ways "Big Brother" can mold us Just watch for the acceptance of green eggs and ham Oh, no What am I saying It's too late

SENTENCE FRAGMENTS AND RUN-ONS

End punctuation errors may result in **sentence fragments** or **run-ons**. A **sentence fragment** is a phrase that is punctuated like a sentence, but it lacks a subject or a verb. To correct these, simply add the missing element. A **run-on** occurs when two independent clauses are joined with no punctuation or connecting word between them. The combining of independent clauses requires either end punctuation, a semi-colon, or a comma (internal punctuation) with a coordinating conjunction.

You have practiced using internal and end punctuation. Now, you can use commas with the following coordinating conjunctions to correct sentence fragments or run-ons: **f**or, **a**nd, **n**or, **b**ut, **o**r, **y**et, **s**o. Remember these words by taking the first letter of each, spelling "**fanboys**."

When writing for a test, you may stop a sentence too soon, or make one sentence blend into the next. As you proofread, make sure each sentence is complete and correctly punctuated.

Practice 15:   Sentence Fragments and Run-Ons

Read the passage below. There are both run-ons and fragments in the story. Decide how to best correct each sentence error. On your own paper, number lines 1 through 10, and write down the corrected sentence. If there is no error, write the word "correct" on the line. Answers may vary.

1. Betsy was not the most graceful or athletic person in our class.

2. Seemed a little klutzy and a natural-born bookworm.

3. In our 7th grade year, however, a vast change.

4. Before, the basketball coach let everyone play he decided to hold team tryouts this year.

5. Appeared to be a challenge to Betsy.

6. She had never been interested in sports now Betsy stayed in the gym after school for weeks before the tryout.

7. Practiced dribbling, passing, and shooting the ball.

8. In classes, bringing books on basketball strategy.

9. Her hard work and single-mindedness got Betsy on the first-string as a guard.

10. We elected Betsy to be the captain of the team she inspired us, on the court and off, in all our years in school.

PHRASES AND CLAUSES

Phrases and **clauses** are two groups of words that help form the structure of sentences. A **phrase** is a group of words that acts as a single unit in a sentence, but it lacks either a subject or a predicate or both. Phrases can function as nouns, verbs, adjectives, or adverbs. A **clause** is a group of words which includes a subject and predicate. There are two kinds of clauses: dependent and independent.

An **independent clause** can stand alone as a sentence. If another independent clause is linked to it, the two clauses must be joined by a comma and a coordinating conjunction (FANBOYS). FANBOYS is an easy way to remember the common coordinating conjunctions: for, and, nor, but, or, yet, so. A **dependent clause** relies on the controlling independent clause in a sentence. The independent clause and the dependent clause are linked together by a relative pronoun such as *which*, *that*, *whose*, or *those*, or by a subordinating conjunction like *while*, *because*, *since*, or *after*.

Being able to recognize these different sentence elements is the first step in learning how to use them in your writing. You may want to review phrases and clauses in American Book Company's *Basics Made Easy: Grammar and Usage Review* (2001) before starting this practice.

Practice 16:   Phrases and Clauses

Read the following passage. On your own paper, write whether the <u>underlined group of words</u> is a **dependent clause**, an **independent clause**, or a **phrase**. (For extra credit, identify the type of phrase: prepositional, appositive, or participial.)

Team Spirit

All sports teams have similar ways <u>of celebrating exciting victories</u>[1]. Even swim teams have big celebrations <u>after they swim for six hours or longer in meets</u>[2]. Popular expressions of group joy, <u>such as head butting and team "dances</u>[3]," however, are not seen beside the pool. Instead, <u>there is cheering, eating, dunking, and body art</u>[4] on display.

<u>The display of body art is actually created</u>[5] with permanent markers. Coaches write a swimmer's schedule of events on the swimmer's wrist <u>with the markers</u>[6]. During the closing two hours of the meet, <u>the swimmers make their own statements</u>[7] on their bare skin, usually their arms, and then their legs, and then their backs. (They need help with that part.) The body art at the beginning of a meet is kept to a minimum <u>because it shows the swimmer's race list and a "Go team."</u>[8] But when a team begins to win, the body art becomes more rowdy and silly. The teams try to outdo each other by inventing funny sayings <u>that won't get them thrown out of the pool area by the coaches</u>[9].

<u>Although the coaches stay busy watching for any problems</u>[10], they manage to lead the cheering and celebrating. Parents, grandparents, and other team members cheer especially loudly <u>when their loved ones are in the water</u>[11]. Coaches often order fresh pizza to celebrate <u>before the last race has been swum</u>[12].

They do this <u>when their teams are winning by a gazzilion points</u>[13]. There is one other big difference between swim teams and other types of sports teams <u>which involves the</u>

party aspect of the sport[14]. While other teams throw water on their coaches after a big win, swimmers throw their coaches into water.

MISPLACED AND DANGLING MODIFIERS

A **modifier** is a word, phrase or clause that helps clarify the meaning of another word by describing it in more detail. However, if a modifier is positioned incorrectly in a sentence, it can confuse and frustrate the reader.

A **misplaced modifier** is positioned in the sentence too far from what it is modifying. This confuses the meaning, as in the following example.

> **Example 1:** The painting had visible brush strokes that I was selling.

In Example 1, it is unclear whether the dependent clause, "that I was selling," describes the painting or the brush strokes. The clause "that I was selling" is a misplaced modifier. To correct this problem, place the modifying clause closer to the word that it describes, as in Example 2.

> **Example 2:** The painting that I was selling had visible brush strokes.

Dangling modifiers are words that modify nothing in particular in the rest of the sentence. They often seem to modify something that is suggested or implied but not actually present in the sentence. They dangle or hang loosely from the rest of the sentence. They frequently appear at the beginnings or ends of sentences. See Example 3.

> **Example 3:** Dangling from a hook, our bird dove for the worm.

Does this sentence make sense to you? What is dangling: is it the bird or the worm? Obviously, the worm would be dangling from the hook, not the bird.

"Dangling from a hook" is a dangling modifier because its position in the sentence makes it look like it is describing the subject, "our bird." However, it should be describing "the worm."

Correctly wording this sentence would mean changing the position of the modifier, so it is closer to the object it is describing, the worm. Notice this correction in Example 4.

> **Example 4:** Our bird dove for the worm dangling from a hook.

Remember, your goal when you are writing is to be clear and logical. Using modifiers incorrectly will confuse your readers. Consider how to make your writing easily understood while using modifiers that add detail and color to your writing. Be aware of the position of modifiers when proofreading.

Practice 17: Misplaced and Dangling Modifiers

Read the following sets of sentences carefully. Then, choose the sentence that is written with correct sentence formation and has no misplaced or dangling modifiers in it.

1. A. We often lose track of each other, being such a large family on trips.

   B. Being such a large family, on trips we often lose track of each other.

   C. Being such a large family, we often lose track of each other on trips.

2. A. They tried their best somewhere near the house to find the hidden treasure.

   B. Hidden somewhere near the house, they tried their best to find the treasure.

   C. They tried their best to find the treasure hidden somewhere near the house.

3. A. Hurrying to make the movie on time, they stopped only long enough to get some popcorn.

   B. They stopped only long enough to get some popcorn hurrying to make the movie on time.

   C. Hurrying they stopped only long enough to get some popcorn to make the movie on time.

4. A. Sitting together on the fountain, we found them feeding some ducks.

   B. We found them feeding some ducks, sitting together on the fountain.

   C. We found them sitting together on the fountain, feeding some ducks.

5. A. Shouting loudly, her face got red and her fists clenched at her sides.

   B. Her face got red and her fists clenched at her sides as she shouted loudly.

   C. Her fists clenched at her sides and shouting loudly, her face got red.

6. A. They listened to all the songs they liked so much on the old turntable swaying with the beat.

   B. Swaying with the beat, they listened to all the songs they liked so much on the old turntable.

   C. Swaying with the beat, they listened to all the songs on the old turntable they liked so much.

CHAPTER 11 REVIEW

A. This exercise will help you with the proofreading plan that you have learned and practiced in the chapter. Read the essay first for content. Then read with an eye for internal punctuation, correct grammar usage, spelling, and sentence formation.

When you find an error, use the proofreading marks which you have seen in the chapter. You may refer to the chart on Page 184 if you wish. Neatly strike through the error, and clearly write the correct form above the error. If there are any problems with the content, note that separately at the end of the extended response.

A local bridal and tuxedo shop is offering a lifetime coupon for a free wedding to the winner of their latest contest. The participants in the contest must write extended responses describing odd places to get married. People used to get married only in religious buildings or court houses; but today, people get married in places such as on an airplane, on the beach, or even under the water. What are odd places to get married?

Odd Places To Get Married

Traditionaly churchs and chapels were the main places for young couples to get wed. In the past twenty years or so people have gone away from the traditional wedding's. To be married where you have meet is not that unusual or bizarre. Many couples have been getting more adventureous in their wedding locations; couples marry where they are happiest too. All of these choices are just that: choices. Weddings need to be meaningfull to the people involved. Four odd places where they get married are underwater, on the beach, on a airplane, and sometimes in their schools.

Getting married underwater involves many factors and variables. First, a scuba-diver lisence needs to be obtained for the bride and groom. So the new couple will need a blood test, and also a swimming test. Second, a good scuba-diving location needs to be found; for example, Key West and the red sea and the Barrier reef is considered the best diving in the world. Third, a pastor or priest with scuba-diving experience need to be found. Those could be a difficult search. Underwater weddings cost the mostest money because of the extra variables. But if that kind of wedding is meaningful to the new couple, I'd say that they should go for it.

Getting married on the beach is a odd, but romantic place to take wedding vows Standing in the sand with the waves roaring, and the sun setting can be romantic. Except for the danger of a jellyfish or stingray alert. Starting the honeymoon after a sting from one of those sea cretures could be unpleasant even with a romantic full moon and thesmell of suntan oil. One advantage of beach weddings is that the wedding and honeymoon can be in the same city. Virgin Islands, Cayman Islands and Jamaica are good examples of places people pick for their meaningful, for them beach weddings.

Airplane weddings have become a odd place for people too get married. Airplane weddings are small due to space. Some people like to parachute out of the plane after taking their wedding vows. Airplane weddings can be very expensive and difficult to plan. Because of having to rent a plane and the skydiving equipment and having to have good whether. There would also need to be a separate place for the the reception or party afterwards. The things that must be considered are: food (airplane food?), flowers (thrown to the winds?), and which hospital is closest (in case the wedding is no longer the main event 'cus of injury). But flying free while being married can be very meaningfull to some couples.

This last example of an odd wedding makes a school wedding seem very respectable. To be married where you have met is very romantic and sweet. If two people can learn to love each other they also need to learn how to live together as a married couple what better place symbolizes that intention than a school. Even if space may be cramped in the hallway, there is always a gym or cafeteria for lying out food and presents. Also most of the guests would be old friends and very familiar with the location; so no maps needed to be printed. All these people could help decorate with posters and streamers, and help mix the party punch. This is a win-win situation. The school is appreciated for it's community service, the new couple has a cheap but happy memory.

Getting married should be fun and a unforgettable memory. Underwater weddings and airplane weddings are more costly than beach and school weddings. People for some time have been looking for odd; yet meaningfull places to get married. The most popular odd places to take wedding vows have been underwater on the beach on airplanes, and in a place of youth, memory and magic; the old school house. Support the two people who want to get married at our school. The media attention will benefit the school and our place in the community. So write letters and call talk shows for the sake of true love and for fame.

B. In Chapter 10, you revised the drafts you wrote for two topics you chose in earlier chapters. Return to those extended responses now. Proofread them based on the skills that you have practiced in this chapter. Use the checklist below to help you. When you are finished, share your work with your teacher.

____ I made my corrections neatly and clearly.

____ I checked for errors in capitalization.

____ I corrected errors in internal punctuation including, commas, colons, semi-colons, apostrophes, and quotation marks.

____ I corrected any errors in grammar and usage, including nouns, pronouns, adjectives, adverbs, negative words, verbs, and subject-verb agreement.

____ I made sure all words are spelled correctly.

____ I looked for errors in sentence formation, including end punctuation, fragments, run-ons, and misplaced modifiers. Share your work with your teacher.

SC EOC English/Language Arts
Practice Test 1

Sunken Treasures

One of the least known facts about Texas history is that a good deal of it lies just beyond the coast. Texas coastlines are dotted with offshore shipwrecks. Historical records indicate many wrecks of ships that came from England, Spain, and France. In most cases however, their exact locations are yet to be discovered. The Texas Historical Commission has identified over 2,000 historically significant shipwrecks in Texas waters. Three of the most important wrecks are the *Belle*, the *Invincible*, and the *Hatteras*.

In 1995, the *Belle* was located in Matagorda Bay. It is one of the most significant underwater finds in North America because the *Belle* is the oldest French colonial shipwreck found in the New World. The wreck was identified as the *Belle* by a bronze cannon on board with the crest of Louis XIV on it. The *Belle* was one of four ships sailed in 1684 by French explorer La Salle to search for the mouth of the Mississippi River. His mission included establishment of a colony at the mouth of the river and trade with the Indians.

In the 1830s, Texas was a separate republic. During that time, hostilities broke out between Texas and Mexico. The government of Texas realized the need for a navy to protect lines of supply from New Orleans to Texas. A bill was passed to purchase four schooners. In January 1836, the Texas Navy was formed. The 125-ton *Invincible* was among the ships purchased.

The *Invincible* proved to be a good ship and helped protect the coast. On August 26, 1837, the *Invincible* escorted another Texas vessel and the Mexican ship they had captured into Galveston harbor. The next day, the *Invincible* was attacked by two Mexican cruisers that pursued the Texas vessels. The *Invincible* attempted to flee after a prolonged battle. Unfortunately, it ran aground and sank. A marine archeology team thought it had found the wreck in 1995. Others disputed the discovery. But historians agree that the ship is still out there, waiting to be discovered.

As the Civil War heated up, one Northern strategy was to blockade Southern ports. By doing this, they could stop supply ships coming through. Several important Civil War shipwrecks have been found in Texas waters. Only one United States warship was sunk at sea in the Gulf. The USS *Hatteras* was purchased by the US Navy in 1861 and converted into a gun boat. After distinguished service in the South Atlantic Blockading Squadron, the vessel was transferred to the Gulf. Early in 1863, the *Hatteras* joined the squadron trying to retake the key port of Galveston.

On January 11, 1863, the *Hatteras* sighted sails on the horizon and chased a ship for four hours, farther and farther from the fleet. At dusk, the Confederate ship *Alabama* finally identified itself and attacked, puncturing the hull of the *Hatteras*. The *Hatteras* surrendered as she sank rapidly. The wreck, discovered in the 1970s about 20 miles off the coast of Galveston, is an integral part of the Civil War story. The fact that its remains are virtually intact makes it an important underwater site.

The shipwrecks off the Texas coast are an important part of history of the state and the country. Most of the discovered shipwrecks in the Gulf of Mexico come from the last few hundred years, but ships have sailed these waters since the 16th century. There are many underwater treasures remaining under the surface to be found.

1. Where would this article most likely be published?   Rd 1.5

    A. in a newspaper
    B. in a magazine for young people who are interested in ships
    C. in a manual for the U.S. Navy
    D. in a book encouraging people to research the locations of famous shipwrecks

2. Which technique does the author use to communicate the information on shipwrecks?   Rd 2.2
    A. interviews with experts   C. quotations from experts
    B. questions and answers   D. statements supported by facts

3. What type of source is the passage?   Rs 2.1

    A. a secondary source because the author did not directly experience any of the events
    B. a secondary source because the author interviewed witnesses of the events
    C. a primary source because the passage is based on eyewitness accounts
    D. a primary source because the author survived a shipwreck

4. Which of the following words is closest in meaning to the word "hostilities" as it is used in the passage?   Rd 3.2
    A. hard feelings   B. fights   C. competitions   D. treatises

5. Which of the following is an inference that can be made based on the passage?   Rd 1.8
    A. No more ships will sink off the Texas coastline.
    B. The Texas Historical Commission will continue to research shipwrecks off the Texas coastline.
    C. The Texas Navy is not responsible for any of the shipwrecks that took place off the coastline.
    D. The number of shipwrecks that take place off the Texas coastline will drastically increase over the next few years.

6. Which of the following best explains the author's credibility?   Rs 2.2
    A. The author is very credible, providing well-researched facts about shipwrecks off the Texas coastline.
    B. The author is not credible, providing hearsay about shipwrecks off the Texas coastline.
    C. The author is somewhat credible; only the information provided by the Texas Historical Commission is valuable.
    D. The author is very credible, providing facts about the history of Texas.

Dietary Supplements: Beyond the Label

Advertisements for dietary supplements bombard consumers when they turn on the television, open a magazine, or surf the Web. Daily vitamin and mineral supplements are products usually taken by mouth. They contain "dietary ingredients" intended to supplement the diet. Dietary supplements may contain, among other things, vitamins, minerals, herbs, and botanicals. There are many other supplements which claim to increase energy, improve athletic performance, and aid in weight loss. How truthful are these claims, and how safe are these products?

Many dietary supplements seem to improve health and well-being. However, some dietary supplements have been shown to cause harm and contribute to death. Others have been shown to be ineffective. Supplements do not have to be approved by the Food and Drug Administration (FDA) before being sold. But the FDA may ban dietary supplements after they have been sold and have been proven harmful. For example, supplements containing ephedra, a substance claimed to promote weight loss, were banned in February 2004. Research showed that ephedra's use was linked to serious health outcomes such as heart attack and stroke.

How can consumers protect themselves against misleading information about such supplements? By thinking critically about the information, asking questions, and performing research, one can evaluate the information and make smart decisions. Some key questions to ask include:

- Is the claim too good to be true? Beware of overly emphatic language.
- Who is making this claim? What is their goal? Are they trying to sell the product?
- What is the source of the information? Does it come from scientific experts?

Perform research. Obtain information from non-biased sources. When in doubt, ask a doctor or other healthcare provider.

7. Which of the following best explains the author's bias?   Rd 1.4
   A. The author is unbiased, objectively describing various dietary supplements.
   B. The author is biased against the use of dietary supplements, believing they should never be used.
   C. The author shows some bias in favor of dietary supplements, explaining their benefits.
   D. The author shows some bias against dietary supplements, warning consumers to be cautious of them.

8. Which of the following is closest in meaning to the word "bombard" as it is used in the passage?
   A. hound   Rd 3.2
   B. stab
   C. elude
   D. blow up

9. Which of the following is a valid inference that can be made based on the passage?   Rd 1.8
   A. The author may have had a bad experience with dietary supplements.
   B. The author works for a company that manufactures dietary supplements.
   C. The author does not believe a doctor should recommend dietary supplements.
   D. The author believes dietary supplements are a great way to gain energy.

10. Which of the following best explains the author's tone?   Rd 2.2
   A. sarcastic   B. cautious   C. sympathetic   D. humorous

From "The Fortune Teller"

by Melville Davisson Post (short story)

Sir Henry Marquis continued to read; he made no comment; his voice clear and even.

It was a big sunny room. The long windows looked out on a formal garden, great beech trees and the bow of the river. Within it was a sort of library. There were bookcases built into the wall, to the height of a man's head, and at intervals between them, rising from the floor to the cornice of the shelves, were rows of mahogany drawers with glass knobs. There was also a flat writing table.

It was the room of a traveler, a man of letters, a dreamer. On the table were an inkpot of carved jade, a paperknife of ivory with gold butterflies set in; three bronze storks, with their backs together, held an exquisite Japanese crystal.

The room was in disorder — the drawers pulled out and the contents ransacked.

My father stood leaning against the casement of the window, looking out. The lawyer, Mr. Lewis, sat in a chair beside the table, his eyes on the violated room.

"Pendleton," he said, "I don't like this English man Gosford."

The words seemed to arouse my father out of the depths of some reflection, and he turned to the lawyer, Mr. Lewis.

"Gosford!" he echoed.

"He is behind this business, Pendleton," the lawyer, Mr. Lewis, went on. "Mark my word! He comes here when Marshall is dying; he forces his way to the man's bed; he puts the servants out; he locks the door. Now, what business had this Englishman with Marshall on his deathbed? What business of a secrecy so close that Marshall's son is barred out by a locked door?"

He paused and twisted the seal ring on his finger.

"When you and I came to visit the sick man, Gosford was always here, as though he kept a watch upon us, and when we left, he went always to this room to write his letters, as he said.

"And more than this, Pendleton; Marshall is hardly in his grave before Gosford writes me to inquire by what legal process the dead man's papers may be examined for a will. And it is Gosford who sends a [servant] riding, as if the devil were on the crupper, to summon me in the name of the Commonwealth of Virginia, — to appear and examine into the circumstances of this burglary.

"I mistrust the man. He used to hang about Marshall in his life, upon some enterprise of secrecy; and now he takes possession and leadership in his affairs, and sets the man's son aside. In what right, Pendleton, does this adventurous Englishman feel himself secure?"

My father did not reply to Lewis's discourse.

11. In the following sentence, which replacement word would give the most appropriate connotation to the word "business"?   Rd 3.4

"He is behind this business, Pendleton," the lawyer, Mr. Lewis, went on.

    A.   idea   B.   meeting   C.   crime   D.   deal

12. Which type of figurative language does the following sentence represent?   Rd 2.2

On the table were an inkpot of carved jade, a paperknife of ivory with gold butterflies set in; three bronze storks, with their backs together, held an exquisite Japanese crystal.

    A.   imagery   B.   euphemism   C.   analogy   D.   metaphor

13. Which of the following is closest in meaning to the word "great" as it is used in the passage?

    A.   old   B.   large   C.   mossy   D.   gnarled   Rd 3.2

14. Which of the following best describes the tone of Mr. Lewis in the passage?   Rd 2.2

    A.   apprehensive   B.   ecstatic   C.   confident   D.   nervous

15. Which of the following dictionary entries correctly defines the word "discourse" as it is used in the pasage?   Rd 3.3

    A.   verbal expression in writing.

    B.   verbal exchange; conversation.

    C.   a formal discussion of a subject, either written or spoken.

    D.   the process or power of reasoning.

From *The Phantom of the Opera* by Gaston Leroux

Chap. 1 "Is it the Ghost?"

And they all began to talk together. The ghost had appeared to them in the shape of a gentleman in dress-clothes, who had suddenly stood before them in the passage, without their knowing where he came from. He seemed to have come straight through the wall.

"Pooh!" said one of them, who had more or less kept her head. "You see the ghost everywhere!"

And it was true. For several months, there had been nothing discussed at the Opera but this ghost in dress-clothes who stalked about the building, from top to bottom, like a shadow, who spoke to nobody, to whom nobody dared speak and who vanished as soon as he was seen, no one knowing how or where. As became a real ghost, he made no noise in walking. People began by laughing and making fun of this specter dressed like a man of fashion or an undertaker; but the ghost legend soon swelled to enormous proportions among the corps de ballet. All the girls pretended to have met this supernatural being more or less often. And those who laughed the loudest were not the most at ease. When he did not show himself, he betrayed his presence or his passing by accident, comic or serious, for which the general superstition held him responsible. Had any one met with a fall, or suffered a practical joke at the hands of one of the other girls, or lost a powder puff, it was at once the fault of the ghost, of the Opera ghost.

After all, who had seen him? You meet so many men in dress-clothes at the Opera who are not ghosts. But this dress-suit had a peculiarity of its own. It covered a skeleton. At least, so the ballet-girls said. And, of course, it had a death's head.

Was all this serious? The truth is that the idea of the skeleton came from the description of the ghost given by Joseph Buquet, the chief scene-shifter, who had really seen the ghost. He had run up against the ghost on the little staircase, by the footlights, which leads to "the cellars." He had seen him for a second—for the ghost had fled—-and to any one who cared to listen to him he said:

"He is extraordinarily thin and his dress-coat hangs on a skeleton frame. His eyes are so deep that you can hardly see the fixed pupils. You just see two big black holes, as in a dead man's skull. His skin, which is stretched across his bones like a drumhead, is not white, but a nasty yellow. His nose is so little worth talking about that you can't see it side-face; and *the absence* of that nose is a horrible thing *to look at*. All the hair he has is three or four long dark locks on his forehead and behind his ears."

This chief scene-shifter was a serious, sober, steady man, very slow at imagining things. His words were received with interest and amazement; and soon there were other people to say that they too had met a man in dress-clothes with a death's head on his shoulders. Sensible men who had wind of the story began by saying that Joseph Buquet had been the victim of a joke played by one of his assistants. And then, one after the other, there came a series of incidents so curious and so inexplicable that the very shrewdest people began to feel uneasy.

16. Which statement best describes a connection or relationship between the excerpt from "The Fortune Teller" and the excerpt from *The Phantom of the Opera*? Rd 1.2
    A. Both selections are narrated by the witness of a ghost.
    B. Both selections describe an elusive troublemaker.
    C. Both selections focus on a character's death.
    D. Both selections concern a failed business deal.

17. Which word best describes Gosford in the excerpt from "The Fortune Teller" and the ghost in the excerpt from *The Phantom of the Opera*? Rd 1.2
    A. mysterious   B. angry   C. bereaved   D. shy

18. How are the excerpt from "The Fortune Teller" and the excerpt from *The Phantom of the Opera* similar in style?   Rd 2.4

    A.   Both contain overly simple sentence structure.

    B.   Neither contains formal language.

    C.   Both contain dialogue.

    D.   Neither contains complex sentence structure.

19. Which statement(s) best compares the time frames of both selections?   Rd 2.6

    A.   Both describe events that took place over the course of several months.

    B.   Both describe events as they are taking place.

    C.   "The Fortune Teller" describes events as they are taking place. *The Phantom of the Opera* describes events that took place over the course of several months.

    D.   "The Fortune Teller" describes events that took place over the course of several months. *The Phantom of the Opera* describes events as they are taking place.

20. Which of the following best describes the tone of Joseph Buquet as he describes the ghost in *The Phantom of the Opera*?   Rd 2.2

    A.   forgetful   B.   joking   C.   sly   D.   fearful

21. Which of the following conclusions can be made about the opera house after reading the excerpt from *The Phantom of the Opera*?   Rd 1.8

    A.   It is definitely haunted.

    B.   Something strange is occurring there.

    C.   The dancers are playing practical jokes.

    D.   A skeleton is hidden there.

22. Which of the following is true about the two selections' genres?   Rd 2.6

    A.   Both are dramas.

    B.   One is written in prose, the other in poetry.

    C.   Both are novels.

    D.   One is a novel; one is a short story.

23. Which of the following dictionary definitions best describes the word "shrewdest" as it is used in the excerpt from *The Phantom of the Opera*?   Rd 3.3

    A.   Characterized by keen awareness, sharp intelligence, and often a sense of the practical.

    B.   Disposed to artful and cunning practices; tricky.

    C.   Sharp; penetrating: *a shrewd wind.*

    D.   Clever; resourceful.

24. Which of the following is an inference that can be made about the excerpt from *The Phantom of the Opera*?   Rd 1.8

    A.   There will be more and more ghost sightings.

    B.   The ghost will never be seen again.

    C.   The ghost will continue to be seen, but only by the female dancers.

    D.   Some of the dancers will disappear.

"When We Two Parted" by Lord George Gordon Byron

When we two parted
In silence and tears,
Half broken-hearted,
To sever for years,

Pale grew thy cheek and cold,
Colder thy kiss;
Truly that hour foretold
Sorrow to this.

The dew of the morning
Sank chill on my brow -
It felt like the warning
Of what I feel now.
Thy vows are all broken,
And light is thy fame:
I hear thy name spoken,
And share in its shame.

They name thee before me,
A knell to mine ear;
A shudder comes o'er me -
Why wert thou so dear?
They know not I knew thee,
Who knew thee too well: -
Long, long shall I rue thee
Too deeply to tell.

In secret we met -
In silence I grieve
That thy heart could forget,
Thy spirit deceive.
If I should meet thee
After long years,
How should I greet thee? -
With silence and tears.

25. Which of the following best explains the purpose of the poem?   Rd 1.5

    A.   The author is encouraging his true love to come back to him.

    B.   The author is describing the loss of a secret love.

    C.   The author is analyzing why his love decided to leave him.

    D.   The author is praising his secret love.

26. In the poem, foretold is to predicted as doubted is to   Rd 3.4
   A. pretended   B. accepted   C. swallowed   D. distrusted

27. Which of the following best explains the narrator's internal conflict in the poem?   Rd 2.8
   A. He is in love with someone but doesn't know how to make his feelings known.
   B. He feels torn between his true love and his career.
   C. He has lost someone he loves but can't tell anyone.
   D. He has to choose between two people who love him.

28. Which of the following is closest in meaning to the word "rue" as it is used in the poem?   Rd 3.2
   A. celebrate   B. mourn   C. gloat   D. pity

29. Which of the following is an example of figurative language used in the poem?   Rd 2.2
   A. allusion   B. rhyme   C. analogy   D. hyperbole

Speech by Wendell Wilkie

In the following speech, former U.S. presidential candidate Wendell Wilkie eulogizes a city and a people destroyed by Nazi tyranny, at Stern Park Gardens, IL, July 12, 1942.

[Wilkie is telling the story of the town of Lidice, Czechoslovakia, where the entire village was destroyed by the Nazis as punishment because a Nazi official (Heydrich) was ambushed and murdered on a road outside of town.]

[…]They came in the night, men in boots and brown shirts, and they took from their homes the bewildered miners and farmers, the tailor and the priest, the boy of seventeen and the old man of seventy, more than two hundred in all, and they shot them, because they could think of no other way to avenge the death of Heydrich. Fifty-six women they took also and killed, and proudly listed their names. The rest of the women they drove into what they called concentration camps; and these women the world will never see again. They herded the pale, terror-stricken children into trucks and carried them off to correction schools where they would be taught that they must honor the murderers of their fathers and the brutalizers of their mothers. The ninety homes, they burned to the ground, the church of St. Margaret they stamped into the earth. And the name of the little town of Lidice, through which ran the street called after a President of the United States, they rubbed out, they thought, from history.

Why did they do this deed, more terrible than anything that has happened since the Dark Ages, a deed not of passion, but of cold, premeditated, systematic murder and rapine? Why? They did it because they are afraid. They are afraid because the free spirit in men has refused to be conquered. Theirs is a system of force and terror, and Lidice is the terrible symbol of that system.

But it is not the only one. Of the five hundred thousand men, women and children who have been shot in Europe by the Nazis, at least twenty-five thousand have perished in mass massacres. Poland, Norway, Belgium, Yugoslavia, all have their Lidices. But this one—a symbol of all we have sworn to remember, if only because the Nazis themselves demand that we forget it. Once more, they have misjudged the human spirit.

Because a hangman was killed, Lidice lives. Because a hangman was killed, Wilson Street must once again be part of a little Bohemian town. Because the lanterns of Lidice have been blacked out, a flame has been lit which can never be extinguished. Each of the wounds of those two hundred men and fifty-six women is a mouth that cries out that other free men and free women must not suffer a like fate. Everywhere, but particularly in our own country, the wave of stubborn, stern resolve rises. Lidice lives. She lives again, thirty-five hundred miles from Wilson Street and St. Margaret's Church, in this little village in Illinois.

I look about me here, and I can see in the distance the black smoke of steel factories, swarming with American workers of all bloods and races. No contrast could be greater than the peaceful Lidice the Nazis thought they had destroyed, and this Illinois country, alive with factories in which the arms of victory are being forged. But I tell you that the two are related. For while such deeds as Lidice are done in another country, we cannot rest until we are sure that they will never be done in our own.

Let us here highly resolve that the memory of this little village of Bohemia, now resurrected by the people of a little village in Illinois, will fire us, now and until the battle is over, with the iron resolution that the madness of tyrants must perish from the earth, so that the earth may return to the people to whom it belongs, and be their village, their home, forever.

30. Which statement best evaluates Wilkie's bias in the speech?   Rd 1.4
    A. Wilkie is unbiased, explaining a situation.
    B. Wilkie is biased in favor of Heydrich, believing he should not have been killed.
    C. Wilkie is biased against the Nazis, explaining their wrongdoings.
    D. Wilkie is biased against his audience, believing they should have helped the citizens of Lidice.

31. Which of the following tones would be most appropriate to use while presenting this speech? C 1.1
    A. relaxed   B. merry   C. hysterical   D. tragic

32. In the speech, which of the following does Wilkie do most effectively?   C 1.3
    A. inspires listeners to stand up against the Nazis.
    B. encourages listeners to consider the Nazis' viewpoint.
    C. presents a positive perspective at a difficult time.
    D. compares viewpoints on a controversial issue.

33. Which of the following dictionary definitions best defines the word "tyrants" as it is used in the speech?   Rd 3.3
    A. Absolute rulers who govern from a foreign country.
    B. Nazi officials who exercise power in a harsh, cruel manner.
    C. People who control small villages.
    D. Oppressors; terrorists

34. If you were giving a speech intended to inform listeners about the wrongdoings of the Nazis, which of the following would most likely serve as an effective conclusion? C 1.5

   A.   Like I said in the beginning, the Nazis were scary, bad people.

   B.   As I stated at the start of this speech, the Nazis were a rather intimidating group of citizens who managed to implement a reign of terror over thousands of innocent lives.

   C.   As you can see, the Nazis were responsible for many wrongdoings. This is one case in which history must not repeat itself.

   D.   Bad things happen to good people.

35. Which of the following best explains the overall purpose of the last paragraph of the speech? C 1.3

   A.   To make sure the listeners don't forget that the Nazis must be fought.

   B.   To stir the listeners' patriotic feelings.

   C.   To scare the listeners into believing the Nazis are coming for them.

   D.   To incite a riot.

36. Which of the following conclusions can be made about Wilkie based on the speech? Rd 1.8

   A.   He was once part of a Nazi organization.

   B.   He believes in fighting for human rights.

   C.   He believes the deaths of the men and women have been vindicated.

   D.   He believes the Nazis will try to take over Illinois.

Versatile Bamboo

  1. Imagine having to cut grass that is over 100 feet tall. **2.** Do you remember the movie *Honey, I Shrunk the Kids*? **3.** Actually, the kind of grass I'm talking about couldn't be cut with a mower; it would take a saw to cut through the stalks. **4.** What kind of grass could this possibly be? **5.** I'm talking about bamboo, one of the most common and useful plants on earth. **6.** Officially classified as a grass and found on every continent except Antarctica, there are over 1,000 species of bamboo to be found. **7.** Bamboo can be found growing in a wide variety of climates from sea level tropical jungles to mountainsides at 13,000 feet. **8.** Many varieties grow very quickly. **9.** Some grow up to a foot per day. **10.** Despite fast growth, some varieties flower every 12 to 120 years. **11.** That means the plant flowers only once in its entire life cycle. **12.** As for usefulness, very few products can match bamboo. **13.** You may have eaten bamboo shoots in Chinese food, and the leaves and tender stalks are used for animal feed. **14.** Paper can be made from the leaves of bamboo, and the wood of the stalk can be used for items from flooring to dinnerware. **15.** For centuries, bamboo has been a favorite subject of artists and writers who celebrate the beauty of the plant in paintings, drawings, stories and poems. **16.** All of these uses add up to a valuable plant that is both practical and useful.

37. Where is the most logical place to put the following sentence? W 1.2

   The most well-known animal to eat bamboo is probably the giant panda.

   A.   after sentence 10   C.   after sentence 13

   B.   after sentence 12   D.   after sentence 15

38. Which sentence interrupts the logical progression of ideas?   W 1.2
    A. sentence 2
    B. sentence 4
    C. sentence 7
    D. sentence 11

39. Which sentence provides the most support for the idea that bamboo can be very useful in the household?   W 1.3
    A. sentence 11
    B. sentence 12
    C. sentence 14
    D. sentence 15

40. Which sentence most effectively combines sentences 8 and 9?   W 1.4
    A. Many varieties grow, up to a foot per day, very quickly.
    B. Many varieties grow very quickly, up to a foot per day.
    C. Many varieties grow up to a foot per day, very quickly.
    D. Up to a foot per day many varieties grow very quickly.

41. Which of the following best explains the author's tone?   Rs 2.2
    A. sad   B. satirical   C. lofty   D. relaxed

42. Which of the following is the correct way to punctuate sentence 15?   W 1.5
    A. For centuries, bamboo has been a favorite subject of artists and writers who celebrate the beauty of the plant in paintings drawings stories and poems.
    B. For centuries, bamboo has been a favorite subject of artists and writers who celebrate the beauty of the plant in paintings, drawings, stories, and poems!
    C. For centuries, bamboo has been a favorite subject of artists and writers who celebrate the beauty of the plant in paintings, drawings, stories, and poems.
    D. Correct as is

43. Which of the following is the best way to revise sentence 6?   W 1.4
    A. Bamboo is officially classified as a grass, and there are over 1,000 species found on every continent except Antarctica.
    B. Except in Antarctica, there are over 1,000 species of bamboo, which is officially classified as a grass, found on every continent.
    C. Bamboo, officially classified as a grass, is found on every continent except Antarctica in its over 1,000 species.
    D. Correct as is

Don't Be Rude!

1. When people travel to another country they expect to see different foods, clothing, and living conditions. 2. But, some people don't know how to act. 3. Some things that Americans find innocent are considered rude in another country or culture. 4. For example, many Americans stand with their hands in their pockets while conversing with friends. 5. In Belgium, Indonesia, France, Finland, Japan, and Sweden, this is considered very rude. 6. In the U.S., whistling is not a big deal. 7. In Europe, whistling is used in jeering or heckling. 8. Also, in India it is considered rude to whistle in public. 9. In the U.S. you may give a person directions by pointing in the way they should go. 10. In Japan and China, you should point with the entire hand to avoid rudeness, and in Malaysia, you should point

with the thumb. **11.** Speaking of thumbs, in Germany the fist with the thumb pointed up is the signal for the number one, but in Japan the same hand signal means the number five. **12.** In the U.S. and England, that signal means "okay" or "good job". **13.** If you're planning a trip to another country, be sure to do a little research so that you can avoid unintentionally being rude while you are there.

44. Which of the following is the best way to revise sentence 6?   C 1.1

   A.   In the U.S., you can whistle.

   B.   In the U.S., whistling is common.

   C.   In the U.S., whistling is a pretty innocent activity.

   D.   Best as is

45. Which of the following sentences contains a spelling error?   W 1.5

   A.   sentence 2   B.   sentence 7   C.   sentence 10   D.   sentence 13

46. Where is the best place to put the following sentence?   W 1.2

      But don't get discouraged; there are ways to avoid a potentially embarrassing situation.

   A.   after sentence 3   C.   after sentence 10

   B.   after sentence 8   D.   after sentence 12

47. Which of the following is a more precise way to write sentence 2?   W 1.4

   A.   But, some people don't know acceptable behaviors.

   B.   However, some travelers are not prepared for the differences in acceptable habits from country to country.

   C.   In addition, some travelers are not prepared for the differences in acceptable habits from country to country.

   D.   Best as is

48. Which of the following is the correct way to rewrite sentence 9?   W 1.5

   A.   In the U.S. you may give a person directions by pointing in the way them should go.

   B.   In the U.S. you may give a person directions by pointing in the way he or she should go.

   C.   In the U.S. you may give people directions by pointing in the way he should go.

   D.   Correct as is

49. Which of the following is the correct revision of sentence 10?   W 1.5

   A.   In Japan and China you should point with the entire hand to avoid rudeness and in Malaysia you should point with the thumb.

   B.   In Japan and China, you should point with the entire hand to avoid rudeness and in Malaysia, you should point with the thumb.

   C.   In Japan and China, you should point with the entire hand to avoid rudeness and in Malaysia you should point with the thumb.

   D.   Correct as is

50. Which of the following is a more precise revision of sentence 3? W 1.4

   A.   Some stuff that Americans find innocent are considered rude in another country or culture.

   B.   Some habits that Americans find innocent are considered rude in another country or culture.

   C.   Some traditions that Americans find innocent are considered rude in another country or culture.

   D.   Best as is

Excerpt from Chapter 5 of *Ramsey Milholland* by Booth Tarkington

...But the new arrivals hooted. *"Fish!"* Ramsey vociferated. "I'll bet a hundred dollars there hasn't been even a minny in this creek for the last sixty years!"

"There is, too!" said Heinie, bitterly. "But I wouldn't be surprised there wouldn't be no longer if you got to keep up this noise. If you'd shut up just a minute you could see yourself there's fish here."

In whispers several of the tamed girls at once heartily corroborated this statement, whereupon the newcomers ceased to gibe and consented to silence. Ramsey leaned forth over the edge of the overhanging bank, a dirt precipice five feet above the water, and peered into the indeterminable depths below. The pool had been stirred, partly by the inexpert pokings of the fishermen and partly by small clods and bits of dirt dislodged from above by the feet of the audience. The water, consequently, was but brownly translucent and revealed its secrets reluctantly; nevertheless certain dim little shapes had been observed to move within it, and were still there. Ramsey failed to see them at first.

"Where's any ole fish?" he inquired, scornfully.

"Oh, my goodness!" Heinie Krusemeyer moaned. *"Can't* you shut up?"

"Look!" whispered the girl who stood nearest to Ramsey. She pointed. "There's one. Right down there by Willis's hook. Don't you see him?"

Ramsey was impressed enough to whisper. "Is there? I don't see him. I can't—"

The girl came closer to him, and, the better to show him, leaned out over the edge of the bank, and, for safety in maintaining her balance, rested her left hand upon his shoulder while she pointed with her right. Thereupon something happened to Ramsey. The touch upon his shoulder was almost nothing, and he had never taken the slightest interest in Milla Rust (to whom that small warm hand belonged), though she was the class beauty, and long established in the office. Now, all at once, a peculiar and heretofore entirely unfamiliar sensation suddenly became important in the upper part of his chest. For a moment he held his breath, an involuntary action; --he seemed to be standing in a shower of flowers.

"Don't you see it, Ramsey?" Milla whispered. "It's a great big one. Why, it must be as long as—as your shoe! Look!"

Ramsey saw nothing but the thick round curl on Milla's shoulder. Milla had a group of curls on each of her shoulders, for she got her modes at the Movies and had that sort of prettiness: large, gentle, calculating eyes, and a full, softly modelled face, implacably sweet. Ramsey was accustomed to all this charm, and Milla had never before been of more importance to him than an equal weight of school furniture—but all at once some magic had enveloped her. That curl upon the shoulder nearest him was shot with dazzling fibres of sunshine. He seemed to be trembling.

"I don't see it," he murmured, huskily, afraid that she might remove her hand. "I can't see any fish, Milla."

She leaned farther out over the bank. "Why, there, goosie!" she whispered. "Right there."

"I can't see it."

She leaned still farther, bending down to point. "Why right th—"

At this moment she removed her hand from his shoulder, though unwillingly. She clutched at him, in fact, but without avail. She had been too amiable.

A loud shriek was uttered by throats abler to vocalize, just then, than Milla's, for in her great surprise she said nothing whatever—- the shriek came from the other girls as Milla left the crest of the overhanging bank and almost horizontally disappeared into the brown water. There was a tumultuous splash, and then of Milla Rust and her well-known beautifulness there was nothing visible in the superficial world, nor upon the surface of that creek. The vanishment was total.

"*Save* her!"

Several girls afterward admitted having used this expression, and little Miss Floy Williams, the youngest and smallest member of the class, was unable to deny that she had said, "Oh, God!" Nothing could have been more natural, and the matter need not have been brought before her with such insistence and frequency, during the two remaining years of her undergraduate career.

Ramsey was one of those who heard this exclamation, later so famous, and perhaps it was what roused him to heroism. He dived from the bank, headlong, and the strange thought in his mind was "I guess *this*'ll show Dora Yocum!" He should have been thinking of Milla, of course, at such a time, particularly after the little enchantment just laid upon him by Milla's touch and Milla's curls; and he knew well enough that Miss Yocum was not among the spectators. She was half a mile away, as it happened, gathering "botanical specimens" with one of the teachers—which was her idea of what to do at a picnic!

51. Which of the following is an inference that can be made based on the passage?   Rd 1.8
    A. Ramsey will jump in the water and try to save Milla.
    B. Milla will drown and never be seen again.
    C. Ramsey will not try to save Milla; instead he will go fishing.
    D. Ramsey and Milla will fall in love.

52. Which of the following best explains the purpose of the passage?   Rd 1.5
    A. To persuade readers that Ramsey is a hero.
    B. To relate an event.
    C. To teach readers how to fish for minnows.
    D. To explain a character's past.

53. Which of the following is an example of irony?   Rd 2.2
    A. Ramsey did not think there were any minnows in the creek, but there really were.
    B. Ramsey suddenly found Milla to be beautiful.
    C. Ramsey's desire for Milla to touch him caused her to be taken away.
    D. Ramsey was expected to save Milla after she fell in the water.

54. Which of the following best explains the effect of the author's choice of narrator?   Rd 2.5
    A. The reader is able to experience Milla's fear.
    B. The reader is kept in suspense about the presence of minnows in the creek.
    C. The reader is unsure if Milla has feelings for Ramsey.
    D. The reader experiences Ramsey's growing feelings for Milla.

55. Which of the following best explains the Milla's tone in the passage?   Rd 2.2
    A. affectionate   B. condescending   C. fearful   D. loving

Informational Passage 1

National Oceanic and Atmospheric Administration (NOAA) and Tsunamis

Tsunamis do not have a season and do not occur regularly or frequently. Yet they pose a major threat to the coastal populations of the Pacific and other world oceans and seas. Nothing can be done to prevent them, but the loss of life and property can be reduced with proper planning.

The National Oceanic and Atmospheric Administration (NOAA) oversees the U.S. Tsunami Program. Its mission is to provide a 24-hour detection and warning system and increase public awareness about the threat of tsunamis. The NOAA National Weather Service operates two tsunami warning centers that continuously monitor data from seismological and tidal stations. They also evaluate earthquakes that have the potential to generate tsunamis. Information and warning bulletins are sent out to government authorities and the public. One of the warning centers is in Palmer, Alaska, and the other is in Ewa Beach, Hawaii. These operational centers form a 24-hour U.S. tsunami warning system for the Pacific Rim area.

General Information about Tsunamis

A tsunami is a series of ocean waves generated by any rapid, large-scale disturbance of the sea. Most tsunamis are created by earthquakes, but they may also be caused by volcanic eruptions, landslides, undersea slumps, or meteor impacts.

The waves radiate outward in all directions from the disturbance and can spread across entire ocean basins. Tsunami waves are distinguished from ordinary ocean waves by their great length between peaks, often exceeding 100 miles in the deep ocean. A second distinguishing feature is the long amount of time between these peaks, ranging from five minutes to an hour. The speed at which tsunamis travel depends on the ocean depth. A tsunami can exceed 500 mph in the deep ocean but slows to 20 or 30 mph in the shallow water near land. In less than 24 hours, a tsunami can cross the entire Pacific Ocean.

In the deep ocean, a tsunami is barely noticeable and will only cause a small and slow rising and falling of the sea surface as it passes. Only as it approaches land does a tsunami become a hazard. As the tsunami approaches land and shallow water, the waves slow down and become compressed, causing them to grow in height. In the best of cases, the tsunami comes onshore like a quickly rising tide and causes a gentle flooding of low-lying coastal areas.

In the worst of cases, a bore will form. A bore is a wall of moving water that can be several meters high and can rush onshore with great destructive power. Behind the bore is a deep and fast-moving flood that can pick up and sweep away almost anything in its path. Minutes later, the water will drain away as the trough of the tsunami wave arrives, sometimes exposing great patches of the sea floor. But then the water will rush in again as before, causing additional damage.

This destructive cycle may repeat many times before the hazard finally passes. Persons caught in the path of a tsunami have little chance to survive. They can be easily crushed by debris, or they may simply drown. Children and the elderly are particularly at risk, as they have less mobility, strength, and endurance.

Tsunamis typically cause the most severe damage and casualties very near their source. There the waves are highest because they have not yet lost much energy to friction or spreading. The nearby coastal population has little time to react before the tsunami arrives. Local residents are often disoriented from the violent earthquake shaking. The largest tsunamis, however, can cause destruction and casualties over a wide area, sometimes as wide as the entire Pacific Basin. These types of Pacific-wide tsunamis may happen only a few times each century.

http://www.publicaffairs.noaa.gov/grounders/tsunamis.html

1. Which of the following best explains the author's purpose in writing the passage?
   A. To explain to readers what they should do in case of a tsunami   Rd 1.5
   B. To persuade readers to stay away from the ocean during tsunami season
   C. To inform readers about the causes and effects of tsunamis
   D. To discuss various tsunamis that have taken place throughout history

2. Which of the following is a conclusion readers could draw after reading the passage?
   A. Though rare, tsunamis can cause great destruction.   Rd 1.8
   B. Tsunamis are especially deadly for ocean creatures.
   C. Tsunamis are always created by underwater earthquakes.
   D. The NOAA will eventually be able to predict all tsunamis.

3. Which of the following best describes the author's tone in the passage?
   A. fearful   C. threatening   Rd 2.2
   B. serious   D. apologetic

4. As it is used in the passage, severe is to insignificant as   Rd 3.4
   A. monstrous is to miniscule   C. open is to agape
   B. deafening is to shrill   D. dangerous is to risky

5. Which of the following best explains the author's credibility?
   A. The author is somewhat credible, using both facts and propaganda.   Rs 2.2
   B. The author is not credible, writing from a clearly biased point of view.
   C. The author is somewhat credible, using information from the NOAA along with sensationalism.
   D. The author is credible, using general information supported by the NOAA.

6. Which technique does the author use to communicate the information on tsunamis?   Rd 2.2

    A.   quotations from experts

    B.   statements supported by facts

    C.   educated guesses

    D.   questions and answers

7. Which of the following words is closest in meaning to the word "hazard" as it is used in the passage?   Rd 3.2

    A.   danger

    B.   pollution

    C.   warning

    D.   waves

8. Where would this passage most likely be published?   Rd 1.5

    A.   in a report containing general information on tsunamis

    B.   in a magazine read by scientists

    C.   in a book supporting research by the NOAA

    D.   in a report predicting the next possible tsunami

9. Which of the following is an inference that can be made after reading the passage?   Rd 1.8

    A.   Earthquakes always harm fewer people than do tsunamis.

    B.   Nature often provides clues that a tsunami is coming.

    C.   The only way to survive a tsunami is to build a raft.

    D.   Tsunamis are rarely deadly.

10. Which of the following best describes the purpose of the passage?   Rd 1.5

    A.   to help tsunami survivors relate to one another

    B.   to show how tsunamis bring out people's creativity

    C.   to teach people how to prepare for a tsunami

    D.   to teach people tips that may help them survive a tsunami

11. Which of the following best explains the author's point of view in the passage?   Rd 2.2

    A. concerned   B. snobbish   C. regretful   D. discouraged

12. Based on the information in this passage, where would a tsunami most likely occur?   Rd 1.4

    A. France   B. Iraq   C. Japan   D. Nigeria

13. Which word best describes the word "trough" as it is used in the passage?   Rd 3.2

    A. vibration   B. low point   C. high point   D. wall

Literary Passage 1

Excerpt from *Robinson Crusoe* by Daniel Defoe

NOV. 17. - This day I began to dig behind my tent into the rock, to make room for my further conveniency.

NOTE. - Three things I wanted exceedingly for this work - viz. a pickaxe, a shovel, and a wheelbarrow or basket; so I desisted from my work, and began to consider how to supply that want, and make me some tools. As for the pickaxe, I made use of the iron crows, which were proper enough, though heavy; but the next thing was a shovel or spade;

this was so absolutely necessary, that, indeed, I could do nothing effectually without it; but what kind of one to make I knew not.

NOV. 18. - The next day, in searching the woods, I found a tree of that wood, or like it, which in the Brazils they call the iron- tree, for its exceeding hardness. Of this, with great labour, and almost spoiling my axe, I cut a piece, and brought it home, too, with difficulty enough, for it was exceeding heavy. The excessive hardness of the wood, and my having no other way, made me a long while upon this machine, for I worked it effectually by little and little into the form of a shovel or spade; the handle exactly shaped like ours in England, only that the board part having no iron shod upon it at bottom, it would not last me so long; however, it served well enough for the uses which I had occasion to put it to; but never was a shovel, I believe, made after that fashion, or so long in making.

I was still deficient, for I wanted a basket or a wheelbarrow. A basket I could not make by any means, having no such things as twigs that would bend to make wicker-ware - at least, none yet found out; and as to a wheelbarrow, I fancied I could make all but the wheel; but that I had no notion of; neither did I know how to go about it; besides, I had no possible way to make the iron gudgeons for the spindle or axis of the wheel to run in; so I gave it over, and so, for carrying away the earth which I dug out of the cave, I made me a thing like a hod which the labourers carry mortar in when they serve the bricklayers. This was not so difficult to me as the making the shovel: and yet this and the shovel, and the attempt which I made in vain to make a wheelbarrow, took me up no less than four days - I mean always excepting my morning walk with my gun, which I seldom failed, and very seldom failed also bringing home something fit to eat.

NOV. 23. - My other work having now stood still, because of my making these tools, when they were finished I went on, and working every day, as my strength and time allowed, I spent eighteen days entirely in widening and deepening my cave, that it might hold my goods commodiously.

NOTE. - During all this time I worked to make this room or cave spacious enough to accommodate me as a warehouse or magazine, a kitchen, a dining-room, and a cellar. As for my lodging, I kept to the tent; except that sometimes, in the wet season of the year, it rained so hard that I could not keep myself dry, which caused me afterwards to cover all my place within my pale with long poles, in the form of rafters, leaning against the rock, and load them with flags and large leaves of trees, like a thatch.

DECEMBER 10. - I began now to think my cave or vault finished, when all of a sudden (it seems I had made it too large) a great quantity of earth fell down from the top on one side; so much that, in short, it frighted me, and not without reason, too, for if I had been under it, I had never wanted a gravedigger. I had now a great deal of work to do over again, for I had the loose earth to carry out; and, which was of more importance, I had the ceiling to prop up, so that I might be sure no more would come down.

14. What is the effect of having the story told in the form of a journal? Rd 2.5
    A. It gives the reader a clear sense that the narrator is telling the truth.
    B. It helps the reader understand why the narrator needs to dig a shelter.
    C. It allows the reader to experience the action as the narrator did.
    D. It gives the reader insight into the narrator's fears.

15. Which of the following is an inference that can be made about the narrator?
    A. He will eventually starve.
    C. He will eventually make a wheelbarrow.
    B. He is quite resourceful.
    D. He is very lonely.

16. Which of the following best explains the narrator's tone?
    A. dramatic
    C. nervous
    B. flippant
    D. objective

17. Which of the following best explains the narrator's conflict?
    A. He must determine the best way to make himself live comfortably.
    B. He must find a way to get rescued.
    C. He wants to be a great inventor.
    D. He needs to learn how to hunt, but dislikes killing animals.

18. Which of the following words is closest in meaning to the word "effectually" as it is used in the passage?
    A. sufficiently
    C. easily
    B. quickly
    D. secretly

Literary Passage 2

Excerpt from *The Mysterious Island* by Jules Verne

"No," replied the reporter; "but if there is a lack of food for want of instruments for the chase?"

"Ah, if we only had a knife!" cried the sailor.

"Well?" asked Cyrus Harding.

"Well! I would soon make a bow and arrows, and then there could be plenty of game in the larder!"

"Yes, a knife, a sharp blade." said the engineer, as if he was speaking to himself.

At this moment his eyes fell upon Top, who was running about on the shore. Suddenly Harding's face became animated.

"Top, here," said he.

The dog came at his master's call. The latter took Top's head between his hands, and unfastening the collar which the animal wore round his neck, he broke it in two, saying,—

"There are two knives, Pencroft!"

Two hurrahs from the sailor was the reply. Top's collar was made of a thin piece of tempered steel. They had only to sharpen it on a piece of sandstone, then to raise the edge on a finer stone. Now sandstone was abundant on the beach, and two hours after the stock of tools in the colony consisted of two sharp blades, which were easily fixed in solid handles.

The production of these their first tools was hailed as a triumph. It was indeed a valuable result of their labor, and a very opportune one. They set out.

Cyrus Harding proposed that they should return to the western shore of the lake, where the day before he had noticed the clayey ground of which he possessed a specimen. They therefore followed the bank of the Mercy, traversed Prospect Heights, and after a walk of five miles or more they reached a glade, situated two hundred feet from Lake Grant.

On the way Herbert had discovered a tree, the branches of which the Indians of South America employ for making their bows. It was the crejimba, of the palm family, which does not bear edible fruit. Long straight branches were cut, the leaves stripped off; it was shaped, stronger in the middle, more slender at the extremities, and nothing remained to be done but to find a plant fit to make the bow-string. This was the "hibiscus heterophyllus," which furnishes fibers of such remarkable tenacity that they have been compared to the tendons of animals. Pencroft thus obtained bows of tolerable strength, for which he only wanted arrows. These were easily made with straight stiff branches, without knots, but the points with which they must be armed, that is to say, a substance to serve in lieu of iron, could not be met with so easily. But Pencroft said, that having done his part of the work, chance would do the rest.

19. Which of the following best explains a connection between the excerpt from *Robinson Crusoe* and the excerpt from *The Mysterious Island*?   Rd 1.2
    A.   Both include a man who has been stranded alone on an island.
    B.   Both involve being stranded and the need to survive.
    C.   Both are written in the form of a journal.
    D.   Both include dialogue.

20. Which of the following themes do both passages have in common?   Rd 2.3
    A.   The strength of love   C.   The will to survive
    B.   The need for friendship   D.   The importance of honesty

21. Which of the following is true of both selections?   Rd 2.6
    A.   They are both biographies.   C.   They are both written as poetry.
    B.   They are both dramas.   D.   They are both written in prose.

22. Which of the following best explains the characters in both selections?   Rd 1.2
    A.   feeble   C.   determined
    B.   foolish   D.   skeptical

23. Which of the following best explains the settings of both passages?   Rd 2.6
    A.   Both take place on a tropical island.
    B.   Both take place in a cold climate.
    C.   Both take place in an isolated location.
    D.   Both take place in the desert.

24. Which of the following dictionary definitions best defines the word "specimen" as it is used in the excerpt from *The Mysterious Island*? Rd 3.3

    A.   An individual representative of a class

    B.   A sample

    C.   An individual; a person

    D.   A bit of tissue or blood or urine that is taken for diagnostic purposes

25. Which of the following is an inference that can be made after reading the excerpt from *The Mysterious Island*? Rd 1.8

    A.   The men must work together.

    B.   The men are in hiding.

    C.   The men are all related.

    D.   The men are unfamiliar with exotic plants.

"The Village Blacksmith" by Henry Wadsworth Longfellow

Under a spreading chestnut-tree
The village smithy stands;
The smith, a mighty man is he,
With large and sinewy hands;
And the muscles of his brawny arms
Are strong as iron bands.

His hair is crisp, and black, and long,
His face is like the tan;
His brow is wet with honest sweat,
He earns whate'er he can,
And looks the whole world in the face,
For he owes not any man.

Week in, week out, from morn till night,
You can hear his bellows blow;
You can hear him swing his heavy sledge,
With measured beat and slow,
Like a sexton ringing the village bell,
When the evening sun is low.

And children coming home from school
Look in at the open door;
They love to see the flaming forge,
And hear the bellows roar,
And catch the burning sparks that fly
Like chaff from a threshing-floor.

He goes on Sunday to the church,
And sits among his boys;
He hears the parson pray and preach,
He hears his daughter's voice,
Singing in the village choir,
And it makes his heart rejoice.

It sounds to him like her mother's voice,
Singing in Paradise!
He needs must think of her once more,
How in the grave she lies;
And with his haul, rough hand he wipes
A tear out of his eyes.

Toiling,—rejoicing,—sorrowing,
Onward through life he goes;
Each morning sees some task begin,
Each evening sees it close
Something attempted, something done,
Has earned a night's repose.

Thanks, thanks to thee, my worthy friend,
For the lesson thou hast taught!
Thus at the flaming forge of life
Our fortunes must be wrought;
Thus on its sounding anvil shaped
Each burning deed and thought.

Read the following lines from the poem.

And the muscles of his brawny arms/ Are strong as iron bands.

26. Which type of figurative language is being used?   Rd 2.2
    A. personification   C. metaphor
    B. oxymoron   D. simile

27. Which of the following dictionary definitions best defines the word "sinewy" as it is used in the poem?   Rd 3.3
    A. possessing excess weight
    B. stringy and tough
    C. lean and muscular
    D. (of meat) full of sinews; especially impossible to chew

28. Which of the following conclusions can be made about the blacksmith?   Rd 1.8
    A. He is wealthy.   C. He is old.
    B. He is a hard worker.   D. He doesn't like children.

29. Which of the following best explains the internal conflict of the blacksmith?   Rd 2.8
    A. He is sad to see his children grow up.
    B. He is tired of working but can't afford to retire.
    C. He feels guilty about once being dishonest.
    D. He misses his wife, but must keep on going.

Read the following line from the poem.

Thanks, thanks to thee, my worthy friend,

30. Which type of figurative language is being used?   Rd 2.2
    A. euphemism   C. onomatopoeia
    B. metaphor   D. alliteration

31. Which of the following best explains the author's tone while describing the blacksmith?   Rd 2.2 / Rs 2.2
    A. praiseful   C. taunting
    B. condescending   D. apologetic

Speech

President Ronald Reagan leads the nation in mourning for the seven astronauts killed in the Space Shuttle Challenger Explosion, Washington, D.C., January 28, 1986.

Ladies and gentlemen:

I'd planned to speak to you tonight to report on the state of the Union, but the events of earlier today have led me to change those plans. Today is a day for mourning and remembering. Nancy and I are pained to the core by the tragedy of the shuttle *Challenger*. We know we share this pain with all of the people of our country. This is truly a national loss.

Nineteen years ago, almost to the day, we lost three astronauts in a terrible accident on the ground. But we've never lost an astronaut in flight; we've never had a tragedy like this. And perhaps we've forgotten the courage it took for the crew of the shuttle. But they, the *Challenger* Seven, were aware of the dangers, but overcame them and did their jobs brilliantly. We mourn seven heroes: Michael Smith, Dick Scobee, Judith Resnik, Ronald McNair, Ellison Onizuka, Gregory Jarvis, and Christa McAuliffe. We mourn their loss as a nation together.

For the families of the seven, we cannot bear, as you do, the full impact of this tragedy. But we feel the loss, and we're thinking about you so very much. Your loved ones were daring and brave, and they had that special grace, that special spirit that says, "Give me a challenge, and I'll meet it with joy." They had a hunger to explore the universe and discover its truths. They wished to serve, and they did. They served all of us.

We've grown used to wonders in this century. It's hard to dazzle us. But for 25 years the United States space program has been doing just that. We've grown used to the idea of space, and perhaps we forget that we've only just begun. We're still pioneers. They, the members of the *Challenger* crew, were pioneers.

And I want to say something to the schoolchildren of America who were watching the live coverage of the shuttle's takeoff. I know it is hard to understand, but sometimes painful things like this happen. It's all part of the process of exploration and discovery. It's all part of taking a chance and expanding man's horizons. The future doesn't belong to the fainthearted; it belongs to the brave. The *Challenger* crew was pulling us into the future, and we'll continue to follow them.

I've always had great faith in and respect for our space program, and what happened today does nothing to diminish it. We don't hide our space program. We don't keep secrets and cover things up. We do it all up front and in public. That's the way freedom is, and we wouldn't change it for a minute. We'll continue our quest in space. There will be more shuttle flights and more shuttle crews and, yes, more volunteers, more civilians, more teachers in space. Nothing ends here; our hopes and our journeys continue. I want to add that I wish I could talk to every man and woman who works for NASA or who worked on this mission and tell them: Your dedication and professionalism have moved and impressed us for decades. And we know of your anguish. We share it.

There's a coincidence today. On this day 390 years ago, the great explorer Sir Francis Drake died aboard ship off the coast of Panama. In his lifetime, the great frontiers were the oceans, and an historian later said, "He lived by the sea, died on it, and was buried in it." Well, today we can say of the Challenger crew: Their dedication was, like Drake's, complete.

The crew of the space shuttle *Challenger* honored us by the manner in which they lived their lives. We will never forget them, nor the last time we saw them, this morning, as they prepared for their journey and waved goodbye, and "slipped the surly bonds of earth" to "touch the face of God."

32. Which statement best evaluates Reagan's bias in the speech? Rd 1.4

    A.   Reagan shows bias in favor of space exploration, believing it is a brave and worthy cause.

    B.   Reagan is unbiased, objectively describing the mission of space exploration.

    C.   Reagan is biased against space exploration, believing it is not worth the loss of human life.

    D.   Reagan is unbiased, describing both the positive and negative aspects of space exploration.

33. Which of the following would be the best presentation strategy for Reagan to use while making this speech? C 1.1

    A.   to speak quietly and look down

    B.   to speak angrily and quickly scan the audience

    C.   to speak solemnly but strongly and make eye contact with audience members

    D.   to speak loudly and avoid making eye contact with audience members.

34. In the speech, which of the following does Reagan do most effectively? C 1.3

    A.   argues for a change in methods used in space exploration

    B.   compares viewpoints of those who both support and oppose space exploration

    C.   explains the recent progress made in space exploration because of the *Challenger* crew.

    D.   comforts family members of the *Challenger* crew.

Rd 2.2

35. Which of the following is the correct denotation of the word "dazzle" as it is used in the speech?

    A.   scare   C.   impress

    B.   bejewel   D.   miss

36. If you were giving a speech intended to persuade people that the *Challenger* crew served a great cause, which would most likely serve as an effective conclusion? C 1.5

    A.   The crew did the best they could.

    B.   As you can see, the *Challenger* crew will be remembered for their brave and important contribution to space exploration.

    C.   So you see now why the *Challenger* crew was pretty cool.

    D.   Throughout the course of history, many people have made important contributions in the area of space exploration.

37. Which source would most likely provide accurate information on the *Challenger* explosion? Rd 2.2

    A.   a novel written about the explosion

    B.   newspaper reports about the explosion

    C.   official records about the explosion

    D.   eyewitness accounts of the explosion

Writing Passage 1

Panda Bears

1 The panda bear or giant panda is one of the endangered species of the world. **2** Less than 1,000 are left in the wild. **3** About another 100 live in various zoos around the world. **4** The native areas that are still home to wild pandas have been reduced to a few bamboo forests, primarily in the mountainous areas of Szechwan province of China. **5** These areas have been designated as nature preserves by the Chinese government. **6** At one time, pandas were found over large parts of China and Myanmar (Burma). **7** The destruction of their natural habitat and uncontrolled poaching has severely reduced the number of pandas. **8** The panda's fur makes it a beautiful animal.

9 Europeans first heard of the giant panda when a Jesuit missionary in China discovered panda furs in 1869. **10** Pandas were not observed in the wild until an expedition in 1914 finally saw them. **11** In the past, scientists had classified pandas as a member of the raccoon family. **12** Today they are classified as a type of bear. **13** Some scientists argue that they should be in a separate classification because many of their characteristics are not like the bear family.

14 Probably the neatest feature of the giant panda is its white and black fur. **15** It has a very recognizable pattern of markings with black patches around both eyes and ears. **16** Another wide band of black covers the shoulders and forelegs, and the back legs are also black. **17** They grow to an average size of about 5 feet in length and about 220 pounds in weight. **18** Although they have a lumbering bear-like gait on the ground, they are very agile tree climbers.

19 They feed primarily on bamboo in the wild, and they even have a special thumb-like structure on their front feet that allows them to grasp and pull up bamboo. **20** A panda spends an average of 10-12 hours a day feeding. **21** They eat 30-60 lbs. of bamboo a day. **22** This is necessary because they actually don't digest it very well. **23** In captivity pandas live mainly on a diet of cereal, milk, and garden vegetables.

Rd 3.2

38. Which of the following is closest in meaning to the word "agile" as it is used in the passage?
    A. clumsy
    B. swift
    C. stiff
    D. smart

39. Which of the following best explains the author's tone in the passage?

Rd 2.2

    A. neutral
    B. mournful
    C. gleeful
    D. worrisome

40. Which of the following is a conclusion that can be made after reading the passage?

Rd 1.8

    A. Giant pandas must have a lot of stomach aches.
    B. Giant pandas do not survive well in captivity.
    C. Poachers of giant pandas are not punished harshly enough.
    D. Without intervention, giant pandas would become extinct.

41. Where is the most logical place to put the following sentence?

W 1.2

    Pandas are known for their eating habits.

    A. after sentence 4
    B. after sentence 12
    C. after sentence 18
    D. after sentence 20

42. Which sentence interrupts the logical progression of ideas?   W 1.2

    A. sentence 3   C. sentence 10
    B. sentence 8   D. sentence 13

                                                                                   W 1.3
43. Which sentence provides the most support for the idea that pandas are in danger of extinction?

    A. sentence 1   C. sentence 5
    B. sentence 3   D. sentence 6

44. Which of the following is a more precise way to write sentence 14?   W 1.4

    A. The giant panda is known for its black and white fur.
    B. The giant panda is distinctive and well known for its creamy white and black fur.
    C. Probably the most distinctive feature of the giant panda is its thick, creamy white and black fur.
    D. Best as is

45. Which of the following is the correct way to rewrite sentence 23?   W 1.5

    A. In captivity, pandas live mainly on a diet of cereal, milk, and garden vegetables.
    B. In captivity pandas live mainly on a diet of cereal milk and garden vegetables.
    C. In captivity, pandas live mainly on a diet of cereal milk and garden vegetables.
    D. Correct as is

The Legend of Lorelei

1 Winding its way through Germany, the Rhine River is one of the most important rivers of Europe and the world. 2 No other river in the world has as many old and famous cities along its banks. 3 Several industrial cities lie along the Rhine. 4 It is a major transport route for all of Europe. 5 The middle section of the Rhine is often considered the most beautiful and picturesque. 6 Towering rock cliffs look over the river, and many ancient castles and fortresses are scattered along the high banks. 7 Near Sankt Goarshausen (St. Goars) is a nearly vertical rock cliff rising over 430 feet above the water level. 8 This is one of the most difficult points of the Rhine to navigate. 9 The river is at its narrowest and deepest here. 10 The rock cliff known as Lorelei overlooks it.

11 The cliff is known as Lorelei because it is connected with one of the most famous legends of Germany. 12 According to the legend, a beautiful young maiden named Lorelei jumped to her death in the river from that rocky point. 13 As with so many legends, her dispair was over a faithless lover, a boatman on the river. 14 Since her death, she sits on the top of the cliff combing her hair and singing songs to all men who pass by on the river. 15 Just like the Sirens of Greek mythology, her singing is so enchanting that the men are caught up in the beauty of the song and in looking up to catch a glimpse of Lorelei. 16 Apparently, this is Lorelei's revenge.

46. Which of the following dictionary definitions best defines the word "vertical" as it is used in the passage? Rd 3.3

    A. being or situated at right angles to the horizon; upright.

    B. of or relating to the vertex of the head.

    C. relating to or involving all stages from production to sale: *vertical integration.*

    D. relating to or composed of elements at different levels, as of society.

47. Which of the following is the correct way to revise sentence 6? W 1.5

    A. Towering rock cliffs look over the river and many ancient castles and fortreses are scattered along the high banks.

    B. Towering rock cliffs look over the river; and many ancient castles and fortreses are scattered along the high banks.

    C. Towering rock cliffs look over the river, and many ancient castles and fortresses are scattered along the high banks.

    D. Correct as is

48. Which of the following is the best way to combine sentences 3 and 4? W 1.4

    A. Several industrial cities lie along the Rhine, and it is a major transport route for all of Europe.

    B. Several industrial cities lie along the Rhine; and it is a major transport route for all of Europe.

    C. Several industrial cities lie along the Rhine and it is a major transport route for all of Europe.

    D. Several industrial cities lie along the Rhine— it is a major transport route for all of Europe.

49. Which of the following is the correct way to revise sentence 11? W 1.5

    A. The cliff is known as Lorelei; because it is connected with one of the most famous legends of Germany.

    B. The cliff is known as Lorelei, because it is connected with one of the most famous legends of Germany.

    C. The cliff is known as Lorelei… it is connected with one of the most famous legends of Germany.

    D. Correct as is

50. Which of the following best combines sentences 9 and 10? W 1.4

    A. The river is at its narrowest and deepest here but the rock cliff known as Lorelei overlooks it.

    B. The river is at its narrowest and deepest here however the rock cliff known as Lorelei overlooks it.

    C. The river is at its narrowest and deepest here where the rock cliff known as Lorelei overlooks it.

    D. The river is at its narrowest and deepest here -- the rock cliff known as Lorelei overlooks it.

51. Which of the following is the correct way to revise sentence 13? W 1.5

    A. As with so many legends, her despair was over a faithless lover, a boatman on the river.

    B. As with so many legends her dispair was over a faithless lover, a boatman on the river.

    C. As with so many legends her dispair was over a faithless lover a boatman on the river.

    D. Correct as is

52. Which of the following is a more descriptive way to write sentence 14?   W 1.4

    A.   Since her death, she sits on top of the cliff combing her long golden hair and singing songs to all the men who pass by on the river.

    B.   Since her death, she sits on top of the cliff combing her long golden hair and singing mysterious songs to all the men who pass by on the river.

    C.   Since her death, she sits on top of the cliff combing her nice hair and singing pretty songs to all the men who pass by on the river.

    D.   Best as is

53. Where is the best place to put the following sentence?   W 1.2

        Because it is such a dangerous part of the river, the men are lured to their rocky deaths.

    A.   after sentence 4   C.   after sentence 11

    B.   after sentence 8   D.   after sentence 15

54. Which of the following best describes the author's tone in the passage?   Rd 2.2

    A.   mysterious   C.   sneaky

    B.   sly   D.   dishonest

55. Which of the following words is closest in meaning to the word "enchanting" as it is used in the passage?   Rd 3.3

    A.   pretty   C.   deceptive

    B.   alluring   D.   funny

NOTES

NOTES

NOTES

NOTES

NOTES

NOTES

NOTES

NOTES

NOTES

NOTES